EUROPEAN HISTORICAL DICTIONARIES
Edited by Jon Woronoff

Historical Dictionary of the Gypsies (Romanies)

Donald Kenrick
with the assistance of Gillian Taylor

European Historical Dictionaries, No. 27

The Scarecrow Press, Inc.
Lanham, Md., & London
1998

SCARECROW PRESS, INC.

Published in the United States of America
by Scarecrow Press, Inc.
4720 Boston Way
Lanham, Maryland 20706

British Library Cataloguing in Publication Information Available

Library of Congress Cataloging-in-Publication Data

Kenrick, Donald.
   Historical dictionary of the Gypsies (Romanies) / Donald Kenrick
  with the assistance of Gillian Taylor.
     p.   cm.—(European historical dictionaries ; no. 27)
    ISBN 0-8108-3444-8 (alk. paper)
    1. Gypsies—History—Dictionaries.   I. Taylor, Gillian.
  II. Title. III. Series.
  DX115.K46   1998
  909′.0491497′003—DC21   97-31419
                                               CIP

♾ ™ The paper used in this publication meets the minimum
requirements of American National Standard for Information
Sciences—Permanence of Paper for Printed Library Materials,
ANSI Z39.48—1984. Manufactured in the United States of America.

Contents

Editor's Foreword

This volume is patently different from the others in our various country series. In nearly all the others, we are dealing with a state and the people living there. In some cases, it is a place that a given people claims as its own, even if it is not generally recognized as a state. Only the Gypsies have refused to be tied to, and defined by, such an artificial barrier as national borders. True, many have settled down and those who continually move about are relatively fewer. But wherever they may be, the Gypsies feel that they are part of a broader people located in many different lands, most of them presently in Europe but others farther afield, while their roots are in India.

This explains an essential variation on the standard format. As usual, the dictionary includes entries on significant persons, events, institutions, organizations and so on. But the crucial entries describe the background and present status of the Romany clans and groups as well as the countries in which they live. The overall situation is neatly summarized in the introduction. The chronology also brings many of the strands together. Of particular interest is the bibliography, which helps readers track down books on multiple aspects of the Gypsies and their history, which are not easily found by the general public.

Writing a historical dictionary of a people dispersed among many countries is harder than presenting a country and its people. Information had to be drawn from many disparate sources and then merged to gain an overall view. This the authors have carefully and competently done.

Donald Kenrick has been involved with the Gypsies for over three decades. Academically he studied linguistics with special emphasis on a Romani dialect. He has lectured and written extensively on the Gypsies. He has also been involved in the Gypsy civil rights movement as secretary of the Gypsy Council and the National Gypsy Education Council. More practically, he served as an interpreter at the four World Romany Congresses.

Gillian Taylor is a freelance writer and researcher who has studied at Auckland and North London Universities where she completed her first degree. She has collaborated for many years in the establishment of a database from which much of the material in the dictionary has been drawn.

This historical dictionary of the Gypsies of Europe is thus an excellent source of information for all those intrigued by the subject, whether beginners or specialists, Gypsies or not.

Jon Woronoff
Series Editor

Preface

This publication is designed to be a tool for all those working in education, culture, civil rights and politics who need more information concerning a name, date or event related to the past and current history of the Gypsy people in Europe. But it will also be of interest for the general reader.

For practical reasons this handbook cannot fulfill the role of a Who's Who, a discography or a directory, although we have mentioned those Gypsies who have become historically significant in their field, many who have excelled in music and entertainment and the representatives of Gypsy organizations. Regrettably few scientists or judges, for example, appear, as often professional people have hidden their Gypsy origin. Conversely, entertainers have proclaimed their roots with enthusiasm.

Nor is this an encyclopedia of Gypsy life. There are no entries for *bori* (daughter-in-law) or "bellows," for instance, though these and many other potential keywords would shed an interesting light on the way of life of the Gypsies.

What we hope we have done is to produce a concise, yet informative, companion that is accessible and promotes an understanding of the history of the Gypsy people in Europe. To assist the process of research, major organizations and museum resources have been listed as an entry into the subject for those who wish to go deeper. Finally, we have included a small selection of current addresses of the main journals (at the end of the bibliography) to help readers get in touch with the vast network available to them.

As the Romani proverb says: It is easy to begin but hard to finish. We welcome corrections and suggestions for inclusion in a second edition.

Acknowledgments

We have drawn heavily on the published literature listed in the bibliography and have found particularly useful the following sources, authors and individuals:

Angus Fraser
Victor Friedman
Reimar Gilsenbach (in particular his *Chronology*)
Milena Hübschmannová
Valdemar Kalinin
Jean-Pierre Liégeois
Elena Marushiakova and Veselin Popov
Pavee Point
Gheorghe Sarau
Diana Tong's *Bibliography*
Etudes Tsiganes
European Race Audit
Folk Roots Magazine
Interface
Journal of the Gypsy Lore Society
Lacio Drom
Romano Centro
Romnet
Rough Guide to World Music
Tocher

The final form of the entries remains the responsibility of the authors.

Notes on Spelling and Terminology

For typographical reasons, Romani words cited are spelled in accordance with general international usage, not in the standard alphabet adopted by the fourth World Romany Congress for writing the language.

č = *ch*	pronounced as in *church*	
š = *sh*	as in *ship*	
ž = *zh*	as in *leisure*	
x	as in *loch* or German *doch*	

rr is a guttural or retroflex *r* (as opposed to trilled or flapped *r*), depending on the dialect.

It has regrettably not been possible to reproduce in one font all the accents used in all the languages of Europe. *Gypsy* and *Traveller* have been capitalized and spelled thus except in citations and book titles. This volume uses the term *Romani* for the Gypsy language and *Romany* for the people. *Gypsy* and *Romany* are used as synonyms throughout the text.

The definition of who is a Gypsy varies. This dictionary includes as Gypsies those who are accepted as such by the community or who proclaim themselves to be Gypsies. A number of non-Gypsies whose life or works are relevant to Gypsy history have been included in the dictionary. They are identified by their nationality. For Gypsies the country of birth or residence is given. Dates of birth and death are not given for non-Gypsies. Where this information could be found, it is included for Gypsies.

Compare a specimen entry for a Gypsy:

Smith, Adam (1929–   ). A musician from England. He has toured widely and made many recordings.

and that for a non-Gypsy:

Smith, George. A contemporary English musician who has used Gypsy melodies in his compositions.

Cross-references in the text are in bold type. Names of countries, *Gypsy*, *Romani* and *Romany* are, however, never printed in bold.

Abbreviations and Acronyms

ACERT	Advisory Committee for the Education of Romanies and other Travellers
AN	Allianza Nazionale (Italy)
ARSS	Council of Romanies in Slovakia
CDCC	Council for Cultural Co-operation
CDMG	European Committee on Migration
CMERI	Centre Missionaire Evangelique Rom Internationale
CIR	Comité International Rom
CIR	Commonwealth of Independent Republics
CIT	Comité International Tzigane
CJPO	Criminal Justice and Public Order Act
CLRAE	Congress of Local and Regional Authorities of Europe
CPRSI	Contact Point on Roma and Sinti Issues
CRT	Centre de Recherches Tsiganes
CSCE	Conference on Security and Co-operation in Europe
GLS	Gypsy Lore Society
hCa	Helsinki Citizens Assembly
IRU	International Romany Union
JGLS	Journal of the Gypsy Lore Society
Kolkhoz	*Kollektivnoe khozyaistvo.* (collective farm).
MBE	Medal of the British Empire
MG-S-ROM	Specialist Group on Roma/Gypsies of the Council of Europe
MP	Member of Parliament
MRG	Minority rights group
MSZMP	A political party in Hungary
NATT	National Association of Teachers of Travellers
ECOSOC	Economic and Social Council (of the United Nations)
ODIHR	Office for Democratic and Human Rights
OSCE	Organization for Security and Cooperation in Europe
PER	Project on Ethnic Relations
PSERM	Party for the Complete Emancipation of Romanies in Macedonia
ROI	Romany Civic Initiative
SR	Slovak Republic

SS	*Schutzstaffel* (Storm Troopers).
STAG	Scottish Travellers Action Group
STAG	Southwark Travellers Action Group
T-LAST	Telephone Legal Advice Service for Travellers
UK	United Kingdom
UNESCO	United Nations Economic and Social Organization
UNICEF	United Nations Children's Fund
UN	United Nations
URPSDR	Union of Roma Political Parties in the Slovak Republic
USSR	Union of Soviet Socialist Republics
WRC	World Romany Congress
WRU	World Romany Union

Chronology of Gypsy History

224–241	Persia. In the reign of Shah Ardashir, Gypsies first come from India to work.
420–438	Persia. Bahram Gur, shah of Persia, brings Gypsy musicians from India.
661	Arab Empire. Indians (*Zott*) brought from India to Mesopotamia.
669/670	Arab Empire. Caliph Muawiya deports Gypsies from Basra to Antioch on the Mediterranean coast.
ca.710	Arab Empire. Caliph Walid resettles Zott from Mesopotamia to Antioch.
720	Arab Empire. Caliph Yazid II sends still more Zott to Antioch.
820	Arab Empire. Independent Zott state established in Mesopotamia.
834	Arab Empire. Zott defeated by Arabs and many of them resettled in border town of Ainzarba.
855	Arab Empire. Battle of Ainzarba: Greeks defeat the Arabs and take Zott soldiers and their families as prisoners to Byzantium.
ca.1050	Byzantium. Acrobats and animal doctors (called *athingani*) in Constantinople.
1192	India. Battle of Terain. Last Gypsies leave for the west.
1290	Greece. Gypsy shoemakers on Mount Athos.
1322	Crete. Nomads reported on the island.
1347	Byzantium. Black Death reaches Constantinople. Gypsies move west again.
1348	Serbia. Gypsies in Prizren.
1362	Croatia. Gypsies in Dubrovnik.
1373	Corfu. Gypsies reported on the island.
1378	Bulgaria. Gypsies living in villages near Rila Monastery.
1384	Greece. Gypsy shoemakers in Modon.

1385	Romania. First recorded transaction of Gypsy slaves.
1399	Bohemia. The first Gypsy is mentioned in a chronicle.
1407	Germany. Gypsies visit Hildesheim.
1416	Germany. Gypsies expelled from Meissen region.
1417	Holy Roman Empire. King Sigismund issues a safe conduct to Gypsies at Lindau.
1418	France. First Gypsies reported, in Colmar.
1418	Switzerland. First Gypsies arrive.
1419	Belgium. First Gypsies reported, in Antwerp.
1420	Holland. First Gypsies reported, in Deventer.
1422	Italy. Gypsies come to Bologna.
1423	Italy. Andrew, duke of Little Egypt, and his followers set off to visit Pope Martin V in Rome.
1423	Slovakia. Gypsies in Spiš.
1425	Spain. Gypsies in Zaragoza.
1447	Catalonia. First report of Gypsies.
1453	Turks capture Constantinople. Flight of some Gypsies westward.
1453	Slovenia. A Gypsy smith in the country.
1468	Cyprus. First report of Gypsies.
1471	Switzerland. Parliament meeting in Lucerne banishes Gypsies.
1472	Rhine Palatinate. Duke Friedrich asks his people to help the Gypsy pilgrims.
1485	Sicily. First reports of Gypsies.
1489	Hungary. Gypsy musicians play on Czepel island.
1492	Spain. First draft of the forthcoming law of 1499.
1493	Italy. Gypsies expelled from Milan.
1498	Germany (Holy Roman Empire). Expulsion of Gypsies ordered.
1499	Spain. Expulsion of the Gypsies ordered (Pragmatica of the Catholic Kings).
1500	Russia. First record of Gypsies.
1501	Belarus and Lithuania. Vasil appointed to be chief of Gypsies.
1504	France. Expulsion of Gypsies ordered.
1505	Denmark. Two groups of Gypsies enter the country.

1505	Scotland. Gypsy pilgrims arrive, probably from Spain.
1510	Switzerland. Death penalty introduced for Gypsies found in the country.
1512	Catalonia. Gypsies expelled.
1512	Sweden. First Gypsies arrive.
1514	England. First mention of a Gypsy in the country.
1515	Germany. Bavaria closes its borders to Gypsies.
1516	Portugal. Gypsies mentioned in literature.
1525	Portugal. Gypsies banned from Portugal.
1525	Sweden. Gypsies ordered to leave country.
1526	Holland. Transit of Gypsies across country banned.
1530	England and Wales. Expulsion of Gypsies ordered.
1534	Slovakia. Gypsies executed in Levoca.
1536	Denmark. Gypsies ordered to leave country.
1538	Portugal. Deportation of Gypsies to colonies begins.
1539	Spain. Any males found nomadizing to be sent to galleys.
1540	Scotland. Gypsies allowed to live under own laws.
1541	Czech lands. Gypsies accused of starting a fire in Prague.
1544	England. Gypsies deported to Norway.
1547	England. Boorde publishes specimens of Romani.
1549	Bohemia. Gypsies declared outlaws and to be expelled.
1553	Estonia. First Gypsies in the country.
1554	England. The death penalty is imposed for any Gypsies not leaving the country within a month.
1557	Poland and Lithuania. Expulsion of Gypsies ordered.
1559	Finland. Gypsies on the island of Åland.
1562	England. Provisions of previous acts widened to include people who live and travel like Gypsies.
1563	Italy. Council of Trent affirms that Gypsies cannot be priests.

1564	Lithuania. Nomadic Gypsies to be expelled.
1569	Lithuania and Poland. Nomadic Gypsies to be expelled.
1573	Scotland. Gypsies to either settle down or leave the country.
1574	Ottoman Empire. Selim II legislates for Gypsy miners in Bosnia.
1579	Portugal. Wearing of Gypsy dress banned.
1579	Wales. First record of Gypsies.
1580	Finland. First Gypsies on the mainland.
1584	Denmark and Norway. Expulsion of Gypsies ordered.
1586	Belarus. Nomadic Gypsies expelled.
1589	Denmark. Death penalty imposed for Gypsies not leaving the country.
1595	Romania. Stefan Razvan, the son of a slave, becomes ruler of Moldavia.
1611	Scotland. Three Gypsies hanged (under 1554 law).
1633	Spain. Pragmatica of Felipe IV. Expulsion.
1637	Sweden. Death penalty for Gypsies not leaving the country.
1692	Austria. Gypsies in Villach.
1714	Scotland. Two female Gypsies executed.
1715	Scotland. Ten Gypsies deported to Virginia.
1728	Holland. Last Gypsy hunt.
ca.1730	Wales. Arrival of Abraham Wood, founder of the Wood clan.
1746	Spain. Gypsies to live in named towns.
1748	Sweden. Foreign Gypsies expelled.
1749	Spain. Round-up and imprisonment of all Gypsies ordered.
1758	Austro-Hungarian Empire. Maria Theresa begins assimilation program.
1759	Russia. Gypsies banned from Saint Petersburg.
1763	Holland. Pastor Valyi is the first to discover the Indian origin of Romani.
1765	Austro-Hungarian Empire. Joseph II continues assimilation program.
1776	Austria. First published article on the Indian origin of the Romani language.
1782	Hungary. Two hundred Gypsies charged with cannibalism.

1783	Germany. Heinrich Grellmann publishes the first academic work establishing the Indian origin of the Romani people.
1783	Russia. Settlement of nomads encouraged.
1783	Spain. Gypsy language and dress banned.
1783	United Kingdom. Most legislation against Gypsies repealed.
1791	Poland. Settlement Law.
1802	France. Gypsies in Basque province rounded up and imprisoned.
1812	Finland. Order to confine nomadic Gypsies in workhouses.
1822	United Kingdom. Gypsies camping on the roadside will be fined.
1830	Germany. Authorities in Nordhausen remove children from their families for fostering with non-Gypsies.
1835	Denmark. Hunt for Travellers in Jutland.
1835	United Kingdom. Highways Act strengthens the provisions of the 1822 Turnpike Act.
1837	Spain. George Borrow translates St. Luke's gospel into Romani.
1848	Transylvania. Emancipation of serfs (including Gypsies).
1849	Denmark. Gypsies allowed into the country again.
1855	Romania. Emancipation of Gypsy slaves in Moldavia.
1856	Romania. Emancipation of Gypsy slaves in Wallachia.
1860	Sweden. Immigration restrictions eased.
1865	Scotland. Trespass (Scotland) Act.
1868	Holland. New immigration of Gypsies.
1872	Belgium. Foreign Gypsies expelled.
1874	Ottoman Empire. Muslim Gypsies given equal rights with other Muslims.
1875	Denmark. Gypsies barred from the country once more.
1884	Sweden. Sonya Kavalevsky appointed professor of mathematics at Stockholm University.
1879	Hungary. National conference of Gypsies in Kisfalu.
1879	Serbia. Nomadism banned.
1886	Bulgaria. Nomadism forbidden.

1886	Germany. Bismarck recommends expulsion of foreign Gypsies.
1888	United Kingdom. Gypsy Lore Society established.
1899	Germany. Police Gypsy Information Service set up in Munich by Alfred Dillmann.
1904	Germany. Prussian Parliament unanimously adopts proposal to regulate Gypsy movement and work.
1905	Germany. A census of all Gypsies in Bavaria is taken.
1905	Germany. Dillmann publishes his *Zigeunerbuch*.
1906	Germany. The Prussian minister issues special instructions to the police to "combat the Gypsy nuisance."
1905	Bulgaria. Sofia conference, demanding voting rights for Gypsies.
1906	France. Identity card introduced for nomads.
1906	Finland. Mission to the Gypsies set up.
1907	Germany. Many Gypsies leave for other countries in western Europe.
1914	Norway. Some 30 Gypsies are given Norwegian nationality.
1914	Sweden. Deportation Act also makes immigration of Gypsies difficult.
1918	Holland. Caravan and House Boat Law introduces controls.
1919	Bulgaria. Istiqbal organization founded.
1923	Bulgaria. Journal *Istikbal* (Future) starts publication.
1922	Germany. In Baden all Gypsies are to be photographed and fingerprinted.
1924	Slovakia. A group of Gypsies tried for cannibalism. They are found to be innocent.
1925	USSR. All-Russian Union of Gypsies established.
1926	Germany. Bavarian state parliament brings in a new law "to combat Gypsy nomads and idlers."
1926	Switzerland. Pro Juventute starts a program of forced removal of Gypsy children from their families for fostering.

1926	USSR. First moves to settle nomadic Gypsies.
1927	Germany. Legislation requiring the photographing and fingerprinting of Gypsies instituted in Prussia.
1927	Germany. Bavaria institutes laws forbidding Gypsies to travel in large groups or to own firearms.
1927	Norway. The Aliens Act bars foreign Gypsies from the country.
1927	Russia. Journal *Romani Zorya* (*Romany Dawn*) founded.
1928	Germany. Nomadic Gypsies in Germany are to be placed under permanent police surveillance.
1928	Germany. Professor Hans F. Günther writes that it was the Gypsies who introduced foreign blood into Europe.
1928	Slovakia. Pogrom in Pobedim.
1929	USSR. Nikolai Pankov's Romani book *Buti I Džinaiben* (*Work and Knowledge*) published.
1929	USSR. Journal *Romani Zorya* (*Romany Dawn*) starts publication.
1930	Norway. A Norwegian doctor recommends that all Travellers be sterilized.
1930	USSR. The first issue of the journal *Nevo Drom* (*New Way*) appears.
1931	USSR. Teatr Romen opens in Moscow.
1933	Austria. Officials in Burgenland call for the withdrawal of all civil rights for Gypsies.
1933	Bulgaria. Journal *Terbie* (*Education*) starts publication.
1933	Germany. The National Socialist Party comes to power. Measures against Jews and Gypsies begin.
1933	Germany. Gypsy musicians barred from State Cultural Chamber.
1933	Germany. Sinto boxer Johann Trollmann was stripped of his title as light-heavyweight champion for "racial reasons."
1933	Germany. Act for the Prevention of Hereditarily Ill Offspring, known as the Sterilization Act.

1933	Germany. "Beggars' Week," many Gypsies arrested.
1933	Latvia. St. John's Gospel translated into Romani.
1933	Romania. General Association of the Gypsies of Romania founded. National conference held.
1933	Romania. Journals *Neamul Ţiganesc* (*Gypsy Nation*) and *Timpul* (*The Time*) founded.
1933	USSR. Teatr Romen performs the opera *Carmen.*
1934	Germany. Gypsies who cannot prove German nationality expelled.
1934	Romania. Bucharest "international" Congress.
1935	Germany. Marriages between Gypsies and Germans banned.
1935	Yugoslavia. Journal *Romano Lil* published.
1936	Germany. The right to vote removed from Gypsies.
June 1936	Germany. Opening of internment camp at Marzahn.
1936	Germany. General Decree for Fighting the Gypsy Menace.
1936	Germany. Racial Hygiene and Population Biological Research Unit of the Health Office begins its work.
1936	Germany. The minister of war orders that Gypsies should not be called up for active military service.
1937	Poland. Janusz Kwiek elected king of the Gypsies.
April 1938	Germany. Decree on the Preventative Fight against Crime. All Gypsies classed as antisocial.
April 1938	Germany. Many Gypsies arrested to be forced labor for the building of concentration camps.
June 1938	Germany. Second wave of arrests to provide labor to build the camps.
Autumn 1938	Germany. Racial Hygiene Research Center begins to set up an archive of Gypsy tribes.
October 1938	Germany. National Center for Fighting the Gypsy Menace established.

December 1938	Germany. Order for the "Fight against the Gypsy Menace."
1938	USSR. Joseph Stalin bans Romani language and culture.
September 1939	Germany. Deportation of 30,000 Gypsies planned.
October 1939	Germany. Settlement Decree. Gypsies cannot travel.
October 1939	Poland. Special identity cards for Gypsies.
November 1939	Germany. Gypsy fortune-tellers arrested and sent to Ravensbrück concentration camp.
November 1939	(German occupied) Czech lands. Nomadism forbidden.
April 1940	France. French government opens internment camps for nomads.
April 1940	Germany. Heinrich Himmler orders the resettlement of Gypsies in the General Government of Poland.
August 1940	Austria. Internment camp built at Maxglan, Salzburg.
August 1940	Czech lands. Labor camps set up in Lety and Hodonín.
October 1940	Austria. Order for the internment of the Gypsies in Burgenland.
November 1940	Austria. Internment camp for Gypsies is set up in Lackenbach.
1941	Croatia. Jasenovac concentration camp opened.
March 1941	Germany. Exclusion of Gypsy children from school begins.
April 1941	Slovakia. Decree on the Organization of the Living Conditions of the Gypsies. They are to be separated from the majority population.
May 1941	Serbia. German military commander's order states that Gypsies will be treated as Jews.
June 1941	USSR. SS Task Forces move into the occupied areas of the Soviet Union and systematically kill Jews and Romanies.
July 1941	Germany. Reinhard Heydrich, SS Chief Himmler's deputy, brings the Gypsies into the plans for a Final Solution to the "Jewish problem."
August 1941	USSR. All the Sinti Gypsy families who lived

	in the Volga Republic are deported to Kazakhstan.
September 1941	USSR. SS Task Forces carry out mass executions of Jews and Romanies in the Baby Yar valley.
October 1941	Yugoslavia. German army executes 2,100 Jewish and Gypsy hostages (as reprisal for soldiers killed by partisans).
October 1941	Czech lands. Decision that Gypsies from the so-called Protectorate are to be sent to a concentration camp.
November 1941	Serbia. German military command orders the immediate arrest of all Jews and Gypsies, to be held as hostages.
October 1941	Poland. A Gypsy camp is set up in the Jewish ghetto of Lodz for 5,000 inmates.
December 1941	USSR. Task Force C murders 824 Gypsies in Simferopol.
December 1941	Latvia. All 101 Gypsies in the town of Libau are executed.
December 1941	Baltic States. State Governor Hinrich Lohse orders that Gypsies should be given the same treatment as Jews.
January 1942	Poland. All Sinti and Romanies from the Lodz ghetto are transported and gassed at Chelmno.
March 1942	Germany. A special additional income tax is levied on Gypsies.
April 1942	Poland. Romanies are brought into the Warsaw ghetto and kept in the prison in Gesia street.
May 1942	Croatia. The government and the Ustasha issue the order to arrest all Gypsies and deport them to the extermination camp in Jasenovac.
May 1942	Poland. All Gypsies in the Warsaw district are to be interned in Jewish ghettoes.
Spring/Summer 1942	Romania. Some 20,000 Romanies are deported to Transdnistria.
July 1942	Poland. Several hundred Polish Romanies killed at Treblinka extermination camp.
July 1942	Germany. A decree of the general staff of the army orders that Gypsies are not to be taken for active military service.

August 1942	Czech lands. 6,500 Gypsies registered by the police on one day.
1942	Bulgaria. Compulsory labor for Gypsies introduced.
August 1942	Serbia. Harald Turner, head of the German military administration, announces that "the Gypsy question has been fully solved."
September 1942	Germany. Himmler and Justice Minister Otto Thierack agree to transfer any Gypsies in prison to concentration camps.
December 1942	Germany. Himmler issues the order to deport the Gypsies in Greater Germany to the concentration camp of Auschwitz-Birkenau.
January 1943	Poland. Gypsies from Warsaw ghetto transferred to the extermination camp at Treblinka.
February 1943	Poland. First transports of Sinti and Romanies from Germany are delivered to the new Gypsy Section in Auschwitz-Birkenau.
March 1943	Poland. In Auschwitz the SS gas some 1,700 men, women and children.
May 1943	Poland. In Auschwitz the SS gas some 1,030 men, women and children.
May 1943	Poland. SS Major Dr. Josef Mengele is transferred at his own request to Auschwitz-Birkenau concentration camp.
July 1943	Poland. Himmler visits the Gypsy Section in Auschwitz and orders the Gypsies to be killed.
September 1943	Germany. Several hundred Gypsy prisoners start work on the production of the V1 and V2 weapons in underground workshops in the Kohnstein Hills.
November 1943	USSR. Minister for the Occupied Eastern Territories orders that all nomadic Gypsies in the territories be treated as Jews.
January 1944	Belgium. A transport of 351 Romanies and Sinti from Belgium is despatched to the Auschwitz-Birkenau concentration camp.
May 1944	Holland. A transport of 245 Romanies and Sinti is sent to Auschwitz concentration camp.
August 2, 1944	Poland. 1,400 Gypsy prisoners are sent from Auschwitz to Buchenwald concentration

	camp. The remaining 2,900 Gypsies are killed in the gas chamber.
Autumn 1944	Slovakia. Romanies join the fight of partisans in the Slovak National Uprising.
January 27, 1945	Auschwitz. At 3:00 P.M. the first Soviet soldiers reach the main camp and find one Romany among the survivors.
May 1945	World War II ends in Europe. All surviving Gypsies freed from camps.
1945	Bulgaria. Gypsy Organization for the Fight against Fascism and Racism set up.
1945	Germany. Nuremburg Trials of Nazi leaders begin. Crimes against Gypsies are included in the charges.
1946	France. Matéo Maximoff's novel *The Ursitory* published.
1946	Poland. Roma Ensemble founded.
1947	Bulgaria. Teatr Roma established in Sofia.
1951	Bulgaria. Teatr Roma in Sofia closed.
1952	France. The Pentecostal movement among Gypsies starts.
1953	Denmark. Gypsies readmitted to the country.
1958	Bulgaria. Nomadism banned.
1958	Czechoslovakia. Nomadism banned.
1958	Hungary. Gypsy organization established.
1960	England and Wales. Caravan Sites Act reduces provision of caravan sites.
1960	France. Communauté Mondiale Gitane established.
1962	German Federal Republic. Courts rule that Gypsies were persecuted for racial reasons.
1962	Norway. Government Gypsy Committee set up.
1963	Ireland. Report of the Commission on Itinerancy published.
1963	Italy. Opera Nomadi education scheme set up.
1963	Yugoslavia. Gypsies move to Shuto Orizari after Skopje earthquake.
1964	Ireland. Itinerant Action Group set up.
1965	France, Communauté Mondiale Gitane banned. Comité International Tzigane set up.
1965	Italy. Pope Paul VI addresses some 2,000 Gypsies at Pomezia.

1966	Britain. Gypsy Council set up.
1967	Finland. Gypsy Association established.
1968	Council of Europe. Rudolf Karway leads Zigeunermission deputation to the Human Rights Commission in Strasbourg.
1968	England and Wales. Caravan Sites Act. Councils to build sites.
1968	Holland. All districts must build caravan sites.
1969	Bulgaria. Segregated schools are set up for Gypsies.
1969	Council of Europe. Assembly passes a positive resolution on Gypsies.
1969	Yugoslavia. Macedonia. Abdi Faik elected as MP for Parliament.
1970	Norway. Report published on proposed work with the Gypsies.
1970	United Kingdom. National Gypsy Education Council established.
1971	England. First World Romany Congress held near London.
1971	Scotland. Advisory Committee on the Travelling People starts work.
1972	Czechoslovakia. Sterilization program for Gypsies begins.
1972	England. Romany Guild founded.
1972	France. Band known as Los Reyes (later Gypsy Kings) is founded.
1972	Sweden. Stockholm's Finska Zigenarförening founded.
1973	German Federal Republic. Three Gypsies shot by farmer in Pfaffenhofen.
1973	Scandinavia. Nordiska Zigenarrådet to link organizations.
1973	Yugoslavia. Macedonia. Radio broadcasts in Romani start from Tetovo.
1975	Council of Europe. Committee of Ministers passes a positive resolution on nomads.
1975	Hungary. The first issues of the magazine *Rom som* (*I am a Romany*) appear.
1977	England and Wales. Cripps Report on Gypsies published.
1977	Holland. Legalization of 500 "illegal" Gypsy immigrants.

1977	United Nations. Subcommission resolution on protection of Gypsies.
1978	Switzerland. Second World Romany Congress in Geneva.
1979	Hungary. National Gypsy Council formed.
1979	Hungary. First national exhibition of self-taught Gypsy artists.
1979	Norway. ABC Romani primer produced for mother tongue teaching.
1979	Romania. Underground publication of St. John's Gospel in Romani.
1979	United Nations. Romany Union recognized by ECOSOC.
1980	Yugoslavia. Romani Grammar in Romani published in Skopje.
1981	Council of Europe. CLRAE resolution on helping nomads.
1981	German Federal Republic. Third World Romany Congress in Göttingen.
1981	Poland. Pogrom in Oswiecim.
1981	Yugoslavia. Gypsies granted national status on an equal footing with other minorities.
1982	France. New Mitterand government promises to help nomads.
1983	Council of Europe. Council of Ministers passes a resolution on stateless nomads.
1983	England. First national Pentecostal convention.
1983	Italy. Gypsy caravans removed from Rome at the start of the Annus Sanctus.
1983	Northern Ireland. Belfast Traveller Education Development Group established.
1983	Yugoslavia. Romani teaching begins in one school in Kosovo.
1984	European Parliament passes a resolution on aiding Gypsies.
1984	India. Chandigarh Festival.
1985	England. Bradford's attempts to make it illegal for nomadic Gypsies to come within city limits overthrown by the courts.
1985	France. First International Exhibition (Mondiale) of Gypsy Art in Paris.
1985	Ireland. Report of the Travelling People Review Body published.

1985	Sweden. Attack on Gypsy family in Kumla with stones and a firebomb.
1986	France. International Gypsy conference in Paris.
1986	Spain. Gypsy houses set on fire in Martos.
1986	Yugoslavia. International Romany seminar in Sarajevo.
1988	Hungary. Organization Phralipe founded.
1989	European Community Council. Resolution on promoting school provision for Gypsy and Traveller children.
1989	Germany. Government intitiates the deportation of several thousand foreign Gypsies from the country.
1989	Germany. Gypsies demonstrate in the ex-concentration camp at Neuengamme against the deportation of asylum seekers.
1989	Hungary. Roma Parliament set up.
1989	Poland. First Romane Divesa Festival.
1989	Romania. Border guards shoot party of Gypsies.
1989	Spain. Gypsy houses attacked in Andalusia.
1990	Macedonia. Egyptians Association set up.
1990	Poland. Permanent exhibition on Romanies opens in Tarnow.
1990	Poland. Fourth World Romany Congress held near Warsaw.
1990	Poland. Standard alphabet for Romani adopted by World Romany Congress.
1990	Poland. Journal *Rrom p-o Drom* (*Romanies on the Road*) founded.
1990	Romania. Miners attack Romany quarter in Bucharest.
1990	Yugoslavia. Kosovo. An Egyptian Association formed.
1991	Czech Republic. Romani teaching starts at Prague University.
1991	Italy. Ostia international conference.
1991	Macedonia. Romanies have equal rights in new republic.
1991	Poland. Pogrom in Mlawa.
1991	Slovakia. Government gives Romanies nationality status and equal rights.

1991	Ukraine. Police attack on settlement of Velikie Beryezni.
1992	Hungary. Arson attack on Gypsies in Kétegyháza.
1992	Poland. Attack on remaining Gypsies in Oswiecim.
1992	Slovakia. Romathan Theater established in Kosice.
1992	Ukraine. Mob atacks Gypsy houses in Tatarbunary.
1992	United Nations. Commission on Human Rights passes resolution on protection of Gypsies. Gypsies recognized as an ethnic group
1993	Bulgaria. A crowd of Bulgarians attacks the Gypsy quarter in Malorad, killing one Romany man.
1993	Council of Europe. CLRAE Resolution on Gypsies.
1993	Council of Europe Assembly. Resolution on Gypsies.
1993	Czech Republic. Tibor Danihel drowns running away from skinhead gang.
1993	Czech Republic. Seven Romanies deported from Uští nad Labem to Slovakia.
1993	Hungary. International Conference in Budapest.
1993	Macedonia. Official introduction of Romani language in schools.
1993	Romania. Three Gypsies killed in pogrom in Hadareni.
1993	Scotland. Scottish Gypsy/Traveller Association set up.
1993	Slovakia. Cyril Dunka beaten up by police after a parking incident.
1993	United Nations. Romany Union upgraded to Category II consultative status.
1994	Britain. Criminal Justice Act. Nomadism criminalized.
1994	Hungary. Budapest OSCE meeting sets up Contact Point for Roma and Sinti Issues, to be based initially in Warsaw.
1994	Hungary. Gypsies vote for their local Romany councils.

1994	Poland. ODIHR organizes Warsaw seminar on Romanies.
1994	Poland. Gypsy boy beaten up and houses inhabited by Romanies attacked in Debica.
1994	Spain. European Congress in Seville
1994	France. At a meeting in Strasbourg, the Standing Conference of Romany Associations is formed.
1995	Austria. Four Gypsies killed by a bomb in Oberwart, Burgenland.
1995	Bulgaria. One Gypsy died following an arson attack on a block of flats in Sofia.
1995	Bulgaria. Angel Angelov shot by police in Nova Zagora.
1995	Czech Republic. Tibor Berki killed by skinheads in Zdár nad Sázavou.
1995	France. Council of Europe in Strasbourg sets up specialist advice group on Romanies.
1995	Hungary. Second International Exhibition (Mondiale) of Gypsy Art.
1995	Hungary. Romany Union organizes "Sarajevo" Peace Conference in Budapest.
1995	Hungary. Gypsies attacked and injured in Kalocsa.
1995	Poland. Gypsy couple murdered in Pabianice.
1995	Poland. Grota Bridge settlement of Romanian Gypsies in Warsaw dispersed by police. Residents deported across the border to Ukraine.
1995	Slovakia. Mario Goral burnt to death by skinheads in Žiar nad Hronom.
1995	Slovakia. Union of Romany Political Parties formed.
1995	Turkey. Zehala Baysal died in police custody in Istanbul.
1996	Albania. Fatmir Haxhiu dies of burns after a racist attack.
1996	Austria. Nicola Jevremović and his wife beaten by police after a traffic incident.
1996	Bulgaria. Kuncho Anguelov and Kiril Perkov, deserters from the army, shot and killed by military police.
1996	Bulgaria. Three Romanies beaten up by skinheads in Samokov.

1996	Bulgaria. Petra Stoyanova shot dead by police in Rakovski.
1996	Czech Republic. Romany children banned from using swimming pool in Kladno.
1996	European Court of Human Rights. The Court rejects the appeal by Mrs. Buckley against the refusal of planning permission in England for her caravan.
1996	France. Second Meeting of the Standing Committee of Gypsy Organizations and first meeting of the Committee of Experts of the Council of Europe in Strasbourg.
1996	Greece. Police raid on camp in Attica.
1996	Greece. Police officer shoots Anastasios Mouratis in Boetia.
1996	Hungary. European Roma Rights Center set up in Budapest.
1996	Ireland. National Strategy on Traveller Accommodation proposed.
1996	Poland. Houses occupied by Romanies attacked in Wiebodzice.
1996	Romania. Twenty-one Romany houses burned down in Curtea de Arges.
1996	Romania. Mircea-Muresul Mosor shot and killed by the chief of police in Valcele.
1996	Serbia. Attack on Gypsies in Kraljevo.
1996	Slovakia. An 18-year old Romany youth was beaten to death by skinheads in Poprad.
1996	Slovakia. Jozef Miklos died when his house was set on fire in Zalistie.
1996	Spain. Romany Union's second "Sarajevo" Peace Conference, in Vittoria.
1996	Turkey. Five thousand evicted from Selamsiz quarter of Istanbul.
1996	Ukraine. Mrs. H. raped by police in Mukacevo.
1996	Ukraine. Two brothers shot by police in Velikie Beryezni.
Jan. 1997	Austria. Mr. and Mrs. Jevremovic given suspended prison sentences for "resisting arrest" (see 1996).
Jan. 1997	Hungary. Fine increased on appeal for the owner of an inn in Pecs who had discriminated against Romanies.

Jan. 1997	Hungary. Symposium on the Legal Defense of the Rights of Romanies held in Budapest.
Jan. 1997	Romania. Mob attacks Gypsy houses in Tanganu village.
Jan. 1997	Turkey. Mob attack Gypsies in Sulukule district of Istanbul.
Jan. 1997	Ukraine. Gypsies beaten by police in four separate incidents in Uzhorod.
Feb 1997	Bulgaria. Killing of three Gypsies by police reported. Police attack the Gypsy quarter in Pazardjik.
Feb. 1997	Czech Republic. Appeals court in Pilsen quashes acquittal of inn owner Ivo Blahout on a charge of discrimination.
Feb. 1997	Hungary. Gypsies beaten up in police station in Szombathely and in a police car in Mandatany in a separate incident.
March 1997	France. Jose Ménager and Manolito Meuche shot dead by police in Nantes.
March 1997	Germany. President Roman Herzog visits the Romany Holocaust Exhibition in Heidelberg.
March 1997	Czech Republic. Four skinheads sentenced to prison in connection with the death of Tibor Danihel (see 1993).
March 1997	Romania. Conference in Bucharest on the Prevention of Violence and Discrimination against Romanies in Europe.
April 1997	Greece. Eviction of 100 families from Ano Liosia. Partial resettlement in a guarded camp.
May 1997	Hungary. Fifth annual International Conference on Culture in Budapest.
June 1997	Poland. Romanies attacked in Wiebodzice.
June 27–28, 1997	Croatia. Seminar on Roma in Croatia today.
August 1997	Czech Republic. Several hundred Romanies fly to Canada to seek asylum.
	Czech Republic. Monument erected at Hodonin to concentration camp victims.
Oct. 23–24, 1997	Pardubice, Czech Republic. Final CLRAE Hearing on Provision for Roma in Municipalities.
Nov. 1, 1997	Bergen, Norway. Ian Hancock receives the Thorolf Rafto Prize on behalf of the Romany people.

Nov. 6–9, 1997	Barcelona, Spain. European Congress of Gypsy Youth.
Nov. 17–30, 1997	Bulgaria. International conference. Gypsy children and their education.
November 1997	Dover, United Kingdom. National Front demonstrate against asylum seekers from the Czech and Slovak Republics.

Introduction

Describing the early history of the Gypsies is like putting together a jigsaw puzzle, when some of the pieces are missing and parts of another puzzle have been put into the box. They suddenly appear in Europe speaking an Indian language, yet there is no trace of their passage across the Middle East. But their language is the key to the route of their travels as they borrowed words from the various peoples they met as they journeyed west.

The Gypsies or Romanies are, in fact, an ethnic group who arrived in Europe around the 14th century. Scholars argue about when and how they left India, but it is generally accepted that they did emigrate from Northern India sometime between the 6th and 11th centuries, then crossed the Middle East and came into Europe. Some stayed in the Middle East and are mentioned in the dictionary under the entry for Nawwar. Their language (closely related to European Romani) also belongs to the north Indian group, alongside Hindi and Punjabi.

The word *Gypsy* is an abbreviation of Egyptian, the name by which the Romany immigrants were first called in Western Europe because it was believed they came from Egypt. The French word *gitan* and Spanish *gitano* come from this etymology. The German word *Zigeuner* and Slav *tsigan* or *cigan* have a different etymology. They come from the Greek word *athinganos,* meaning a "heathen." This term was originally used of a heretical sect in Byzantium and, because the Gypsies who arrived in Europe were not Christians, they were given the name of this sect.

The Gypsies' name for themselves is "Rom" (with a plural "Roma" in most dialects). This is generally considered to be cognate with the Indian word *dom,* whose original meaning was "man." Even groups (such as the Sinti) who do not call themselves Rom still preserve this word in their dialect in the sense of "husband."

Over four million Gypsies or Romanies live in Europe, and they form a substantial minority in many countries. The vast majority have been settled for generations. Most still speak the Romani language. As the Gypsies are an ethnic group and not a class, individuals pursue various professions; some are rich and others poor. It is only in Western Europe that Gypsies are seen as a nomadic people and that the term Gypsy is loosely used for nomadic Travellers who are not of Indian origin.

History

The ancestors of the Gypsies of Europe began to leave India from A.D. sixth century onward. Some left voluntarily to serve the rich courts of the Persian and later Arab dynasties in the Middle East. Others were brought as captives. A third, smaller group, who were nomadic, found that their way back to India had been cut off by conflict and instead moved westward.

The first Gypsy migration into Europe during the 14th and 15th centuries included farmworkers, blacksmiths and mercenary soldiers, as well as musicians, fortune-tellers and entertainers. They were generally welcome at first as an interesting diversion in the dull everyday life of that period. Soon, however, they attracted the antagonism of the three powers of the time: the state, the church and the guilds. The civil authorities wanted everyone to settle legally at a permanent address, to have a fixed name, and to pay taxes. The church was worried about the heresy of fortune-telling, while the guilds did not like to see their prices undercut by these newcomers who worked at all hours of the day and night, with wives and children helping, trading from tents or carts.

Other factors also led to feelings of mistrust toward the newcomers. They were darkskinned, itself a negative feature in Europe, and they were suspected in some countries of being spies for the Turks because they, too, had come from the East. Some problems were also caused by small groups of Gypsies who claimed to be Christians fleeing from Muslim invaders from Turkey and who lived by begging.

It was not long before these feelings of antagonism and mistrust led to a reaction. As early as 1482 the assembly of the Holy Roman Empire passed laws to banish the Gypsies from its territory. Spain introduced similar legislation 10 years later, and other countries soon followed. The punishment for remaining was often death. This policy failed in most cases, as the countries to which they were deported often expelled them in turn. Only the Scandinavian countries and Holland managed to efface all visible trace of Gypsies for over two centuries. Most countries finally had to try a new policy—enforced integration or assimilation.

In Spain in 1499 and in Hungary in 1758, new laws required Gypsies to settle down or leave the country. They had to become land workers or be apprenticed to learn a craft. But they also had to be assimilated into the native population. Everywhere laws forbade Gypsies to wear their distinctive colorful clothes, to speak their language, to marry other Gypsies or to ply their traditional trades. As a result of these settlement policies, today large populations of settled Gypsies are in Spain and Hungary, while in Romania, Gypsy land workers and craftspeople were reduced to a status below that of serfs, to virtual slavery.

The latter part of the 19th century saw a new migration westward as

Romania released its Gypsies from bondage. Many thousands emigrated, some as far as America, Australia and South Africa. Well over a million Gypsies live in North and South America today, with the Kalderash clan forming the majority.

The nomadic Gypsies, however, have survived as a distinctive group until the present day. The reason for this was partly the inefficiency of local constabularies but also because the Gypsies developed as a fine art living on the border of two countries or districts and slipping over the border when the forces of law and order approached. Also, the nobility and large landowners throughout Europe protected the Gypsies. They encouraged seminomadic families to stay on their land and were able to employ the men as seasonal laborers. The women could serve in the house or sing and dance when guests came.

In the 19th and 20th centuries in Western Europe, Gypsies encountered problems finding stopping places. Camping on the side of the main roads was made difficult by laws such as the United Kingdom Highways Act of 1835. Large shantytown settlements developed on wasteland, but then the authorities stepped in and evicted the families. Such incidents occurred in England in the Epping Forest eviction of 1894. In this way many families who would have settled down were forced into nomadism.

Discriminatory laws (on language and dress) fell into abeyance, but laws against nomadism remained a threat, in both Western and Eastern Europe, to those Gypsies practicing traditional crafts. Studies from all over the world have shown that sedentary peoples have an inherent fear of the nomad, even when the latter performs useful services. The policy of banning nomadism without helping the nomads to settle proved a failure throughout Europe, and Gypsy nomadism continued unchecked until World War II.

The Holocaust

When the Nationalist Socialist Party came to power in Germany in 1933, the nomadic Gypsies were already subject to restrictions. But the Nazis regarded Gypsies as a race and made both nomads and sedentaries subject to the Nuremberg Laws of 1935. These forbade marriages between Gypsies and "Aryan" Germans. Adolf Hitler's Germany saw the Gypsies as no less a danger to the purity of the German race than the Jews and set about their isolation and eventually their destruction.

This policy of exclusion was a contrast to the assimilationist policies practiced in the past. Gypsies were not allowed to practice music as a profession, and boxers were similarly barred from competition. Next, Gypsy children were excluded from school. Camps were set up for nomads on the edge of towns. They were guarded, and the inmates were not allowed to practice their traditional trades but were put into labor gangs. Sedentary Gypsies were removed from their houses and placed in these internment camps.

In 1939 it was decided to send all the 30,000 Gypsies from Germany and Austria to Poland. In May 1940 the first steps in this program were taken, with the expulsion of over 3,000. The deportations were stopped largely because of a shortage of transport. In 1942 Heinrich Himmler (head of the SS) signed the so-called Auschwitz Decree, and in the following year some 10,000 German Gypsies were sent to Auschwitz. A sterilization campaign was undertaken both within and outside the camps. The slave labor of the Gypsies was needed, for example, in the underground factories where the V1 and V2 rockets were made, but they were not to be permitted to reproduce.

In the occupied countries of Eastern Europe, the Task Forces— *Einsatzgruppen*—massacred Gypsies in the woods outside the towns where they lived. Then extermination camps were opened, the four largest being Belzec, Chelmno, Sobibor and Treblinka. Gypsies were brought to these camps—often in their own caravans—and shot or gassed, alongside Jews. It is estimated that between a quarter and a half million Gypsies were killed during the Nazi period.

After 1945

In the first years following the end of the Nazi domination of Europe, the Gypsy community was in disarray. The small educational and cultural organizations that had existed before 1939 had been destroyed. The family structure was broken with the death of the older people—the guardians of the traditions. While in the camps, the Gypsies had been unable to keep up their customs—the *Romanía*—concerning the preparation of food and the washing of clothes. They solved the psychological problems this presented by not speaking about the time in the camps. Only a small number of Gypsies could read or write, so they could not tell their own story. But also they were unwilling to tell their stories to others, and few others were interested anyway. In the many books written describing the Nazi period and the persecution of the Jews, Gypsies usually appear as a footnote or small section.

It was hard for the Gypsies to come to terms with the Holocaust, for a persecution on this scale had never occurred before. There had been executions of smaller numbers, but nothing like this. A group of survivors in Munich began collecting evidence of the Gypsy genocide, but it was not until 20 years after the downfall of Hitler that Jewish writers such as Miriam Novitch, Ben Sijes and Sylvia Steinmetz made available to the public a documentation of the fate of the Gypsies under the Nazis. No global reparations were made, and not many individuals received restitution. Eventually those Gypsies who held German citizenship did receive compensation for their suffering.

In both Eastern and Western Europe, a return to nomadism was discouraged if not suppressed. After 1945 those Gypsies who tried to continue to nomadize met with opposition, though many Yugoslav Romanies came West as migrant workers. In Western Europe the supply of empty land for caravans has diminished. The increasing speed of motor traffic makes living on the side of the road, whether in a horse-drawn wagon or a truck-drawn caravan, too dangerous. Gypsies were largely seen as a social problem to be integrated into the wider community. A term often used was "resettlement," although most of the nomads concerned had never been settled. Pressure from central governments to set up camp sites was largely ignored by the local authorities, the Netherlands being an exception.

In the East they were one more minority likely to cause trouble to the monocultural states created by communism. Here, where some four million Gypsies lived under totalitarian rule, they were not allowed to form organizations, and their language was again suppressed. In most countries of Eastern Europe, the Gypsy population was very large (see the table in Appendix A), and policies were evolved to meet the challenge of this large, unassimilated minority. In the case of the Soviet Union, Stalin had decided that the Gypsies had no land base and therefore could not be a nation, and their status as a nationality was not recognized. Assimilated Gypsies were encouraged to change the "nationality" in their passports to that of the majority and answer the census questions, for example, as Serbs or Russians. The few activists were sent into internal exile or imprisoned, such as the parliamentarian Shakir Pashov in Bulgaria.

In Eastern Europe, too, the small numbers of nomads were forcibly prevented from traveling by laws and by measures such as shooting or confiscating their horses and removing the wheels from their caravans. Here and there, however, Gypsy national sentiment was still alive. In Czechoslovakia organizations were formed and began to demand their rights—a demand temporarily squashed after Soviet troops entered Prague in 1968.

In the West after the end of World War II, the communities were smaller in number and largely continued or returned to being nomadic. But it was in the West that the foundations of an international Gypsy organization could be formed. The real beginning was the committee known as the Comité International Tzigane, set up in Paris by Vanko Rouda. This body organized the first World Romany Congress, and since then, three further international congresses have been held. The fourth Congress in Warsaw in 1990—as the political changes in Eastern Europe began—saw the attendance for the first time of delegations or individuals from Romania, the Soviet Union and even Albania.

The idea of "Romanestan," a homeland for the Gypsies, emerged in Poland in the 1930s, clearly influenced by the Zionist movement. Since l945 this has not been seriously considered, though many intellectuals are fostering the link with the "Motherland" of India. Two festivals have been held in Chandigarh (Punjab) to which Gypsy intellectuals and musicians were invited from Europe. Some Gypsy writers have introduced Hindi and Sanskrit words into their poetry.

With the fall of the totalitarian regimes in Eastern Europe came a new freedom to form organizations. The new opportunities for travel both from and to Eastern Europe have enabled the holding of international Gypsy festivals such as those in Bratislava and Gorzow, in addition to formal conferences. Newspapers opened as fast as sidewalk cafes. The Gypsies, who had never completely forgotten how to trade privately, were the first to set up small businesses. Their ability to survive the changes better than their compatriots led to jealousy and an outbreak of anti-Gypsy violence. The road to capitalism was not as smooth as had been expected, and with no Jews to act as scapegoats, the population turned to the Gypsies as the reason for their real or imagined troubles.

Freedom has also meant freedom for right-wing racists to organize, and this movement was facilitated by a falling away of the control exercised by the police. As early as January 1990, a crowd of 700 Hungarians and Romanians attacked the Gypsy quarter in Turu Lung in Romania. Thirty-six of the 42 houses belonging to Romanies were set on fire and destroyed. Two similar incidents took place that year in Romania, resulting in the death of four Gypsies. In September 1990, skinheads attacked Romany houses in Eger and Miskolc in Hungary. The following year saw a pogrom in Mlawa, Poland, where nine houses were destroyed, and Bohemia (Czechoslovakia), where a Gypsy was killed during an attack by skinheads on a Romany club. Between January 1990 and August 1991, 88 attacks were reported against Gypsies in Eastern Europe during which 20 Romanies were killed. In Rostock in Germany, a refugee center inhabited by Romanies among others was burned down by right-wing rioters. These attacks have continued to the present day, and a selection is listed under each country entry and in the chronology.

In Hungary, Czechoslovakia, Romania and Macedonia, Gypsy political parties stood in the elections, and Gypsies were elected to Parliament by the votes of their own people. In Bulgaria "ethnic" parties are banned, while the surviving population in Poland is too small to have any political influence, though there are musical groups and cultural centers.

Many Romanies, particularly those from Poland and Romania, have sought asylum in the West, but very few have been granted refugee status. At the end of 1996, the German government announced plans to repatriate 30,000 Gypsies to Romania, from where they had fled to avoid racist attacks during which many houses had been burned. Less has been heard about an earlier repatriation program from Germany to the ex-Yugoslav republic of Macedonia.

The comparatively smaller Gypsy populations in most Western countries saw a revival of national feeling as they came into contact with the Romani-speaking communities of the East. These had retained their traditions, and under the new regimes found it easier to travel and to invite other Gypsies to their festivals and competitions. The Romani language has been revived by the influx of immigrant and refugee families, for whom it is still the dominant community language.

The European Communities, now called the European Union, and the Council of Europe began to take an interest in the Gypsies by inviting their organizations to send representatives to meetings and passed resolutions to work toward improving the living conditions of Gypsies. The overall effect was that Gypsy people have been recognized by cross-national bodies as a minority in their own right, and measures have been introduced, if not implemented, in most countries toward improving their situation.

The sedentary Gypsies of Eastern Europe have quite different needs from the nomadic Gypsies, who want secure stopping places. In spite of years of compulsory education, their children had not managed to acquire many new skills or paper qualifications. They were the first to go in the new capitalist climate in the East when factories began to shed surplus labor. They have found it the hardest to obtain new jobs because of discrimination.

It is noteworthy that the large Spanish Gypsy population has not felt any great desire to migrate—at least no farther than the south of France. Under Francisco Franco, they were treated as second-class citizens, and the end of official discrimination merely brought a new unofficial discrimination. The Spanish Gypsies, or *gitanos,* are still at the bottom of the ladder for housing and jobs. Their children are not easily accepted into schools. However, even the accession of Spain to the European Union has not caused any noticeable emigration of Gypsies from Spain.

In the West some young Gypsies are coming out of houses and taking to the caravan life again. In Eastern Europe the Romani language is beginning to be taught in schools, and intellectuals of Gypsy origin are refinding their roots and reaffirming their identity. Writers have been, pessimistically or optimistically, predicting the disappearance of the Gypsies each generation since they came to Europe at the beginning of this millennium, but they have survived as an ethnic group and will do so into the foreseeable future.

The Dictionary

A

ABDI, FAIK. A contemporary political activist and member of the Macedonian Parliament. He was born in Skopje. Faik attended the first **World Romany Congress** and later came to England to be part of a delegation that met Prime Minister Indira Gandhi of India during her visit to London. After Abdi's initial term as an MP, from 1969 to 1974, the Communist authorities deprived him of his passport for five years, to prevent his participation in international meetings.

ACKOVIĆ, DRAGOLJUB (1952–   ). A journalist and broadcaster. He was born in Serbia and studied at Belgrade University. From his youth, he took part in the drive for the advancement of the Gypsies and participated in international gatherings. He has published many articles and two books—one on the history of the Gypsies in Yugoslavia and the other on the Jasenovac concentration camp. He currently works as a journalist with Radio Belgrade and has been responsible for broadcasts in Romani. He is also president of the Romano Kulturako Klubi in Belgrade.

ACTON, THOMAS. A contemporary British sociologist and author who is professor of Romany studies at Greenwich University. He has been active in the Gypsy Council and National Gypsy Education Council.

ADAM, GEJZA. The president of the Únia Rómskej Obcănskej Iniciatívy (Romany Union Citizens Initiative) in Slovakia. He is currently a music teacher in Kosice.

ADJAM,TIKNO. A resistance fighter and poet. He was a mythical figure during World War II.

ADVISORY COMMITTEE FOR THE EDUCATION OF ROMANIES AND OTHER TRAVELLERS (ACERT). In 1988 the **National Gypsy Education Council** split, with some of the committee forming

ACERT. The committee has widened its mission from education to include planning for caravan sites.

ADVISORY COMMITTEE ON TRAVELLERS. Scotland. The committee was set up in 1971 to advise the secretary of state for **Scotland**, mainly on the provision of camping sites for Travellers. It has published a series of reports with recommendations.

ALBAICÍN, MARIA. The sister of **Rafael Albaicín**. She was a film star in Spain in the 1920s whose films included *La fuente magica, Los pianos mecanicos*, and *Cafe de Chinitas*.

ALBAICÍN, MIGUEL. A dancer in Spain and brother of **Rafael** and **Maria Albaicin**. Miguel appeared in the film *El Amor Brujo*, directed by Antonio Roman.

ALBAICÍN, RAFAEL. A 20th-century bullfighter in Spain. He appeared in several films including *La fiesta sigue, Maria Antonia* and *La Caramba*.

ALBANIA. Estimated Gypsy population: 95,000. The first Gypsies probably arrived in Albania during the 14th century. From 1468 to 1912, the country was part of the **Ottoman Empire**. Music and craftwork were common occupations of the Romanies in the area. Around 1920, an Albanian law stopped Gypsies from dancing in public for money. From 1934—the previous regulation having failed to stop the practice—dancers had to pay a special fee to license their performances. During World War II, the Italians who were mainly in control seem to have ignored the Gypsy population as did the postwar Communist government.

The fall of communism, as elsewhere in eastern Europe, led to the emergence of anti-Gypsy sentiments. Early in 1996 stories appeared in the Albanian press of Gypsies killing their children to sell their organs for transplants. These reports seem to have followed a court case where some Romanies in Durres were accused of selling their children for adoption. In July 1996 Fatir Haxhiu, a 15-year-old boy, died as a result of being burned during a racist attack.

The Gypsies of Albania are mainly Muslim and speak Balkan or **Vlah** dialects of Romani. A branch of the cultural association Romani Baxt (Romany Fortune) has been formed, and Albanians have taken part in the Romani **Summer Schools**.

ALPHABET. It seems probable that the Gypsies did not bring any writing system with them when they came to Europe. The alphabet given in Jean-Paul Clébert's book *The Gypsies* is spurious. Publications in Romani in the 20th century have used the Latin or Cyrillic alphabets. The first **World Romany Congress** recommended a broad phonetic alphabet based on Latin letters, and most literature produced since then has been in the Latin alphabet. At the fourth **World Romany Congress** in Warsaw in 1990, a writing system elaborated by the linguist **Marcel Cortiade** was adopted. Its purpose was to enable speakers of different dialects to use the same spelling system to represent different dialect pronunciations. The presidium of the International **Romani Union** approved the alphabet on April 7, 1990. Later a meeting of the Language Commission of the Union, meeting during the Helsinki **Summer School,** recommended that no change be made in the alphabet for a period of 10 years. It has been adopted in Holland and Romania for educational purposes and has been used in a number of publications.

The alphabet of the first World Romany Congress was as follows: a b č čh d e f g h ȟ i j k kh l m n o p ph r s š t th u v z ž

At the second congress *ȟ* was replaced by *x*.

The alphabet accepted at the fourth congress was as follows: a b č c ç ćh d e f g h i j k kh l m n o p ph r rr s š t th θ u v x z ž ʒ

The letters ç and θ are used morphophonemically, that is, they always represent the same grammatical form but are pronounced differently. So, in *raklesθe* (to the boy) and raklenθe (to the boys), θ is pronounced "t" in the former word and "d" in the latter.

The letters ćh and ʒ are pronounced differently according to the dialect. Most speakers of **Vlah** dialects would read them as /shy/ and /zhy/ (approximately the sound in English "treasure"), while speakers of Balkan dialects would read them as aspirated "tch" and (English) "j."

AMADOR, RAIMUNDO. A flamenco dancer in Spain.

AMAYA, CARMEN (1920–). A flamenco dancer. She was born in Granada but emigrated to America at the time of the Spanish Civil War. Her metallic, harsh voice and powerful dancing gained her success in the New York nightclub scene and a biography, *A Gypsy Dancer,* was published in 1942.

AMAYA, LORENZA FLORES. Using the stage name La Chunguita, a flamenco dancer in Spain from about 1965.

AMAYA, MICAELA. Using the stage name La Chunga, a popular flamenco dancer in Spain from about 1960 and the elder sister of **Lorenza Flores Amaya.**

AMAYA, PEPE. A flamenco dancer who took part in the Paris Exhibition of 1900.

AMENZA KETANE. A music group in Austria. Their latest cassette contains traditional Lovari songs together with more modern songs from the pen of Hojda and **Ceija Stojka**.

AMICO ROM. An international competition for Romany literature and the arts, founded in Italy in 1994.

ANDO DROM. A contemporary folk-rock band in Hungary.

ANTHEM. See NATIONAL ANTHEM.

ANTONIO. See SOLER, ANTONIO RUIZ.

APPLEBY FAIR. A horse fair in the north of England established by a royal charter (1685) that takes place from the second Wednesday in June. It is a popular meeting place for English Gypsies, including those still traveling in horse-drawn **caravans**.

ARLIA. See ERLIA.

ARMENIA. Estimated Gypsy population of the Armenian Republic: 10,000. The Romanies came into contact with Armenian speakers on their way from India to Europe as they passed through the Caucasus and what is now northeastern Turkey. Quite a number of Armenian words were borrowed by Romani at this time. Some Gypsies remained in Armenia and Turkey, and they are known as Bosha or Lom. They speak a variety of Armenian known as Lomavren.

ART. See PAINTING.

ARPAD, TONI. A contemporary **cimbalom** player in Hungary. He has played with Muszikas and other folk bands.

ARTEMIS. A database for Gypsy and Traveller education based in Preston, United Kingdom.

ASOCIACIÓN SECRETARIADO GENERAL GITANA. A Catholic-oriented organization operating from Madrid, Spain. It works for improvements in the educational and employment prospects for Gypsies. It publishes the bulletin *La Senda*, devoted to training and employment.

ASSOCIATION INTERNATIONALE DES ÉCRIVAINS TZIGANES. Founded 1964. This group is no longer active, but see ROMANI PEN ZENTRUM.

ASSOCIATION OF GYPSIES/ROMANI INTERNATIONAL. A nonprofit making association with the intention of giving glory to God, of preserving and maintaining the Gypsy race.

ASSOCIATION OF GYPSY ORGANIZATIONS. Formed by ex-members of the **Gypsy Council** in 1977, it linked a number of Gypsy and Gypsy support organizations. The Secretary was Roy Wells. It ceased activity around 1981.

AŠUNEN ROMALEN. (Listen, Romanies). A radio program broadcast from Belgrade (1981–1987).

ATHINGANI. A heretical Christian sect that lived in the Byzantine empire during the eighth and ninth centuries. When the Gypsies arrived from the East, they did not practice Christianity but were probably—if anything—still following Hinduism or Zoroastrianism. As a result, they were called *athingani* (heathens). This name has survived in the names given to the Gypsies in many countries, including *çingene* (Turkey), *tsigan* (most Slav countries), the German word *Zigeuner,* and French *tsigane.*

"ATKINS" REPORT. United Kingdom. The report on the working of the 1968 Caravan Sites Act prepared for the government in 1991 by a firm of private consultants W. S. Atkins Planning and Management Consultancy. The researchers were G. Clark and D. Todd. The report accepts that the 1968 **Caravan Sites Act** was intended to enable Gypsies to continue their traditional way of life while using official caravan sites, and criticizes local councils for not carrying out the provisions of the act (which has since been repealed). The report also accepted the idea of "designation" by which Gypsies were barred from certain areas of England and Wales.

AUSCHWITZ. A Nazi concentration camp in Poland. Auschwitz (Oświęcim) was opened in 1940, and Gypsies were among the first prisoners. Several transports of Czech Gypsies arrived in the camp in 1942. A satellite camp was opened nearby at Auschwitz-Birkenau, and in March 1943 a Gypsy Family Section was created within the wires of this camp. Between March 1943 and August 1944, over 20,000 Romanies were brought to the camp and held in poor conditions. The death rate from disease and malnutrition was high, especially among the children. In 1944 a number of internees were sent to other camps to work, and the remaining prisoners, some 2,800 women, children and elderly men, were gassed on the night of August 2–3, 1944. The memorial to the several million people killed in Auschwitz has an inscription in Romani.

In the town of Oświęcim itself, there was a small Gypsy population after 1945, but in 1981 local Poles organized a pogrom against them and most of them left the town.

AUSCHWITZ DECREE (*Auschwitz-Erlass*). In December 1942, Heinrich Himmler, head of the German police, issued an order that Gypsies from Germany and a number of other, mainly Western European countries should be sent to the new **Auschwitz**-Birkenau Camp. Certain categories of Gypsies were to be exempted—for example, those who had served in the German forces and those **Sinti** who were considered to be of pure Gypsy blood and capable of forming a small company of nomads that would be preserved as a form of living museum. When the instructions to the police were published early in 1943, these exemptions had mostly disappeared so that when it finally came to arrest the Gypsies and deport them to the concentration camp, no exceptions were made.

AUSTRIA. Estimated Gypsy population: 25,000. Gypsies probably first reached Austria in the 15th century. From 1758 **Maria Theresa** began a policy of settling nomads and assimilating them. She prohibited Gypsies from living in tents, wandering, dealing in horses, speaking in Romani and marrying other Gypsies. All of these decrees were ignored by the Gypsies, or "New Hungarians," as she wished them to be called. By 1938, however, the majority of the Gypsies were semisettled.

In 1924 a Gypsy primary school opened in Stegensbach (**Burgenland**) and seems to have operated successfully after a difficult start. No provision was made in the school program for classes in Romani, German being the only language used. But it did include special subjects like the violin and Gypsy history, also a subject entitled "Die Zigeuner als Landplage" (The Gypsies as a National Menace). The Nazis closed the school in 1938.

Austria was annexed to Hitler's Germany in 1938. The measures already operating against Gypsies in Germany were applied to Austria. Gypsies were fingerprinted and forbidden to leave the country. Sporadic arrests began in June 1938 of Romany men who were sent to Dachau concentration camp. In autumn 1939 several hundred women were arrested and sent to Ravensbrück camp. An internment camp was then set up at Salzburg (Maxglan) to hold Gypsies in readiness for a planned deportation to Poland that was not to happen in the event until much later. In November 1940 a forced labor camp was opened at Lackenbach. The families were permitted to live together, but conditions in many ways resembled a concentration camp. The highest total of inmates was 2,300 in November 1941. Many died in the early years from the poor conditions and were buried in the nearby Jewish cemetery. In 1941 transports containing 2,000 persons were sent from Lackenbach to the Jewish **Lodz ghetto**, mainly women and children. No one survived. A further 2,600 Gypsies were sent from Austria to **Auschwitz**, including many from the Salzburg camp, which was closed. One bright spot in this sad story was the action of Baron Rochunozy, who was determined that none of the families who worked for him should fall into the Nazis' hands. He helped them to escape across the frontier to Hungary and was later forced to flee himself. Toward the end of the war, conditions were improved in Lackenbach camp as the prisoners were put to work helping the German war effort, and many were able to survive. Two-thirds of the some 11,000 Austrian Romanies and **Sinti** are estimated to have perished during the Nazi period.

After 1945, those Gypsies who had been imprisoned in Lackenbach or Salzburg-Maxglan did not get any compensation until 1961. It was not until 1988 that they were put on the same basis as those who had been in the concentration camps of Auschwitz.

The small number of Romanies and Sinti surviving the **Holocaust** has been augmented by immigrants coming to work, in particular from Yugoslavia, and more recently by refugees from Eastern Europe. Considerable anti-Gypsy feeling persists among the Austrian population at large. This sentiment surfaced in 1995 when a sign appeared near the Romany settlement of Oberwart in Burgenland reading (in German) "Romanies back to India." When four Gypsies tried to remove it, a bomb blew up, killing all four. The Austrian playwright Elfrieda Jeleneck wrote a play on the subject but, because of the racist attacks on her, decided the play should have its performances in Hamburg and not in Vienna. So far no one has been charged with the bombing.

The first Gypsy organization, Verein Roma, was founded in 1989 in Oberwart and was followed by other groups. In 1993 some Gypsies were given recognition as a *Volksgruppe* (ethnic group)—a status shared, for example, by the Hungarians and Croats. There is now a Romany advisory council (which includes non-Romany representatives) that advises the prime minister. The 5,000 or so Gypsies recognized as the ethnic group are those who belong to families who have been in Austria for three generations. They have some legal rights as a result of this status. The remaining Gypsies are in a precarious situation as they are affected by a number of laws for aliens (Asylum Law of 1992, Aliens and Residence Laws of 1993). Neither the police nor the authorities have been particularly helpful to these Gypsies. The **Romano Centro,** Vienna, acts as a cultural and advice center for many Romanies. Other associations, including the Kulturverein Öster-reichischer Roma (Cultural Association of Austrian Romanies), are also in Vienna.

AUTONOMIA FOUNDATION. A voluntary organization in Hungary that includes work with Romanies, among its activities.

AVEN AMENTZA FOUNDATION. A cultural and welfare organization in Romania. *Aven amentza* means "Come with us."

B

BAGLAENKO, VALENTIN. A contemporary singer from the Crimea. He sang with the Gypsy Circus and finally in 1967 joined the **Teatr Romen**. He has toured in Europe with the Kharkov Operetta, performed as a horserider and dancer, as well as making several recordings.

BAIRD, REVEREND JOHN. The leader of a mission to reform Gypsies and Travellers in Scotland in the 19th century.

BAJRAMOVIĆ, ŠABAN. A singer and composer from Serbia. He has often sung on radio and has recorded his songs.

BAKO, MARIA. Born in Hungary, the star of the Italian film *Una alma dividita in due* by the director Silvio Soldini. She was invited to the Venice Festival of 1993 but was refused entry by the immigration authorities at Milan airport, who suspected her of being an illegal immigrant.

BALÁZS, GUSTAV. A contemporary musicologist and dance teacher from Hungary. He has studied the Gypsy form of the czardas in Hungary and Transylvania and teaches a dance summer school each year in Hungary. He is currently resident in Holland.

BALÁZS, JÁNOS (1905–1977). A naive artist in Hungary. He began to draw as a child but was discouraged by his parents. He took up painting again in 1968. His first solo show was in 1977 at Salgótarján, and he has exhibited since in Hungary and abroad. He said that his paintings show distorted figures because their basic source stems from our own distorted world.

BALIĆ, SAIT. An engineer by profession and a political activist in Serbia. He was a sometime member of the Serbian Parliament and was elected president at the third World Romany Congress.

BALLARDO, MANERO (1940–). Born in Montpellier, France, where he still lives. He is a cousin of **Manitas de Plata**. He works as a builder and sings flamenco largely for his own entertainment.

BALOGH, KÁLMÁN (1959–). A **cimbalom** player from Miskolc in Hungary. He was taught by his uncle Elemér, also a famous player in his time, and then studied classical music in Budapest. With a wide repertoire, he has played with many bands such as Teka and Muszikas and has recorded as a soloist. He is also a teacher of his instrument.

BALT-SLAVIC ROMANI. A name given by scholars to a cluster of **Romani** dialects spoken in Belarus, Lithuania, Poland and Russia by over 800,000 persons. They include Belarus, in Belarus and Lithuania; the dialect of the north Russian Romanies, including those of Siberia, and the Lowland Romani of Poland.

BALTZAR, VEIJO (1942–). An author writing in Finnish. As a child he shared a tiny cottage with his horse-dealer father, mother and nine sisters and brothers. He describes Gypsy life and culture from inside his own group in his first novel *Polttava tie* (Burning Road), published in 1968. The story tells of young Gypsies struggling in the crisis of changing times. This work was translated into Swedish. The second novel *Verikihlat* (The Blood Engagement) published the following year, describes the consequences of a vendetta. His third novel, *Mari*, published in 1973, is the story of a woman's role in Gypsy society. He also wrote a fable for adults and has branched out into writing articles on the social conditions of his own people and on prejudices against them. He is also a talented painter.

BAMBERGER, JAKOB (?–1989). A runner-up in the German national flyweight championships. He was a member of the Olympic team in 1936. In 1940 he was arrested in Prague and sent to the Flossenburg and Dachau concentration camps.

BANAT. A province in the Balkans bordering Romania that has at different times been under Hungarian (ca. 850–ca. 1550), Ottoman (ca. 1550–1718), and Austrian (1718–1920) rule. Records exist of Gypsies in the 18th century engaged in charcoal burning, gold washing, bear leading, horse trading and coppersmithing. They performed valuable services for the villagers, which was recognized in an edict of 1757 to stop tax collectors from driving Gypsies out of the villages by extortionate taxation. In 1763 a census recorded some 5,000 Gypsies. Angus Fraser has suggested, on linguistic grounds, that the **Kalderash** coming into Western Europe in the 19th century had emigrated from the Banat and not from Wallachia and Moldavia, as others maintain. In 1920 the Banat was divided between Hungary and Yugoslavia. During World War II, the Yugoslav Banat was under direct German military rule, and persecution of the Gypsy minority began toward the end of the war.

BANGA, DEZIDER (1939–   ). A poet in Slovakia who writes in Slovak and Romani. A collection of his works in Slovak—*Piesen nad vetrom* (Songs of the Wind)—was published in 1964.

BANJARA. A tribe in India who live a similar life to that of the nomadic Gypsies of Europe. They are also known as Lambadi, and their language is called Gor-Boli. A Banjara delegation attended the second **World Romany Congress**.

BARGOENS. A variety of Dutch spoken by **Travellers** in Belgium and Holland (the **Woonwagenbewoners).** Some of the vocabulary is of Romani origin, e.g., *lobie* (money).

BARI, KAROLY (1952–   ) A poet. He spent 16 years collecting and publishing Gypsy tales and songs from Hungary, where he lives, and Transylvania.

BARRETT, FRANK (1977–   ). An Irish Traveller and the amateur light welterweight champion of Ireland. He took part in the 1996 Olympic Games.

BARTOSZ, ADAM. The director of the regional **museum** in **Tarnów**. He has researched, documented and popularized the culture of Polish Romanies. In 1979 he introduced a collection of Gypsy artifacts to the museum, which was transformed into a permanent exposition devoted to Gypsy history in 1990. He has also published a book: *Do Not Fear a Gypsy*. Annual summer folklore events are held at the Tarnów museum in collaboration with the Center of Romany Culture.

BARULLO (EL). Manuel Moneo. A young flamenco singer from the Moneo family of Jerez, Spain. He has recorded with the guitarist Moraito.

BAYASH, BEYASH. A Gypsy clan living in east Hungary and Transylvania. They do not speak Romani, but an archaic form of Romanian.

BELARUS. Estimated Gypsy population: 17,000. The first document referring to Gypsies on the territory of present-day Belarus dates from 1501 when Earl Alexander of Lithuania gave the Gypsies a certain autonomy under their chief Vasil, in Belarus, Lithuania and Poland. In 1586, however, the Parliament of Lithuania-Poland issued a decree expelling all Gypsies who refused to settle down. This applied to Belarus. There was still some measure of self-government, as in 1778 when Jan Marcinkiewicz was appointed the chief of the Gypsies in the area around Mir, and he continued in this role until 1790. At that time there was a famous academy where bear trainers were educated at Smorjan. In 1780 the Polish king Stanislaw II authorized a non-Gypsy, Jakob Zniemarowski, to be king over the Romany people in Belarus (as well as Lithuania, Ukraine and Poland). He continued to rule until 1795, when Belarus was annexed by the Russian Empire. From then until 1991, the history of Gypsies in Belarus followed that of **Russia** and the **Union of Soviet Socialist Republics**.

During the German occupation (1941–1944), half of all the Gypsies in Belarus were killed by the Task Forces (***Einsatzgruppen***) and army units in concentration camps, such as Polask and Trastiniets, as well as in the woods near their homes. Others, including Admiral Kotslowski, served in the Soviet armed forces or the partisans.

After the end of World War II in 1945, little cultural activity took place, though from 1987 to 1989 **Valdemar Kalinin** ran the folk group Belvelitko (Evening Party). The official 1989 census recorded only 10,762 Gypsies with 82 percent speaking Romani as their mother tongue. The major dialect is similar to that of northern Russia and had been used during the 1930s for literacy purposes. Since the breakup of the Soviet Union, racist incidents have increased, including a pogrom at Sitlagorsk.

BELGIUM. Estimated Gypsy population: 10,000 (excluding **Travellers**). The territory of present-day Belgium saw its first Gypsies possibly as early as 1400, but certainly in 1419 in Antwerp and in 1420, with the arrival of Duke Andrew of Little Egypt, in Brussels. In 1421 they came to Bruges. Duke Andrew said he and his followers had been expelled from their homes by the Turks, and he was given money and food. Later opinion turned against these "pilgrims." In 1504 the bailiff of Rouen was told by King Louis XII of France to chase any "**Egyptians**" across the frontiers and out of the country. A period likely followed when very few Gypsies were in the country. Decrees in 1856 and 1900 said that foreign nomads should not be included in the population registers. In 1872 foreign nomads were to be stopped from entering the country, and those already there, expelled. In 1933 the Foreigners Police was set up, and one of its tasks was to issue special passes for nomads. In 1941 the occupying German forces withdrew these passes and introduced the nomad's card (*zigeunerkaart*), which was not abolished until 1975.

At the outbreak of World War II, perhaps only 20 extended families were living permanently in Belgium together with others who had been trapped there by the outbreak of war. Nomadic Gypsies were arrested under the orders of the Germans from October 1943 in both Belgium and northern France, which was administered from Brussels. The encampments were surrounded and everyone taken. No serious effort was made to seek out house-dwelling Gypsies. The nomads were held in local prisons and gradually transferred to Malines. On January 15, 1944, a party of 351 of mixed nationality were handed one piece of bread and loaded into cattle trucks for the journey to **Auschwitz**. Some 300 died or were killed in that camp. The remainder were transferred to other camps, and 12 of these survived until the end of the war.

Current figures are 4,000 for Flanders, with a smaller number in the French-speaking part of Belgium. There are four groups; (1) **Vlah** Romanies who came to Western Europe from Romania in the 19th century and the beginning of the 20th; (2) Romanies who came from Eastern Europe (especially Yugoslavia) after 1945; (3) **Manouche** and **Sinti** who have lived for several centuries in Belgium, France or Germany; and (4) non-Romany Travellers (known as **Woonwagenbewoners** or Voyageurs), some of whom speak **Bargoens.**

Many Romanies of the first two groups still travel, whereas the Manouche, Sinti and Travellers mostly live on caravan sites and many are moving into houses. Most live from recycling or house to house sales of craftwork. There has been no long-term Gypsy organization in Belgium, although individual lawyers and others have helped with individual casework. Keree Amende was a center for Gypsies in Merksem around 1977. The Association des Roms de Belgique no longer functions.

BELUGINS, ALEKSANDR (LEKSA MANUŠ) (1949–1997). A researcher at the Academy of Sciences. Born in Moscow, he was a poet and translator. His writings include a translation (published in Chandigarh) of the Indian classic *The Ramayana*. Many of his poems have been published in the journal *Roma*. He was also the editor of an anthology of Gypsy poetry.

BENG. The Romani word for the Devil. It is likely that it was already used by the Romanies for reptiles inhabiting the Hindu version of

Hell and transferred to the Devil they saw being killed by St. George in Byzantine icons.

BERBERSKI, SLOBODAN (1919–1989). A poet from Belgrade. He was elected president of the **World Romany Congress** at the first congress in 1971. He served until the second congress.

BERGITKA ROMA. The so-called mountain Gypsies of Poland. They are later arrivals and speak a different dialect from the lowland Gypsies.

BESSARABIA. A territory belonging to Russia (1812–1917) and Romania (1917–1940). After 1945 it was retained by the USSR and divided between the Moldavian and Ukrainian republics. Aleksandr Pushkin's epic poem *The Gypsies* is set among the nomads of Bessarabia, while Kishinev had a large settled Gypsy population. There are reports of a thousand nomadic Bessarabian Gypsies being driven to the death camp at Treblinka during the Nazi period.

BIALYSTOK. A major town in Poland. Large numbers of Gypsies were assembled there during the Nazi period for deportation to **Auschwitz**. The deportees on two large transports numbering some 2,500 were gased on or soon after arrival at the concentration camp in contrast to other Gypsies who remained in the camp for up to 18 months until the liquidation of the Gypsy camp.

BIBLE. The first time a complete gospel was translated into Romani was in 1837, by George Borrow. Verses 30–37 of Luke, Chapter 10, had been translated into Czech Romani by Anton Puchmayer in 1821 and published in his book *Romani Chib*.

A list of post-1945 translations can be found in the bibliography (in the section "Literature in Romani").

BIENNALE KLEINERE SPRACHEN. See ZIGEUNERLEBEN.

BIHARI, JÁNOS (1764–1827). Musician in Hungary. He composed **Verbunkos** music and led his own band. In 1808 he wrote the piece *Krönungs-Nota* for the coronation of Empress Maria Louisa and collaborated in the composition of the *Rakoczy March,* later to become the Hungarian national anthem. He was one of the Gypsy musicians who influenced **Franz Liszt**.

BISMARCK, OTTO VON. In 1886, as newly appointed Chancellor of the Second German Empire, Bismarck sent a letter to all the states comprising the empire to unify, at least in practice, the various valid decrees against Gypsies. Bismarck recommended the expulsion of all foreign Gypsies to free the territory of the country completely and permanently from this "plague."

BLACK VIRGIN. A number of churches where there is a statue of a Black Virgin have been the object of pilgrimages by Gypsies. In 1471 Duke Paul of Egypt went to visit the statue of Our Lady the Black Virgin of Guadalupe at Compostela in Spain. Some scholars believe that the Gypsies saw in the Black Virgin a reminder of the Indian goddess **Kali**.

BLAIRGOWRIE. A small village in Scotland famous for its berries and music. In season many Travellers and townspeople come to help in the picking, and many informal musicmaking sessions take place in the evenings after the picking is over. An annual music festival is also held. **Belle Stewart** and her family are closely associated with Blairgowrie, and Stewart wrote the song *The Berryfields o' Blair* as long ago as the 1920s.

BLOCH, JULES. French scholar of Indian studies. In 1953 his book *Les Tsiganes* was published in the series *Que sais-je?* This book has been superseded in the collection by a new book with the same title written by N. Martinez.

BLOCK, MARTIN. A German professor of linguistics at Marburg University. He wrote in 1936 the book *Die Zigeuner: ihr Leben und ihre Seele* (The Gypsies: their Life and their Soul) which summarized what knowledge there was at the time among outsiders of the Gypsies' life and beliefs. It is believed that he died in a German concentration camp.

BLYTHE, JAMES. Chief of a clan of Scottish Travellers in the south of Scotland.

BOORDE, ANDREW. An Englishman who authored an encyclopedia entitled *The Fyrst Boke of the Introduction of Knowledge* (1547). It had a chapter on Romani, which includes some of the earliest specimens of the language, probably collected in Calais.

BORROW, GEORGE. A 19th-century English writer and linguist. He lived with Gypsies in England and visited Spain to learn the language of the Gypsies there. He translated St. Luke's Gospel into Spanish **Caló.** Borrow also wrote several works on the Gypsies, in particular

The Bible in Spain (1843), *Lavengro* (1851), and *The Romany Rye* (1857).

BOSNIA-HERZEGOVINA. Estimated Gypsy population before the recent conflict: circa 80,000. An unknown number of Bosnian Romanies have sought refuge in other countries since 1992. The 1971 census recorded 1,456 Romanies.

Before 1428, the Gypsy population of Bosnia would have consisted of no more than a couple of families, but no records from that time exist. In the period 1428–1875 Bosnia was under the rule of the **Ottoman Empire**. Under Turkish rule the Gypsies were treated as any other non-Turkish ethnic group, with some discouragement of nomadism, largely because of the difficulty of raising taxes from nomads. In 1574 Sultan Salim II decreed that the Gypsies who worked in the Bosnian mines were to be exempted from certain taxes and had to choose a headman for each group of 50 adults.

From 1875 to 1918 the country was under the de facto (or de jure rule) of the Austro-Hungarian Empire. In 1918 it became part of the newly established Yugoslavia and then in 1941 the puppet fascist state of **Croatia**.

In the federal state of Yugoslavia, which was reestablished after 1945, the Romanies were recognized as a national minority in the Republic of Bosnia and Herzegovina. They were allowed to run their own organizations and use the Romani language. The population was between 50,000 and 100,000. In 1986 the **Sarajevo Conference** was held, which was a landmark in the development of Romany culture.

After 1992 in the Bosnia-Herzegovina Republic (Muslim-Croat Bosnian Federation), Romany populations survived in Tuzla and Sarajevo and other towns during the war, though many fled to Western Europe. As Gypsies were living in all areas of the country, men were conscripted for military service by all three warring parties. Men from Zavidovici formed an all-Romany unit called Garavi Vod that fought alongside the Bosnian government forces. It is thought that some 80 Romanies were killed in the Serbian-run concentration camp at Manjaca. At least 500 were killed during the fighting in Bihać, Sarajevo, and Zvornik. There was no functioning Romany organization in Bosnia during the war period except in Sarajevo.

Some 300–400 Gypsies are living in what was the Serbian district of Ilidža in Sarajevo, and others are in Gorica. The Gypsy population of all Sarajevo is between 1,000 and 2,000, with a high proportion of children. Some six active organizations operate in Bosnia. Braca Romi (Romany Brethren) functions locally in Sarajevo, as do other bodies in Kiseljak (SAE Roma), Visoko, and Zenica. However, several deputations visiting Tuzla and other towns found that the Romanies were at the bottom of the list for receiving humanitarian help from outside agencies. At the time of this writing, several thousand Romany refugees from Bosnia are in Germany, and smaller numbers live in other Western countries. Some are being sent back to Bosnia, though there are some doubts whether the new constitution will allow all the Gypsies who once lived in Bosnia to become citizens of the new federation, as they may not all be able to establish residence (because they were born in or spent long periods in other republics of the former Yugoslavia). A fact-finding mission under the auspices of the Council of Europe visited Bosnia in May 1996. It recommended that both parts of the Republic (Bosnia-Croatia and Republika Srpska) recognize Romanies as a nationality. See also REPUBLIKA SRPSKA.

BOSWELL, SYLVESTER GORDON. He was born in the large Gypsy camp on the North Shore, Blackpool, the 11th son of Trafalgar Boswell. He served in World War I in the Royal Veterinary Corps. He then married and traveled across the British Isles, later settling in Lincolnshire, near Spalding. Boswell was a close friend of members of the **Gypsy Lore Society**. He succeeded in saving and expanding the threatened **Appleby Fair**. In 1970 *The Book of Boswell,* his autobiography, was published from a transcript of a tape recording made by him. It contains a lively account of his life in the army and on the road.

BOSWELL, GORDON. A member of the well-known Boswell extended family. He has opened a privately run museum of caravans and other traditional items in Lincolnshire, England.

BRATSCH. A popular non-Gypsy band in France that sings in Romani as well as Yiddish, Kurdish and other languages. Their CD, somewhat misleadingly entitled *Gypsy Music from the Heart of Europe*, contains three Gypsy songs.

BRIAVAL, COCO. A musician in the Django Reinhardt style. His music has been recorded with the title *Musique Manouche.*

BRITAIN. See separate entries for ENGLAND, SCOTLAND and WALES.

BRITISH ROMMANI UNION. An organization established in the 1990s by the poet Tom Odley. It had a strong Romany nationalist position.

BRNO. The town of Brno in the Czech Republic is the home of a **museum** of Romany culture founded in 1991. The museum publishes a journal and books as well as offering public lectures. The director is Ilona Laznickova.

BROTHERTON COLLECTION. Part of the Leeds University Library, United Kingdom. It is one of the largest collections of books on Gypsy subjects. The original collection was donated by Mrs. McGrigor Phillips in 1950, and an endowment enables its continued progress.

BRUSSELS DECLARATION. A roundtable on the Roma/Gypsies was held in the European Parliament in Brussels on July 12, 1996, attended by representatives from the major Romany organizations and those working with Gypsies. The declaration adopted by the participants called for recognition for the Romani language and way of life in the school system. It also asked for special attention to be paid to creating employment possibilities for Gypsies as well as health care. The Gypsy organizations said they needed support and asked for the international bodies in Europe to each appoint someone as an official representative of the Romany people.

BRYNNER, YUL. An actor and film star whose trademark was his shaved head. He played the king of Siam in the Broadway (1951) and film version (1956) of Rodgers and Hammerstein's *The King and I.* He also gained critical acclaim for his role as leader of the Magnificent Seven in the film of the same name in 1956. In a June 1978 interview published by the *New York Times*, he said it was uplifting to hear the refrain *Upre, Roma!* (Arise, Romanies!) at the second **World Romany Congress,** of which he was patron, and announced that he intended to go to the forthcoming **Chandigarh festival**. However, his claim in this article to be of mixed Gypsy, Swiss and Mongolian descent was overturned by his son Rock's autobiography (*The Man Who Would Be King*), which states that his father was brought up with Gypsies but was not one himself.

BUCHAREST CONFERENCE. This 1934 conference was organized by Lăzărescu Lăzurică and the Uniunea Generala a Romilor din Romania (General Union of the Gypsies of Romania). There were a number of invitees from abroad. Its final declaration asked for equal civil rights for Gypsies and help with education and employment. It has been considered as the first international meeting of Gypsies.

BUFFALO (*Bubalus bubalis*). The Asian buffalo played an important part in the migration of the Romanies from India to Europe. Many were brought by the Arabs as captives from India to serve as herds-men in Mesopotamia and from there to the coast of the Mediterra-nean. Gypsies were recorded as nomadizing with buffalo in Turkey. They were photographed and painted with buffalo in the 19th century in "Rumelia" and Transylvania. It is likely that they accompanied herds of buffalo from Turkey into the Balkans under the **Ottoman Empire**.

BULGARIA. Estimated Gypsy population: 750,000. The town of Sliven has a Gypsy population of around 40,000. The first historical refer-ence, in 1378, is to sedentary Gypsies, living in huts near Rila Monas-tery. By 1396 Bulgaria had become part of the **Ottoman Empire**. The Gypsies were treated generally as other ethnic groups by the Ot-tomans, provided they paid their taxes. There were many craftsmen and farm workers. Some of the Bulgarian Gypsies converted to Islam, while other Muslim Gypsies arrived with the Turkish conquerors.

In 1878 Bulgaria was liberated from the Ottoman Empire. In 1886 the new government instituted a decree forbidding nomadism, and the Frontier Law could be used to prevent the immigration of Gypsies. As a result of economic (rather than legal) pressure, many Gypsies took jobs in the newly opened factories—in textile factories in Sliven, for example. Others continued to nomadize until well after World War II.

A census taken in 1887 put the official Bulgarian Romany popula-tion at 50,000. The central government wished to prevent Gypsies from voting under the new constitution. A conference of Gypsies in Sofia in 1905 was organized to protest against this law.

Between the wars, Christian missionaries were active among the Gypsies in Bulgaria. In the 1930s the Scripture Gift Mission pub-lished brochures in two dialects of Romani, and in Pazardjik a local Gypsy from the Tinners' clan translated two gospels into his dialect of Romani.

In Sliven, however, the Gypsies were working in factories and turn-ing toward socialism. Romany trade unionists in Sliven were to take a lead in 1927 in organizing a petition to the U.S. government against the execution of the two anarchists, Nicola Sacco and Bartolomeo Vanzetti. Gypsies had also taken part in the largely peasant uprisings against the government in 1923. A journal in Turkish for the Muslim Gypsy population, *Istikbal* (Future), was published from 1923 to 1925, when it was banned by the government. The organization Istiq-bal (founded in 1919) was banned in 1934 along with all nonstate organizations. The last census before the World War II was in 1926 and gave a figure of 135,000, perhaps half of the real total.

During World War II, many Gypsies from the towns were rounded up and sent to work in labor camps. Others, however, served in the army, and yet others joined the partisans. Dimiter Nemtsov from Sliven, who was serving with the Bulgarian army of occupation in Yugoslavia, deserted and joined the local resistance movement. In May 1942 a decree was issued providing for Gypsies to be directed to compulsory employment. A year later Gypsies from Sofia had been sent to a labor camp in Dupnitsa. Those who remained were refused access to the center of the town and use of the trams.

After 1945 the Gypsies were at first encouraged by the Communist government to develop their own ethnicity. A magazine was set up under the aegis of the Communist Party, and the Theater Roma was established in Sofia in 1947. The magazine was at first given the Romani name *Romano Esi* (Romany Voice). The name was changed to *Nevo Drom* (New way) in 1949, then in 1957 to *Neve Roma* (New Romanies), and finally given a Bulgarian title *Nov Put* (New Way). The first editor was **Shakir Pashov**. It proclaimed assimilation as the desirable aim for the Gypsies and was to cease publication with the fall of the Communist regime. In 1945 the Gypsy-led Organization for the Fight against Fascism and for Raising the Cultural Level of the Gypsy was founded. Shakir Pashov was its head. It was soon closed and absorbed into the Otechestven Front, a mass organization allied to the Communist party. The Romany theater in Sofia was closed in 1951 and its director, **Romanov Manush**, sent into internal exile. Pashov was interned in a labor camp on the island of Belen.

The government was determined to end nomadism. This was banned in 1958. A circular in the following year referred to 14,000 traveling Gypsies and also stressed the need to get the Gypsies to assimilate to the Bulgarian majority and not align themselves with the Turkish minority. The government opened many boarding schools for Gypsy children, mainly those of previously nomadic families. From 1954 onward, Muslim Gypsies were pressured to adopt Bulgarian names. Gypsies accused of nationalist deviation during this period were sent to labor camps in Lovech and Skraventsa.

When the Communist party fell from power in 1989, Gypsies were allowed once more to have their own journals and organizations. Four acknowledged Gypsies were elected to the first democratic Parliament.

The collapse of the Communist regime, on the other hand, led to a rise in anti-Gypsy articles in the press and racist attacks. Skinheads attacked Gypsies in Pleven at the end of 1995. Others have attacked homeless children who sleep in the Sofia railway station. In March 1995 one Romany died when a block of apartments was set on fire in Sofia. There have also been reports of police brutality. In June 1996 Amnesty International issued a report documenting the death of five

Romanies in police custody during 1995 and 1996; they included Iliya Gherghinov, Zaharie Aleksandrov, Angel Angelov and Iliyan Veselin Nikolov. No action has been taken against the police regarding these deaths. In two other cases, however, action has been taken in respect of persons beaten up by police. In June 1992 Kiril Yosifov from Pazardjik was beaten. In December 1995 the regional court ordered the Ministry of Internal Affairs to pay compensation to Yosifov. In March 1996 police officers from Pleven were given a suspended sentence of eight months in prison for beating two boys in Vidin. Heavy-handed police raids took place in March 1996 in Russe and in April in Barkach.

In December 1991 circular 232 of the Council of Ministers permitted Romani to be taught up to four hours a week on a voluntary basis, and an alphabet book was produced. From 1997, however, an experimental program of Romany culture is offered in some schools to all children, Romany or not.

The Gypsy population of Bulgaria today is mixed, Christian and Muslim. The recently settled nomads speak a variety of dialects, both **Vlah** and non-Vlah, while the sedentaries in the west speak mainly **Erlia**. There are probably some 30 distinct dialects. Thanks mainly to compulsory education in the communist period, Gypsies are found at all levels of society, from surgeons to laborers. Music is a popular profession.

BUNYAN, JOHN. The English author of *Pilgrim's Progress* (1678). He said he came from a **tinker** family, but there is no evidence that he was an ethnic Gypsy. The surname, with the spelling Bonyan, was recorded as used by Gypsies in the 1590s in England.

BURGENLAND. A province in the east of Austria. Many Gypsies were settled there by **Maria Theresa**. During the 1930s their economic position as casual farm workers was becoming difficult, and friction arose with local Austrians competing for work. They were among the first to be interned by the National Socialists after Germany annexed Austria in 1938. Most perished in **Auschwitz**, Buchenwald, Chelmno and Ravensbrück. There is a small surviving population, but few of the children speak Romani. A cultural center was set up in recent years. Attempts are being made to develop the dialect (known as Romano) as a written language.

BURMAN, RAHIM (1949–). Born in Skopje, Macedonia, a theater producer and actor with the **Pralipe** company.

BURTON, RICHARD. A writer, voyager and linguist. One of his books was *The Jew, the Gypsy and El Islam* (1898). In spite of his being probably partly of Romany descent, he painted a bad picture of Gypsies in this work.

BYZANTIUM. Byzantium is the name given to the Greek Empire, which covered modern Greece and what is now Turkey. The first Gypsies are recorded in Byzantium in 1054 in Constantinople (present-day Istanbul). They were magicians, fortune tellers and veterinary surgeons. It is thought these Gypsies entered Europe across the Bosphorus. Others crossed the Mediterranean to the Greek islands and mainland.

C

CALCUTTA ASIATIC SOCIETY. Founded by Sir William Jones in 1784. Around this time, scholars found a link between Latin and Sanskrit, and European interest in Indian languages grew. This was to lead to the recognition of the Indian origin of the Romani language and the Gypsies.

CALDARAS, HANS. A contemporary singer and composer of mainly traditional music in Sweden. He has recorded in Swedish and Romani.

CALÓ. (i) A variety of Spanish with many Romany words. It replaced Romani as the language of Spanish Gypsies. **George Borrow**'s translation of the Bible is in Caló. (ii) Sometimes used instead of *gitano* to describe a Spanish or Portuguese Gypsy. It is a Romani word meaning "black." See also *KALO*.

CAMMINANTI. Non-Romany Travellers in Sicily. Their speech is a variety of the Sicilian dialect of Italian, with many words disguised by inserting a meaningless syllable.

CANNSTADT CONFERENCE. In 1871 during the Wurtemberg annual festival, the editor of a Stuttgart paper played a trick announcing that a Gypsy parliament would be held. Many curious people went to see this event. The trains coming to Cannstadt were apparently packed. In January 1872 the *Times* published a notice about the parliament as did the *Evening Standard* a month later. From these false reports the conference slipped into some books about Gypsies.

CANT. The term used for the language used by Irish and Scottish Travellers. These are two distinct varieties of English. The syntax and grammar are English, but the vocabulary comes from many sources, including the medieval vocabularies known as **Shelta** and **Gammon**. The vocabulary is taught from birth alongside the English equivalent, and as the children grow up they learn which words are used by their community and which are the general English words. There is some overlap between Irish and Scottish Travellers' cant. Most Travellers know some 400 words. These words are used within the community to give a sense of identity and sometimes so that the Travellers can speak without being understood by outsiders. In the Scottish Highlands and Islands, a third variety of speech is used—again a special vocabulary, but in this case with the syntax and grammar of Scottish Gaelic.

Examples of cant:
Irish Travellers: *Bug muilsha gather skai*. [Give me a drink of water]. Lowland Scottish Travellers: I *slummed* the *pottach* in the *gowl* and then I *bing'd avree*. [I hit the boy in the stomach and then I went out]. Highland and Islands Scottish Travellers: *S'deis sium a meartsacha air a charan*. [We are going on the sea].

CANTEA, GEORGI. See KANTEA, GEORGI.

CARAVAN. The horse-drawn caravan was not invented by the Gypsies but rapidly adopted by them in the 19th century. The horse-drawn caravan first appeared in France and northern Europe about 1800. The earliest picture of a caravan in England dates from 1804. In 1817 van Gogh painted Gypsy caravans in France.

There are a number of different types such as the Reading wagon. The horse-drawn caravan is called a *vardo* in the Romani language.

CARAVAN SITES ACT OF 1960. This United Kingdom act introduced new planning controls on **caravan** sites in England and Wales. As a result, it became difficult to open new sites, and many existing sites were closed if they had not been operating for a certain number of years before 1960. The act gave local authorities the power to build sites for Gypsies, but very few did so.

CARAVAN SITES ACT OF 1968. This United Kingdom act placed a duty on county councils in particular to build sites for Gypsies "residing in and resorting to their area." At the same time, new powers were introduced to make parking a **caravan** in an area illegal when the area was "designated" as having provided enough caravan pitches or when the government judged it was not "expedient" for the area to do so. Progress under the act was slow, and by 1994 only some 30 percent of Gypsies were housed on official caravan sites. Others had obtained permission for private sites in accordance with a number of circulars that followed the passing of the 1968 Caravan Sites Act. The act was repealed in 1994 by the Criminal Justice and Public Order Act.

CARI, OLIMPIO. A painter from Italy who exhibited at the second **Mondiale of Gypsy Art** in Budapest (1995).

CARINTHIA. Now a province of Austria, previously (1276–1918) part of the Austro-Hungarian Empire. Gypsies are mentioned in the area for the first time in 1692 at Villach. There was a small Gypsy population of Romanies and **Sinti** in the period up to the World War II. Many of them were transported to Lackenbach internment camp and others put on a train heading in the direction of Tschenstochau. It is possible that they never reached Tschenstochau as the route passed near **Auschwitz**. Plans are under way to erect a memorial in Villach to the victims of the Nazi regime.

CARMEN. *Carmen*, the fictitious story of a Spanish Gypsy, was written by Prosper Merimée (1846) after visiting a Spanish cigarette factory and turned into an opera by Bizet (1875). It is said that Merimée wrote the story in just eight days. The story (of a love triangle, or quadrilateral, if we count Carmen's husband) has been filmed, by Cecil B. De Mille, Carlos Saura, Francesco Rosi and Jean-Luc Godard. It has recently been turned into a flamenco opera (by Antonio Gades) and an ice show—the latter with a sequence of Irish stepdancing on skates, which has no parallel in the original story or opera. It was adapted to be the musical *Carmen Jones*—with a black heroine—in 1943 (and later filmed). In 1997 James Robinson produced a play at the Court Theater in Chicago based on Merimée's original novel with moderate success.

CATALONIA. In 1447 the first Gypsies were recorded in Catalonia. In 1512 they were ordered to leave the region. Catalonia became administratively part of **Spain** later in the 16th century.

CENTER FOR CENTRAL AND EASTERN EUROPEAN ROMA. The offices of the center are in Brno, Czech Republic, and the director is Karel Holomek.

CENTRE DE RECHERCHES TSIGANES. The center holds a database of organizations, books and articles and publishes the journal *Interface*. Three research and action groups are managed by the center—on history, education and language. The Interface book collection and a planned **encyclopedia** is also a part of the center's work. The director is **Jean-Pierre Liégeois.**

CENTRE MISSIONAIRE ÉVANGÉLIQUE ROM INTERNATION-ALE (CMERI). A Pentecostal group, mainly **Kalderash**, that split from the Vie et Lumière group in 1995 and formed its own association. They have a central church in Bondy (France) and some 65 churches, mainly in Germany and Sweden. They use the Romani language in services. The President is Loulou Demeter.

CENTRO STUDI ZINGARI. An Italian cultural and educational organization founded in 1966. It publishes the journal *Lacio Drom* and has organized several international meetings, including the **Ostia Conference**. Mirella Karpati has been the leading figure at the center.

CHACHIPE, CAYI DE (ca.1920–   ). A Gypsy dancer in Spain who began his career performing for tourists in Albaicín. At the age of 8 he went to Paris, and by the time he was 15 he had danced in the major cities of Spain and throughout South America.

CHANDIGARH FESTIVALS. The contemporary Indian scholar **W. R. Rishi** organized two festivals so that European Romanies could come to their original homeland India and meet their long-lost cousins. Meeting the European delegates at the 1984 festival was one of the last public engagements of Indira Gandhi before her assassination.

CHAPLIN, CHARLES (1889–1977). Born in London, Chaplin was a film star whose hits included *The Great Dictator* and *Limelight*. In his autobiography he wrote that his mother was half-Gypsy and that her mother's maiden name was Smith. According to other sources, she was called Mary Ann Terry, and yet a further possibility is that his maternal grandfather Charles Frederick Hill, a shoemaker, was an **Irish Traveller**. Chaplin's biographer, Joyce Milton, felt that Chaplin was well aware of his Romany heritage and that his tramp character recalled the image of the eternal Romany wanderer.

CHERENKOV, LEV. A contemporary cultural activist in the Soviet Union and later in Russia. For many years after World War II, he corresponded with Western scholars and through them contributed to learned journals on the subject of Romani.

CHERGASHI or CHERHARI (tent dweller). The name given to a number of Gypsy clans: (1) The Chergashi of Bosnia. Many emigrated to Western Europe after 1966. On their visits to London, flower selling was a major source of income. A peculiarity of their dialect is that the retroflex "r" sound has become a guttural /x/—the sound in Scottish *loch* or German *doch*. (2) The Cherhari of East Hungary who speak a **Vlah** dialect.

CHINCHIRI, HASSAN (1932–1994). A bandleader, singer and composer in Bulgaria after 1945. He made several recordings before the clampdown on Romany culture in that country.

CHUHNI. A dialect of **Romani,** spoken in Latvia. Some speakers of Chuhni have emigrated recently to Lithuania. The total number of speakers is perhaps 10,000. A translation of John's Gospel into the Chuhni dialect was made in 1933, and a translation of Luke's gospel is in preparation. The earlier translation is in the Kurzimiaki subdialect of Chuhni and the current translation in the Vitsemyaki subdialect, although the differences between the two are minor.

CHUNGA, LA. See AMAYA, MICAELA.

CHUNGUITA, LA. See AMAYA, LORENZA FLORES.

CHURARI. A Gypsy clan that evolved in Romania. Later many emigrated after the end of serfdom in the 19th century. The term is derived from the Romani word *churi* (knife).

CIBULA, JAN. A surgeon born in Czechoslovakia but currently resident in Switzerland. He served as president of the **World Romany Congress** from 1978 to 1981.

CIMBALOM. It is thought that the cimbalom was brought to Europe by the Gypsies. It is a stringed instrument played with sticks and is related to the Indian *santur*. In the 19th century it was enlarged and provided with legs, which is the way it is played in Hungary today, though elsewhere in the Balkans it is still hung from the neck.

CIOABĂ, IOAN (1935–1997). An elder of the **Kalderash** clan and a Romanian political leader. He kept in contact with the **Comité International Tzigane** and agitated for Gypsies' rights during the Communist period. In 1986 he was jailed under a trumped-up charge of cheating the government on a copper contract. After the fall of Nicolae Ceauşescu, he was a member of the Provisional National Council. He and his son Florin ran for the senate in 1995 but were not elected. In September 1992 in Romania he was proclaimed King of All of the Gypsies. His authority as king was limited to the Kalderash clan, but many other Romanian Gypsies saw him as their spokesman. His daughter Lucia is married to the son of Iulian, who was crowned Emperor of All the Gypsies in August 1993, while his daughter **Luminiţa Mihai Cioabă** is a well-known writer.

CIOABĂ, LUMINIŢA MIHAI (1957–   ). Daughter of **Ioan Cioabă.** A journalist and poetess, she won first prize for poetry in the second **Amico Rom** contest. Her poetry includes the Romeo and Juliette-style ballad *Mara thai Bakro* and the poetry collection *Die Wurzel der Erde* (The Roots of the Earth) (in Romani, Romanian, German and English).

CIVIC UNION OF ROMA. An umbrella organization of groups in Hodonin and other towns in the Czech Republic. Its program includes preschool activities and a music festival.

CLAN. (i) This term is used in the dictionary in preference to "tribe" as a collective noun for groupings of Gypsies sharing a cultural and linguistic heritage. These include the **Sinti** and the **Romanichals,** who do not use the word *Rom* as a self-ascription as well as for those groups that in addition to the general word *Rom* call themselves by names related to their traditional trade, for example, **Kalderash** or **Sepedji.** Some clans have a geographic name (e.g., Istriani Sinti)**.**
   (ii) In Spain the word *clan* is used—by the press in particular—to describe extended families of Gypsies.

CLINTON, WILLIAM (BILL) JEFFERSON. The current president of the United States of America, elected in 1993 and descended from Scottish Gypsies. Mr. Clinton was originally called William Jefferson Blyth. Charles Blyth, who held the title of Charles I of the Gypsies, was crowned at Kirk Yetholm in 1847. He is Clinton's great-great-great-great-uncle. Charles's brother Andrew settled in the American south, and his son Andrew Jefferson Blyth was born in 1801 in South Carolina. He is the great-great-grandfather of Bill Clinton.

COLOCCI, ADRIANO. An Italian Gypsylorist. He met Gypsies during a visit to the Balkans and wrote a book about them *Gli Zingari: storia di un popolo errante* (Gypsies: The Story of a Wandering People)(1889). He was later elected as president of the **Gypsy Lore Society**. He was not just an amateur student of Gypsy lore, for he also took up the defense of the Gypsies in 1911 at the First Ethnographic Congress in Rome, where he denounced intolerance against Gypsies. He also opposed a proposal in the Italian Parliament to ban the immigration of Gypsies.

COLOGNE CONFERENCE. In February 1989 a conference and arts festival was held in Cologne attended by more than 450 persons, mainly Romanies, from towns in Germany and elsewhere. A new group was formed at the end of the conference—the Cologne Appeal for the Implementation of Human Rights for Sinti and Roma.

COMBAYS. A trio from Zaragoza playing rumbas. They made one record in Spain and were the support for the **Gypsy Kings** at the Nimes Festival in 1989. The trio no longer plays together.

COMITÉ INTERNATIONAL ROM. See COMITÉ INTERNATIONAL TZIGANE.

COMITÉ INTERNATIONAL TZIGANE (CIT; International Gypsy Committee). Formed in Paris in 1965, it sought to overcome religious and clan differences to create a united body. Muslim, Catholic, Orthodox and Protestant all worked together. The CIT formed several branches in other countries and adopted non-Gypsy strategies, such as demonstrations, to gain publicity for its aims. These aims included preserving Gypsy culture and language and promoting the right of Gypsies to travel. It then went on to launch the first **World Romany Congress**, near London in 1971. It later changed its name to Comité International Rom (CIR). The CIR's international role was gradually taken over by the **World Romany Congress** and the **Romany Union**. The CIR continues to operate on a small scale in Paris.

COMMITTEE FOR THE DEFENSE OF MINORITY RIGHTS. The Bulgarian partner in a contemporary project under the auspices of the **Minority Rights Group**, United Kingdom. The committee has created three curriculum working groups to create educational materials about the Romanies' history, literature and music. The Bulgarian Ministry of Education has recently agreed that some of these materials can be used in schools.

COMMUNAUTÉ MONDIALE GITANE (CMG). The organization founded early in the 1960s by **Vaida Voevod III**. It was banned by the French government in 1965, and most of its work taken over by the **Comité International Tzigane.** The CMG nevertheless continued to operate at least until 1984.

CONFERENCE ON SECURITY AND CO-OPERATION IN EUROPE (CSCE). Established in 1975 at a meeting of world leaders in Helsinki. One of its aims was to increase democracy in Europe. A development of this has been the protection of minority rights. Both the participating states and the associated nongovernmental organizations have taken on board the Gypsy issue. At the CSCE follow-up meeting in Helsinki in 1992 and the CSCE Council meeting in Rome in 1993, it was decided that the **Office for Democratic Institutions and Human Rights** (ODIHR)—an institution of the CSCE—would organize a number of specialized meetings. The seventh of these seminars dealt with Gypsies in the CSCE region and took place in Warsaw in September 1994. A consolidated summary of the discussions was published by the CSCE. In 1994 it became the **Organization for Security and Co-operation in Europe.**

CONGRESS OF LOCAL AND REGIONAL AUTHORITIES OF EUROPE (CLRAE). The CLRAE works as part of the **Council of Europe**. It was among the first international bodies to concern itself with Gypsies. In 1979 its Cultural Committee organized a hearing on the subject of the problems of populations of nomadic origin.

In 1981 a Resolution on the Role and Responsibility of Local and Regional Authorities in regard to the Cultural and Social Problems of Populations of Nomadic Origin (Resolution 125) contained a number of recommendations mainly directed at the Council of Europe and other bodies. They included:

- the designation of a mediator for the problems of nomads
- the recognition by countries of the Romanies and the Sami as an ethnic minority
- the provision of camping and housing facilities
- the provision of more information by the traveling people about their cultural and social identity and
- the drawing up of a map showing caravan sites open to traveling people.

In July 1991 a second hearing was held in Strasbourg with representatives of Gypsy communities from 12 European countries. One of the results of this hearing was the setting up of the **Standing Conference** for Co-operation and Coordination of Romany Associations in Europe.

In 1993 the CLRAE passed a resolution specifically on the Gypsies. This was Resolution 249 on Gypsies in Europe, concerning the role and responsibility of local and regional authorities. It called on various authorities to:

- integrate Gypsies into their local communities by providing camping sites and housing
- provide comprehensive information to counteract prejudice suffered by Roma/Gypsies
- consider the possibility of launching a European Gypsy Route as part of the European Cultural Routes program and

- launch a network of municipalities concerned with the reception of Gypsy communities.

CONNORS, JOHNNY "POPS." A contemporary Irish Traveller civil rights activist and songwriter, active in the early days of the **Gypsy Council**. His songs and fragments of his autobiography (*Seven Weeks of Childhood*) have been published in various ephemera.

CONTACT POINT ON ROMA AND SINTI ISSUES (CPRSI). The contact point was set up by the Budapest meeting of the **Organization for Security and Co-operation in Europe** in 1994. The coordinator for the Contact Point is Jacek Paliszewski, who is based in Warsaw, helped by interns. The CPRSI newsletter is published by the **Office for Democratic Institutions and Human Rights**. The CPRSI logs all reported instances of violence against Romanies and Sinti and informs the national authorities in the respective countries. In January 1996 the CPRSI organized a Workshop on Violence against Roma in Warsaw attended by representatives of 35 Romany and Sinti organizations and nongovernmental organizations. On November 21 and 22, 1996, the Contact Point and the **Council of Europe** held a meeting in Budapest with representatives of governments and Romany organizations to discuss minority rights and the legal situation of Romanies. This meeting appears to have taken place simultaneously with that of the **Standing Conference** for Co-operation and Coordination of Romany Associations in Europe in Vienna, which shows perhaps the numbers now involved in self-defense activities. It is preparing a special report on violence against Gypsies for the OSCE Permanent Council.

CORFU. In the 14th century, Gypsies were already living on Corfu under the leadership of one of their own clan.

CORTES, JOAQUÍN (1969–   ). A dancer and choreographer, born in Cordoba, Spain. His passion for dance was inspired by his uncle, Cristobel Reyes, who performed flamenco in local bars and persuaded Cortes to study ballet. His grandfather was the flamenco singer **Antonio Reyes**. Cortes joined the Spanish National Ballet at 15 and soon became the principal dancer but left at 20 to pursue a solo career. In 1992 he established his own company and began to develop his individual style. Combining ballet and flamenco, he caused an instant sensation in the Spanish national press but was also criticized for diluting Gypsy culture. He has insisted that his style is in fact a combination of "precision and passion, symbolizing the pride of a marginalized tribe, and that just as the younger generation of Gypsies is now adapting to white culture and wants to be absorbed, so Gypsy culture is adapting too." He has appeared in two major films: *The Flower of My Secret* and *Flamenco*. His first show as producer and choreographer was *Cibayi*, followed by *Pasión Gitana*, which went on a world tour during 1995–1997.

CORTES, LUIS. A contemporary sculptor, born in Spain. He is currently living and working in Italy.

CORTIADE (COURTHIADE), MARCEL. A contemporary linguist and translator from Occitania in France. He is vice president of the International **Romany Union**. He has been active in promoting a standard **alphabet** and a common language for literary purposes and organizes the annual language **summer schools.**

COUNCIL FOR CULTURAL CO-OPERATION (CDCC). The CDCC has organized since 1983 a series of training courses and seminars for teachers on schooling for Gypsy and Traveller children. It commissioned from **Jean-Pierre Liégeois** an expanded edition of a Council of Europe publication on the Gypsies of Europe, which has now appeared under the title *Roma, Gypsies and Travellers* (with a number of translations). The CDCC has also supported the **Centre de Recherches Tsiganes** in Paris in the production of a primer in common Romani.

COUNCIL OF EUROPE. The Council of Europe, based in Strasbourg, first took an interest in Gypsies in 1969 when the Consultative Assembly adopted Recommendation 563 on the Situation of Gypsies and other Travellers in Europe. It recommended to the Committee of Ministers (of the Council) that it urge member governments to stop discrimination, provide a sufficient number of equipped caravan sites and houses, set up special classes where necessary, support the creation of national bodies with Gypsy representation and ensure that Gypsies and other Travellers have the same rights as the settled population.

Six years later, in 1975, the Committee of Ministers adopted Resolution 13, containing recommendations on the Social Situation of Nomads in Europe. This again stressed the need to avoid discrimination, provide caravan sites, education and training for adults, and ensure that nomads could benefit from welfare and health services.

In 1983 the Committee of Ministers adopted Recommendation R1 on Stateless Nomads and Nomads of Undetermined Nationality, recommending the linking of such nomads with a particular state.

In 1993 the Parliamentary Assembly adopted Recommendation

1203 on Gypsies in Europe. It again proceeded by making recommendations to the Committee of Ministers. Recognition was given to the existence of large, settled Gypsy populations in many countries. These recommendations were far-reaching, covering the teaching of music and the Romani language, training of teachers, the participation of Gypsies in processes concerning them, the appointment of a mediator and programs to improve the housing and educational position of Gypsies.

A first reply was given by the Committee of Ministers to the Assembly in January 1994. The committee then instructed the European Committee on Migration to conduct an in-depth study of the situation of Gypsies in Europe. Further, in September 1995 the Committee of Ministers replied again to Recommendation 1203 adopted in 1993. The report of the study was declassified and made available to the assembly. The Committee of Ministers has transmitted the Committee on Migration's report to the European Commission against Racism and Intolerance and other bodies.

In 1996 the Council of Europe set up a **Specialist Group on Roma/Gypsies**, chosen from nominees by the different member states. The first meeting was held in March in Strasbourg. The council now has a co-ordinator of activities on Roma/Gypsies, John Murray who is based in Strasbourg. A newsletter is published regularly giving an account of the council's work in respect of Gypsies. See also CONGRESS OF LOCAL AND REGIONAL AUTHORITIES OF EUROPE.

CRABB, JAMES. An English clergyman in the 19th century who set up a number of educational projects for Gypsies. He opened a center for Gypsies in Southampton and tried to promote Christianity among them.

CRETE. Gypsies were recorded in Crete in 1322, living in black tents. It is likely that they returned to the coast of present-day Lebanon. Others came later, and the presence of Gypsies, living in poverty, was noted again in 1528.

CRIMEA. See UKRAINE.

CRIPPS REPORT. The Labour Government in the United Kingdom in 1977 commissioned John Cripps (later to be Sir John Cripps) to write a report on the working of the 1968 **Caravan Sites Act.** He wrote a detailed report with many recommendations. Some of these were incorporated in a new Caravan Sites Bill that, however, was never passed owing to the fall of the Labour government in 1979.

CRIS. See KRIS.

CRISS. See RROMANI CRISS.

CROATIA. Estimated Gypsy population: 100,000. The first written record of Gypsies on the territory of present-day Croatia dates from 1362 and refers to two Gypsies in Dubrovnik. Other early arrivals noted in the next century were a trumpeter and a lute player.

Until 1918 Croatia was associated with the Austro-Hungarian Empire. It then became part of **Yugoslavia**. During World War II, after the German occupation of Yugoslavia, a puppet state was set up covering Croatia and Bosnia-Hercegovina under the control of the fascist Ustashe movement and Ante Pavelió. For the Ustashe Gypsies, Jews and Orthodox Serbs were the enemy. Muslim Gypsies had a certain amount of protection from the Muslim authorities because Germany wanted the friendship of Muslim leaders in the Middle East. Under Decree No. 13–542 of the Ministry of the Interior, all Gypsies had to register with the police in July 1941. They were forbidden to use parks and cafés. By 1943 most of Croatia's Gypsies were put in the Ustashe-run concentration camps: **Jasenovac**, Stara Gradiska, Strug and Tenje. At the creation of the Independent State of Croatia, there had been over 30,000 Gypsies, either nominally Orthodox or Moslem. At least 26,000 perished between 1941 and 1945.

Croatia became part of Yugoslavia from 1944 to 1991. At the end of the war very few Gypsies survived in Croatia itself, but there was a steady immigration from other parts of Yugoslavia.

Croatia became independent in 1991. During the 1991–1995 war in ex-Yugoslavia, many Romanies who did not manage to escape from Baranja (in western Slavonia) were killed by the Serbian occupiers. On November 31, 1991, Serbian irregular units burnt down the Gypsy quarter of the village of Torjanici and killed the remaining 11 inhabitants. Because the Gypsies were Catholics, they were accused of collaborating with the Croats. In 1993 Romanies were driven out of a suburb of Zagreb called Dubac by Croats returning from fighting the Serbs and have had to resettle elsewhere in Croatia.

Official census figures were 313 Gypsies in 1961, rising to 1,257 in 1971, 3,858 in 1981, and 6,695 in 1991. Various sources give estimates for the real figures ranging from 35,000 to 150,000.

The Cidinipe Romano ani Croatia (Romany Society in Croatia) was founded in 1991 with its headquarters in Virovitica. Its president is Vid Bogdan. In 1994 the bulletin *Romano Akharipe /Glas Roma* (*Romany Voice*) was established. In 1994 also the first summer school was organized in Zagreb for Romany children. Other Romany associations are in Rijeka, Zagreb (Zajednica Roma Grada Zagreba and Cidinipe Roma ani Zagreb) and elsewhere.

CSARDAS (czardas). A popular couple dance in Hungary and Romania. The Gypsy csardas is traditionally danced with the man and woman not holding hands. The dance may go on for some time with a new man or woman taking over the role of one of the partners.

CYPRUS. Estimated Gypsy population: 4,000 (in both parts of the island). The first recorded presence of Gypsies on the island is from 1468, but it is thought that they were there some years earlier. In 1549 a report described them earning their living from making and selling nails and belts. In this century they trade in jewelry and meat skewers, tell fortunes, and sell donkeys. They also travel to different parts of the island to help with the harvest. Many villages and towns allocated sites where the nomadic Gypsies could stop.

Since 1974 Cyprus has been divided into two parts. In that year Muslim Gypsies fled to the Turkish-held part of the island and Christian Gypsies to the Greek part, whereas previously both groups had circulated freely throughout Cyprus. Shortly after Turkish troops entered Cyprus, rumors circulated that the Turkish Government was bringing in large numbers of Gypsies. This proved to be false—the new immigrants were Laz (a Turkic group). The traditional circuit for harvest work in the west of the island for carob and olives and then to the east for grapes has been stopped by partition.

All reports suggest that the small Gypsy population in Greek Cyprus lives in comparative harmony with the Greek-speaking population, although there is little social mixing. In Greek they are known by two names: Yieftos (**Egyptians**) and Tsignos (from **athingani**).

Asylum seekers from Turkish Cyprus state that the situation of several thousand Gypsies, known as Gurbet (or çengene), there is not as good as in the Greek part. There is a great deal of racism and discrimination in employment. Many have tried to seek asylum in Britain to join relatives who came legally as citizens of Cyprus when it was a British colony. In 1994 over 350 Gypsies sought asylum on one day and all were refused. In 1994, too, some Turkish airline companies refused to sell tickets to Romanies, saying they gave Turkey a bad name by seeking asylum in the West. A well-known personage in the community is the painter Asik Mene. The majority of the Gypsies in Turkish Cyprus live in the town of Guzelyurt.

CZECH REPUBLIC. Estimated Gypsy population: 300,000. The Czech Republic was established in 1993 when Czechoslovakia became two separate states. Most of the families had come from **Slovakia** after

1945. Some of these had difficulties in obtaining Czech citizenship and were in danger of becoming stateless. The new law stated that applicants for citizenship had to have had a clean criminal record for at least five years. This requirement has been criticized, as many Romanies have been punished for acts that would not have been considered crimes in a democratic state. Young unmarried women, for example, who stayed at home were sentenced as work-shy, and others obtained a criminal record by committing the "crime" of moving from one town to another without permission.

Prejudice against Gypsies persists and incidents of discrimination and harassment have been reported. Attacks on Gypsies by skinheads and right-wing elements that began before the breakup—as early as 1990—have increased and have led to many deaths. At least 12 Romanies are known to have died in racist violence since 1992 in Czechoslovakia. Two Romanies were killed in 1993 in the space of one week in September. Also in 1993 Tibor Danihel was drowned, fleeing from a skinhead gang. In 1994 skinheads threw Molotov cocktails into the homes of Romanies in Jablonec nad Nisou. In 1995 skinheads attacked Gypsies in Breclav and on a train from Chomutov to Klasterec. Tibor Berki was killed in May 1995 in Zdár nad Sázavou. Roman Zigi was killed in the same year. Further attacks took place in Prague, Hlubaha nad Vltava, Jablonec nad Nisou, Olomouc, and elsewhere. In 1995 altogether more than 80 attacks by skinheads and right-wing groups on Romanies were reported, twice as many as in 1994. A band of 13 skinheads attacked two Romany couples in Pilsen, Bohemia early in 1996. Accusations have been made of police harassment. In June 1994 Martin Cervenak died in police custody. The Ministry of the Interior has issued special instructions for police searching Romany dwellings. There is also discrimination in admission to restaurants and discotheques throughout the country. Segregation in hospitals and schools has also been reported. The right-wing Republican party has attacked Gypsies in speeches.

The 1991 census (taken before the two countries split) only recorded 33,000 Romanies. The new freedom to form organizations, travel, and publish after the fall of communism in 1989, however, led to a flourishing of activities. The **Museum** in **Brno** obtained its own building and several journals are published. Romani was introduced as a degree subject in Prague University in 1991, taught by **Milena Hübschmannová,** and two radio programs aimed at the Gypsy population are broadcast. There are many Romany and pro-Romany organizations operating in the Czech Republic, such as the Foundation for the Renewal and Development of Traditional Romany Values and the Dr. **Rajko Djurić Foundation.** See also CZECHOSLOVAKIA.

CZECHOSLOVAKIA. In 1399 the first Gypsy on the territory of Bohemia is mentioned in a chronicle. There are further references, and then in 1541 Gypsies were accused of starting a fire in Prague.

In general, while the provinces were under the **Habsburgs** and the **Holy Roman Empire**, Gypsies were semi-nomadic in Bohemia and Moravia. They were largely protected over the centuries against central legislation by noblemen who found their services useful on their estates even though Leopold I in the 17th century, for example, had declared that all Gypsies were outlaws. He had ordered them to be flogged and then banished if found in the country. In Slovakia they were pressed to settle by **Maria Theresa** and **Joseph II**.

The modern state of Czechoslovakia was formed in 1918. In 1921 Gypsies were recognized as a minority and able to organize some sports clubs. However, both the nomads and those living in settlements were viewed with mistrust by the majority population. Nineteen Gypsies were tried for cannibalism in Kosice in 1924 (and eventually found not guilty). In 1928 there was a pogrom against Gypsies in Pobedim after some crops had been pilfered. Slovak villagers killed four adults and two children and wounded 18 more.

Nomadism by **Vlah** Romanies was strongly discouraged. Law 117 of July 19, 1927, placed controls on a wide variety of nomadic tradesmen. All Romany nomads had to carry a special pass and be registered if they were over the age of 14. Over the next 13 years, the number of identity cards issued reached nearly 40,000. Local regulations prohibited Gypsies from entering certain areas.

Germany invaded Czechoslovakia in 1938. The country was divided, and the Czech lands (Bohemia and Moravia) became a German protectorate in 1939. The first anti-Gypsy decree during the Nazi occupation by the Protectorate Ministry of the Interior on March 31, 1939, prohibited nomadism in the border zones and in groups larger than an extended family. In May 1942 a further decree was passed (on the Fight to Prevent Criminality) by which Gypsies were not allowed to leave their residence without permission and all Gypsies could be taken into "protective custody." A count of Gypsies on August 2, 1942, registered 5,830 "pure and half-breed" Gypsies. Two existing work camps at Lety and Hodonín were turned into concentration camps for Gypsies. Gypsies were also sent to the main camp at **Auschwitz** in December 1942 and January 1943. The Lety camp received a total of over 1,200 prisoners, and Hodonín a similar number. Conditions in these camps were poor. Food and medical attention were in short supply and the guards brutally beat the inmates. Over 500 prisoners died in the camps before they were closed in 1943, and the majority of the inmates transferred to the Gypsy Family Camp in Auschwitz, together with over 3,000 Gypsies who had been left in supervised liberty. Only some 600 persons all told survived the Nazi occupation of the Czech lands.

In contrast to the multinational state that had existed before World War II, Czechoslovakia in 1945 was restored as a state for the Czechs and Slovaks, and there was no place in it for the Romanies as a nationality or even as an ethnic group. Little changed with the takeover in 1948 by the communists who decided on a policy of assimilating the Gypsies.

The first step was to end nomadism and a law to this effect was passed in 1958. The penalty for disobedience was imprisonment. The some 10,000 nomads' horses were taken away and the wheels removed from their **caravans**. In 1958, too, the Communists issued a statement saying that Gypsies constituted a socioeconomic group (not an ethnic group), which had to be approached in a specific manner. In 1965 the government passed the Resettlement Law. It was decided that no town or village should contain more than 5 percent Gypsies. This meant that large numbers would have to be resettled from Slovakia to the Czech lands. Both the Gypsies and the potential host communities resisted this transfer, although some Romanies had moved west in search of work in the postwar years.

The government did allow the setting up of the Svaz Cikan Rom (Union of the Romany Gypsies) in 1968, operating throughout Czechoslovakia. Some 20,000 members joined in the first two years. The Union established a recommended orthography for the Romani language and for a time a number of publications were produced. A Czechoslovak delegation attended the first **World Romany Congress,** but no one was allowed to travel to the second or third congresses. Lessons in Romani for teachers were organized from 1971 to 1974.

The Soviet invasion of 1968 led, however, to a change in the liberal policy, under Husak's government. In 1973 the Gypsy organizations were wound up, the magazines ceased to appear, and from then until 1989 there were to be very few publications in Romani.

The next attempt to control the Gypsy population was a sterilization program linked to a decree of 1972. Hints were passed on by word of mouth to social workers and doctors that Gypsies should be encouraged to be sterilized. Special inducements were offered to Romany women—classed as "socially weak" under the decree. After bearing a fourth child a Czechoslovak woman could be sterilized on payment of 2,000 crowns. Romany women, on the other hand, were offered 2,000 crowns to be sterilized after the second child. Some women were treated without them being aware that the operation was irreversible. The civil rights movement Charter 77 organized protests against this program. It is believed that 9,000 Romany women were sterilized during the program, including some who had had no children.

In the last years of the Czechoslovak Republic, a revival of organizations and publications took place. In the 1990 elections the Roman Civic Initiative (ROI) gained two seats in the federal parliament. See also GERMANY for legislation for Czech territory in the Middle Ages, SLOVAKIA for the World War II period there, and the CZECH REPUBLIC and SLOVAKIA for the new states after 1993.

CZIFFRA, GYÖRGY (ca.1915–1970). A classical pianist in Hungary.

CZINKA, PANNA. See PANNA, CZINKA.

D

DANIEL, ANTONIN (1958–1996). Born in **Brno**, Czechoslovakia. He was a teacher, writing in Romani.

DANIEL, BARTOLOMĚJ. A contemporary historian working at the **museum** in **Brno**, Czech Republic.

DANIHEL, VINCENT (1946–   ). A cultural worker and writer in Slovakia.

DARÓCZI, AGNES. A contemporary Hungarian civil rights activist. She was active in the cultural association Amalipe and is now part of the teams preparing the regular radio and TV broadcasts aimed at the Romany population.

DARÓCZI, JÓZSEF CHOLI. A contemporary poet, translator and cultural activist. He has translated the four gospels into Romani as well as **Federico Garcia Lorca**'s *Romancero Gitano,* which has appeared in a trilingual edition in Budapest (Romani, Hungarian, Spanish). He was a presidium member of the **Romany Union**. In 1979 he became the head of a new political organization for the Romanies in Hungary—the Orzsagos Cigánytanacs (National Gypsy Council).

DAVIDOVÁ, EVA. A sociologist in the Czech republic. She helped to keep Romany culture alive during the years 1958–1989 and was one of the founders of the **Brno Museum**.

DĘBICJI, EDWARD. A Gypsy poet in Poland. His brainchild is the Gypsy music festival in Gorzów Wielkopolski, which has run annually since 1989. In addition to music, it has featured films, exhibitions, and book promotions and, more recently, seminars related to Gypsy culture. He is also director of the Gypsy music group Terno and has written *Tel nango boliben* (Under the Open Sky) published in 1993 (available in Polish and Romani).

DENMARK. Estimated Gypsy population: 1,750. The first recorded Gypsies in Denmark came from Scotland in 1505 and then moved on to Sweden. They had a letter of recommendation from King James IV of Scotland to King Hans of Denmark, his uncle. In 1505 other Gypsies came across the border from Germany. Junker Jørgen of Egypt came to Jutland and got a letter of safe conduct from Duke Frederik. In 1536, however, *tatere* (Gypsies) were ordered to leave Denmark in three months. This order was not obeyed. In 1554 King Christian III circulated a letter accusing many noblemen and others of supporting the Gypsies, although they were believed to be "wandering around and deceiving the people." Anyone who gave them refuge would be punished, anyone who killed a Gypsy could keep his property, and any local authority official who did not arrest the Gypsies in his area would have to pay for any damage they did. The main effect of this letter was that the Gypsies started traveling in smaller groups. A further letter was issued in 1561 by Frederick II, in a milder form than Christian's. A certain Peder Oxe was sent to arrest all Gypsies in Jutland and bring them to Copenhagen to work as smiths or in the galleys.

In 1578 the Bishop of Fyn told his priests not to marry Gypsies and to have them buried outside the churchyard as if they were Turks. In 1589 the original edict, ordering Gypsies to leave the realm inside three months, was reissued with the addition of capital punishment for those who remained. With the end of immigration and strong laws, the Gypsies resident in Denmark merged with the indigenous nomadic population forming a group of Travellers, popularly still called *tatere*. There was a small immigration of **Sinti** and **Jenisch** families at the beginning of the 19th century. The laws against Gypsies were eased in 1849 and reimposed in 1875 with the threat of a large-scale immigration of **Vlah** Romanies. From 1911 this law was carried out more effectively with the creation of a national police force. A traveling musical group known as Marietta's gang were probably the last to be expelled, in 1913, and by 1939 very few families of Gypsies, if any, lived in Denmark, and the Travellers had all but disappeared.

After 1945, the government banned anyone who had not been born in a caravan from nomadizing. Around 1970 there was a camping site at Islands Brygge near Copenhagen that was used by Scandinavian

Travellers and Gypsies, and from time to time by Dutch Travellers. After the repeal of anti-Gypsy legislation in 1953, small numbers immigrated from Eastern and Central Europe. They are settled in houses and flats in Copenhagen and Helsingor. Stevica Nikolić was the representative of the **Comité International Rom** until he moved to Holland.

DERBY. A horse race in England. It has for a long time been one of the important events in the Gypsy calendar. Gypsies have gathered there for many years from the Sunday before the race (known as Show Sunday). Apart from being a source of income for fortune-tellers and racing tipsters, it is also a social gathering. Gypsies maintain that they were the first to race on the Epsom Downs where the Derby takes place. Since 1937 several attempts have been made to stop Gypsies from attending. In that year Gypsies camped instead on the land of a sympathizer, Lady Sybil Grant. Currently a fenced-in field has been allocated for Gypsy families and their **caravans**, while the fortune-tellers park separately. It is likely that the moving of the Derby from Wednesday to Saturday (when it clashes with the **Appleby Fair**) will lead to a reduction in the number of Gypsies attending.

DEVEL (DEL). The Romani word for "God." It is cognate with Latin *Deus* and Greek *theos*. Early writers on Gypsies were confused by the similarity of *Devel* and "Devil" and thought the Gypsies worshipped the Devil. The Romani word for "Devil" is *Beng*.

DEVLIN, BERNADETTE. See McALISKEY, BERNADETTE.

DIMIĆ, TRIFUN. A contemporary writer in Serbia. He has translated the New Testament and the *Epic of Gilgemish* into Romani. He has also translated and produced a first reader for children.

DIMITRIEVITCH, VALJA. A singer, formerly living in Russia. She is married to the Brazilian consul in France.

DJURIĆ, RAJKO (1947–   ). A journalist and poet, born in Malo Orasje near Belgrade. Djuric studied in the Faculty of Philosophy at Belgrade University from 1967 to 1972. In 1985 he was awarded a doctorate for his thesis on the culture of the Romanies in Yugoslavia. Until 1991 he was editor of the cultural section of the daily newspaper *Politika*. As an opponent of the government and the war in Bosnia, he had to flee in October that year to Germany, where he still lives. He has written poetry and prose in both Romani and Serbo-Croat. At the third **World Romany Congress**, he was elected secretary, and at the fourth Congress he became president. *Zigeunerische Elegien* (Gypsy Elegies) is a bilingual edition of his poetry in German and Romani, published in 1989.

DODDS, NORMAN. A Labour member of Parliament in the United Kingdom who fought for Gypsy rights. At one time he opened a **caravan** camp on his own land. He was to die before seeing the fruits of his efforts in the **Caravan Sites Act of 1968**.

DOM. Dom is an earlier form of the word *Rom*. Originally in Sanskrit it meant "man" and was the self-ascription of many tribes, some of whom emigrated west and helped to form the Romany people. However, in some parts of India it now has a pejorative meaning, referring to a lower caste person. Members of a clan of Indian origin in the Middle East known as Dom or **Nawwar** occasionally visit Europe.

DOONANS, THE. **Irish Traveller** musicians.

DORAN, FELIX (?–1972). An **Irish Traveller,** piper and brother of **Johnny Doran**. He won the first prize for the pipes at Fleadh Ceoil na h-Eireann, the national competition. He moved to Manchester where he became a haulage contractor and continued to play and record.

DORAN, JOHNNY (1907–1949). An **Irish Traveller**, piper and brother of **Felix Doran**. Johnny and Felix were descendants of John Cash, a famous piper in Wicklow in the 19th century. Johnny traveled in a horse-drawn caravan throughout Ireland but principally in County Clare, before he was killed in an accident.

DORTIKA. A variety of Greek with Romani words.

DOUGLAS, CHARLES MBE (Member of the Order of the British Empire). A **Scottish Traveller**. He was an activist in the 1970s, including setting up the Scottish Gypsy Council, which worked in cooperation with the **Gypsy Council**. He has been one of the representatives of Travellers on the Advisory Committee for the secretary of state for Scotland.

DRAKHIN (Grapevine). A web site for Romanies conducted in the Romani language.

DRAMA. The establishment of the **Teatr Romen** in Moscow led to the writing of plays in the USSR celebrating the transmutation of nomadic Gypsies into collective farmers and factory workers. After 1945, a few writers have created original plays in Romani. The works of **Romanov Manush** in Bulgaria were unfortunately confiscated by the police some years after the Sofia Gypsy theater was closed. See GINA, ANDREJ; KRASNICI, ALI; LACKOVA, ELENA.

DRINDARI. Quiltmakers' clan in Kotel, Bulgaria. Their name comes from the sound made by a mallet carding wool for quilts. They are also known as *Musikantsi* (Musicians) and *katkaji*—as they use the word *katka* (here) in their dialect as opposed to the majority of Bulgarian Gypsies who say *kate*. Bernard Gilliatt-Smith described their dialect in the *Journal of the Gypsy Lore Society*.

DUBLIN TRAVELLERS' EDUCATION AND DEVELOPMENT GROUP. Formed in 1983. Part of its program includes legal advice and training courses for young adults. It is now known as **Pavee Point**, after the name of its headquarters and to reflect its nationwide role.

DUENDE. A Spanish term describing a mysterious power held by some **flamenco** singers and dancers.

DUO Z. The professional name used by the singers **Rudko Kawczynski** and Torando Rosenberg from 1979. The Z stood for the concentration camp designation of Gypsies (*Zigeuner*). Their aim was to sing for the non-Gypsies to confront them with the problems of their people. One of their successes was a reworking of the German folk song *Lustig ist das Zigeunerleben* (Gypsy Life is Carefree) with words referring to the persecution during and after the **Holocaust**.

DŽENO FOUNDATION. A foundation in the Czech Republic that aims at the renewal and development of traditional Romany values. Among its activities are collecting and analyzing media reports and running training courses. It made a presentation to the Prague seminar on the media in September 1996. It publishes a quarterly magazine called *Romani Duma* (Romany Word).

E

EAST ANGLIAN GYPSY COUNCIL. A regional body operating in England under the leadership of Peter Mercer.

ECONOMIC AND SOCIAL COUNCIL OF THE UNITED NATIONS (ECOSOC). In 1979 the **Romany Union** was recognized as a non-governmental organization representing Gypsies and **Travellers**. In 1993 it was upgraded to category II status. **Etudes Tsiganes** is also recognized by ECOSOC. See also UNITED NATIONS.

EGYPTIANS. (i) The name first given to Gypsies when they reached Western Europe, as it was thought they came from Egypt. (ii) A number of groups in the Balkans previously thought to be Romany Gypsies but who no longer spoke the Romani language began in the last few years to claim that they were not Gypsies but descendants of Egyptian immigrants to Europe. They number several thousand and are found in Albania, Kosovo and Macedonia. In Albania they are known as Evgjit or Jevg. There, their non-Romany origin has been accepted for longer. There is a tale of an Egyptian shipwrecked on the coast near Durres around the year 825, being able to converse—in Coptic, presumably—with local Egyptians.

EINSATZGRUPPEN. The Nazi Task Forces that murdered some 20,000 Gypsies in the occupied regions of the Soviet Union between 1941 and 1943. Their primary targets were "Jewish Bolshevists." During a visit to Minsk in August 1941, Heinrich Himmler extended the original orders of the Task Forces to kill all Gypsies—men, women and children.

ENCYCLOPEDIA. The fourth **World Romany Congress** set up an Encyclopedia Commission with the remit of preparing an encyclopedia in Romani. The work has been taken over by a working party under the auspices of the **Centre de Recherches Tsiganes**. Some draft entries and a call for contributors were circulated with **Interface** early in 1997.

ENGLAND. Estimated Gypsy population (in **caravans** and houses): 110,000. It is likely that the first Gypsies came to England from France around 1480. The first written record dates from 1514 and refers to a fortune-teller from Lambeth who had left England some time previously. Further references occur between 1513 and 1530. A distinctive costume was common knowledge in England early in the 16th century, as we have records of court ladies dressing up as Gypsies as early as 1517. There were soon a large enough number of Gypsies to worry the authorities, and the first anti-Gypsy law was passed in 1530 under Henry VIII. This banned "**Egyptians**" from entering the country and ordered those already there to leave within 15 days. In 1540 a group of Gypsies was released from Marshalsea

Prison and put on a ship bound for Norway. Others were expelled to Calais, still an English colony. In 1554 and 1562 the law was strengthened, with the death penalty imposed for anyone consorting with the Gypsies. In 1577 in Aylesbury, six persons were hanged under this law, and a further five in Durham in 1592. Nine more Gypsies were executed in York in 1596. At least 13 more Gypsies were hanged under this law before it, and most legislation concerning Gypsies, was repealed in 1783.

Between 1598 and 1868, many Gypsies were deported to the colonies in Australia and America under the 1598 Act for the Punishment of Rogues, Vagabonds and Sturdy Beggars. In some parts of the country, however, no action was taken against Gypsies, and they were also protected by landowners who found it useful to have Gypsies available for entertainment and casual work.

Fortune-telling was evidently an important occupation. In 1602 **William Shakespeare**'s Desdemona refers to a handkerchief that an Egyptian woman who could read minds had given to her mother. The wife of the diarist Samuel Pepys went to see Gypsies at Lambeth with a friend to have their fortunes told. However, a male was apparently burned at the stake in Warwickshire for telling fortunes, if the story is to be believed.

The policy of expulsion from the country failed, and in the 19th century settlement and assimilation became the aim. Various Christian missions took an interest in the Gypsy nomads, and special schools were opened. In 1815 John Hoyland was commissioned by the Society of Friends to collect information about Gypsies with a view to improving their condition. This was the first survey made and gave **James Crabb**, among others, the impulse to start his mission. Assimilation was the aim, but this was thwarted by police and local authorities who continued to move Gypsies on. In 1822 and 1835 (the Highway Act) penalties were introduced for Gypsies camping on the highway. Attempts by **George Smith** to control the nomadic Gypsies with the **Moveable Dwellings Bills** in Parliament failed, however, owing to the opposition of circus and fair owners. The Gypsy population around this time has been estimated at about 10,000.

Popular novels in England—as elsewhere—featured Gypsies who stole children or pronounced curses that could not be avoided. In the late 19th century **Gypsylorists** emerged.

A new immigration started in the second half of the 19th century and there are reports of "foreign Gypsies—certainly belonging to **Vlah** clans. At the beginning of this century, England was visited by bear trainers, "German Gypsies" (probably **Lovari**) and the first of the **Kalderash** families who were to become regular visitors. Legislation against "aliens" aimed at Jewish immigrants from Eastern Europe, was used to prevent Romanies landing and to expel them rapidly. Nevertheless, in the 1930s the Kalderash Stirio and Yevanovic families established themselves in England, and their descendants form a compact Romani-speaking community today. **Irish Travellers** have been coming to England and the rest of Britain, particularly since the middle of the 19th century. They number some 6,000 in England.

Between the two world wars (1918–1939) much legislation was enacted affecting the nomadic Gypsies. The 1936 Public Health Act (Sec. 268) defined tents, vans and sheds as "statutory nuisances." In 1937 the first of many attempts to stop the Gypsies' annual gathering for the **Derby** horse race failed. During both wars Romanies served in the armed forces, and many were awarded medals for valor.

In the highly industrialized England that arose after 1945, nomadic Gypsies found life much harder. Their traditional camping places were built on, and, with increased and faster traffic, stopping on the roadside became dangerous and—in many cases—banned. The 1947 and 1950 Town and Country Planning Acts restricted the use of land by **caravans** and then the **Caravan Sites Act of 1960** led to the closure of many sites.

A civil rights movement began to emerge in the 1960s with the Society of Travelling People in Leeds (1965) and Tom Jonell in the south. In 1966 the **Gypsy Council** was founded at a meeting in Kent. Under its secretary **Grattan Puxon,** it began a campaign of passive resistance to the forced moving-on of caravan, which obtained considerable press and television publicity. It organized the first caravan school at Hornchurch aerodrome, with volunteer teachers including **Thomas Acton**. Others followed.

Under pressure from **Norman Dodds**, a member of Parliament, the central government began to take an interest in Gypsies. The Ministry of Housing and Local Government produced a report, *Gypsies and other Travellers* (1967), which was the first official study of Gypsies in England and Wales. With pressure from inside and outside Parliament, the **Caravan Sites Act of 1968** was passed, applying to England and Wales only. This act placed a duty on county councils in particular to provide caravan sites. However, areas of the country could then be "designated" as areas where Gypsies could not park their caravans unless they found a pitch on the official sites. The first of these designations were made in 1973.

In 1980 the Local Government Planning Land Act removed the word "Gypsy" from the 1835 Highway Act. This was no longer necessary because of the provisions of the 1968 Caravan Sites Act. Gypsies were no longer singled out for punishment for camping on the roadside, unless it was a "designated" area. In 1994 the Criminal

Justice and Public Order Act imposed stronger penalties for camping anywhere in England and Wales outside official sites. At the same time the duty on councils to provide such sites was removed, and Gypsies were told that they had to buy land, get planning permission and make their own caravan sites. The census figures for January 1997 show some 6,000 caravans on official council sites, over 3,500 on authorized private sites and 2,500 illegally parked.

In 1996 it was estimated that 50,000 nomadic children aged 0–16 lived in England. This figure includes some **New Age Travellers**. The majority of primary age children (5–11) attend school but the situation is not so satisfactory for secondary school children (age 11–16). Over 3,000 schools are in receipt of special grants for the children of "Travellers," who are defined as nomads or recent nomads. These grants are available for work with caravan dwelling families and those who have recently moved into housing. Continuing education after the age of 16 is not common. It is thought that three Gypsies or Travellers were attending college in 1996.

Gypsies in England today are mainly self-employed with such trades as recycling metal, landscape gardening and house repairs. As musicians they are known in folk club circles but not to the general public. See also SCOTLAND and WALES.

EPSOM DOWNS. A gathering place for English Gypsies at the time of the **Derby**. Howard Brenton wrote a play *Epsom Downs* that was first performed by the Joint Stock Company at the Roundhouse, London, in 1977.

ERKÖSE BROTHERS. Ali (zither), Barbaros (clarinet) and Salahaddin (lute) are contemporary folk musicians, originally from Bursa in Turkey. They have played concerts abroad and have recorded.

ERLIA, ARLIA. A term used by Romanies in the Balkans to describe sedentary Gypsies and their dialects, as opposed to nomads. The derivation is from the Turkish word *yerli* (local).

ESMA. See REDJEPOVA, ESMA.

ESSEX, DAVID (Albert David Cook) (1947–). A singer and actor who in 1971 took the part of Jesus in *Godspell* and in 1978 Che Guevara in *Evita*. He assisted at the official opening of the office in Essex of the **Gypsy Council for Education, Culture, Welfare and Civil Rights** (of which he is patron) in 1995. He has recorded the poems of **Charles Smith**.

ESTONIA. Estimated Gypsy population: 1,000. The first record of a Gypsy in the territory of present-day Estonia dates from 1533 when the presence of at least two Gypsies in Tallinn was noted. Estonia was under the rule of various countries until 1918, and their laws would have applied. Numbers have never been high, and, during the Nazi period, the German occupiers murdered almost all the Gypsies in the years 1941–43. The dead included the whole of the Lajenge Romanies, a distinct clan with their own dialect of Romani. The Estonian writer Tuglas Friedbert is of Romany origin.

ÉTUDES TSIGANES. An organization with mainly non-Gypsy members, founded in Paris after World War II. Since 1955 it has published the journal of the same name (current editor: Alan Reyniers) and has held two scientific conferences—the first in Sèvres in 1986 and the second in the Centre Pompidou in Paris. Most of the papers delivered at these conferences have been published, either in special volumes or in the journal.

EUROM. A Gypsy organization founded in 1990, following a meeting in Mülheim. Its members were mainly in Germany and Hungary.

EUROPEAN COMMISSION AD HOC ROMA PROJECT. The European Commission is a body of the European Union. It instigated a newsletter with project partners in Bulgaria, Poland, Slovakia and the **Minority Rights Group** (MRG) in London. The newsletter's purpose is to inform anyone involved in Romany rights and education.

EUROPEAN COMMISSION ON HUMAN RIGHTS. Established by the Council of Europe in 1950 it merged into the European Court of Human Rights in 1993.

EUROPEAN COMMITTEE ON MIGRATION (CDMG). On the instructions of the Committee of Ministers of the **Council of Europe,** the CDMG carried out an in-depth study in 1994 on the situation of Gypsies in Europe.

EUROPEAN COMMUNITIES. See EUROPEAN UNION.

EUROPEAN CONGRESS. Held in Seville, Spain, in 1994 this congress was organized originally with the primary purpose of looking at education, but its remit expanded and it took on the air of an international congress. The king and queen of Spain patronized the proceedings.

EUROPEAN PARLIAMENT. See EUROPEAN UNION.

EUROPEAN ROMA RIGHTS CENTER. An autonomous nongovernmental human rights organization in Budapest, Hungary, governed
by a nine-member board to monitor and defend the human rights of
Romanies in Europe. It was founded in March 1996. The chair is
Andreas Biro, and the director is Dimitrina Petrova. Initial funding
came from the **Open Society** Institute. The center's publications include *Divide and Deport: Roma & Sinti in Austria* (1996). In January
1997, together with the **Autonomia Foundation** and the **Human
Rights Project,** it organized a four-day symposium of lawyers and
human rights activists to discuss the legal developments in the field of
human rights for Romanies. The symposium highlighted the difficulty
Romanies meet in trying to get redress for violence and discrimination against them.

EUROPEAN UNION. The European Union (previously known as the
European Communities), based in Brussels, has taken a number of
initiatives in Gypsy matters.

On May 24, 1984, the European Parliament passed a resolution
on the situation of Gypsies in the Community. It called on member
states:
- to eliminate existing discriminatory provisions that may exist in
  their legislation
- to coordinate their reception of Gypsies
- to make it easier for nomads to attach themselves to a state (in
  accordance with recommendation R(83)1 of the **Council of Europe**) and
- to draw up programs to improve the situation of Gypsies and
  subsidized from Community funds, after representation from
  Gypsy organizations has been sought.

On May 22, 1989, the council passed a resolution on School Provision for Gypsy and Traveller Children. The program of action to be
taken included the following:
- support for educational establishments
- experiments with distance learning
- training and employing Gypsies and Travellers as teachers wherever possible
- encouragement of research on the culture of Gypsies and Travellers and
- exchange of experience by meetings at Community level.

The Union has financed a number of projects in the spirit of these
recommendations. Governments were to let the European Union
know the results of their measures so that a combined report could

be presented to the Council by December 31, 1993. The report was eventually published in 1996.

EUROROMA. A civil rights program run by the **Autonomia Foundation** in Hungary. It covers Bulgaria, Slovakia, Hungary and Romania and is financed by the **European Union**. Its aim is to foster self-help initiatives among the Romany communities in the partner countries. The first meeting of the partner organizations from the four countries took place in Budapest in January 1996.

EVANGELICAL CHURCH. See CENTRE MISSIONAIRE ÉVANGÉLIQUE ROM INTERNATIONALE; PENTECOSTALISM.

EVENS, REVEREND GEORGE BRAMWELL (?–1943). Known as "Romany." He was the son of Tilly Smith—the sister of **Rodney Smith**—and Salvation Army lieutenant George Evens. He was a broadcaster of BBC *Children's Hour* programs in Manchester from 1933 to 1943, when he unexpectedly died. His wife, Eunice Evens, published a biography of her husband entitled *Through the Years with Romany.*

EVGJIT. See EGYPTIAN.

EYNARD, GILES. An activist in France. He was a member of the committee of the Comité Rom de Provence and the West European Gypsy Council. He is currently treasurer of **Tchatchipen**.

EXPERT GROUP (of the **Council of Europe**). See SPECIALIST GROUP ON ROMA/GYPSIES.

F

FAA. The surname of several **Scottish Traveller** families. The name was also adopted by some Romanies who came to Scotland.

FAA, JOHNNY. A **Scottish Traveller** who, according to legend, rescued two sisters from the clutches of their uncle in 1470. The uncle had thrown them into a cellar to make off with their inheritance.

FABIANOVÁ, TERA (1930–   ). A writer in the Czech Republic who was one of the first to write in Romani.

FAMULSON, VICTOR. A **Vlah** Romany living in Finland and vice-president of the International **Romany Union** (elected 1990).

FAYS, RAPHAEL (1959–). An Italian Manouche guitarist and the son of the guitarist Louis Fays. He plays classical as well as jazz and Latin American music. He is currently playing in the **Django Reinhardt** style with a trio.

FELDITKA ROMA. A term used for the Lowland Gypsies in Poland.

FERKOVÁ, ILONA (1956–). Writer of tales in Romani, born in **Rokycany**, in the Czech Republic. Ferková began to write in Romani after getting acquainted with the works of **Tera Fabianová** and **Margita Reiznerová**.

FERRÉ, BOULOU. A contemporary Gypsy jazz guitarist and the son of **Matelo Ferré**. Both he and his brother Elios tour widely as a duo in the style of **Django Reinhardt**. They have made several recordings.

FERRÉ, MATELO (1918–). A jazz guitarist. He is the last survivor of the senior Ferré brothers. A *Gitano* living in Paris, he and his brothers composed many waltzes. His three sons—**Boulou,** Elios and Michel—all follow in his footsteps as musicians.

FICOWSKI, JERZY. A contemporary Polish writer and authority on Romany history and culture. His first major publication was *Cyganie Polscy* (The Gypsies of Poland) in 1953. He has since published several books in Polish and *Gypsies in Poland, History and Customs* in English. Ficowski was instrumental in introducing the Romany poet Papusza (**Bronislawa Wajs**) to the Polish public.

FILM. Many films have been made by non-Gypsies with the theme of Romanies, for example:
Angelo My Love (United States,1982).
Gypsy (Great Britain, 1936)
The Gypsy and the Gentleman (Great Britain, 1957)
Gypsy Wildcat (US, 1944).
I Even Met Happy Gypsies (Skupljace perja) (Yugoslavia, 1967).
   Some other films have been made by Gypsies or with their involvement at production level:
   The Raggedy Rawney (Great Britain, 1987)—**Bob Hoskins** directed and starred in the title role (an army deserter dressed as a Gypsy girl).
   The Time of the Gypsies (Yugoslavia, 1989)—**Rajko Djuric** was the advisor.
   A large number of documentaries have also been produced, includ-

ing a trilogy by **Tony Gatlif**—*Les Princes, Latcho Drom* and *Dinilo Gadjo.*

We should also mention *Into the West* (Irish Republic, 1992), a film featuring **Irish Travellers**.

FINLAND. Estimated Gypsy population: 8,000. From approximately 1200 to 1809, Finland was under Swedish control. Eight work horses were confiscated from Gypsies on the island of Åland in 1559—the year of their arrival. They were reputedly the first Gypsies in Finland. Many of this group were sent back to Sweden. The first record on the mainland dates from 1580. In the 1600s Finland's Romany population grew with immigration occurring from the east as well as from Sweden. In 1660, the ruler Per Brahe settled 140 Gypsies on farms in the Kajaani Castle area. These were farms abandoned by Finnish peasants after the crops had failed. He wanted the Gypsies to serve as spies and guard on the eastern border. It seems then that they did not settle down, and in 1663 Per Brahe issued a warning that if they did not settle by the next year on the plot of land given to them, they would be banished from the whole of the Swedish empire. The Swedish law of 1637, which applied to Finland, too, stated that all Gypsies should be banished or hanged, but this was ineffective. The Gypsy population carried out traditional nomadic trades in Finland—horse selling, veterinary care, castration of pigs, ironwork, smithing, making and selling lace, fortune-telling and seasonal agricultural work.

In 1809 Russia occupied Finland. In 1812 a decree was issued that all the disabled, wandering **Tartars**, Gypsies and other vagabonds of poor reputation who were not capable of ordinary work were to be dispatched to workhouses. In 1863, any Gypsies in ordinary workhouses were removed and placed in special stricter workhouses in Hameenlinna. The year 1862 saw Gypsies arriving from abroad being sent back even if holding genuine passports. A census in 1895 recorded 1,551 Gypsies, a figure seen as too low.

Finland became independent in 1917. In 1906 a Gypsy mission had been founded by Oskari Jalkio, whose aim was to remove Gypsy children from their families and give them a normal education. The first attempts to set up children's homes in the 1920s were not successful. By 1953 a new commission was set up with various recommendations, including once again the use of children's homes and enforcing school attendance. By 1963 five homes were established, and 100–150 children lived in them.

After World War II, the industrialization of Finland decreased the demand for the Gypsies' trades, and seasonal work was no longer available. In addition, the Gypsy community of Karelia, taken over by the Soviet Union, decided to migrate from their former living areas into Finland proper. Gypsies had to move into towns where they soon found themselves living on welfare benefits. In 1960 a report of the Helsinki City Special Committee published a survey of the situation.

In 1967 the Suomen Mustalaisyhdistys Ry (Finnish Gypsy Association) was formed, with the aim of bringing pressure on the government to improve the standard of living of the Gypsies and to stop discrimination in Finnish society. For several years the magazine *Zirickli* (The Bird), edited by Kari Huttunen, was a mouthpiece for Gypsy civil rights.

In 1968 the State Committee for Gypsy Affairs was re-established. The committee included three members representing the association and two from the Lutheran Gypsy Mission. They set about making two studies, one on the social needs of Gypsies and one on housing, which were published by the committee. In 1970 an act of Parliament prohibited racial discrimination. In 1971 the Social Welfare Act was reformed, and the government then refunded half of any welfare assistance that the local authorities gave to their Gypsy population. At this time, three-quarters of the Gypsies were receiving welfare payments and faced diminished health, family breakdown and unemployment. The aim of the reform was to make it easier to obtain welfare payments and provide more systematic and better planned support to promote assimilation. The Ministry of Education encouraged adults to join classes in literacy and technical subjects, as well as studying Gypsy history. The National Board of Education then printed a history book for the Gypsies. The Work Group for Vocational Training set up by the Ministry of Labor proposed in 1972 linking vocational and basic education into one course.

In the 1980s, 2,000 Finnish Gypsies emigrated to Sweden. Most left for better housing and employment conditions, and the Finnish Romany Association in Stockholm was created to assist the Gypsies there. Meanwhile, living conditions in Finland itself improved.

At the end of the 1960s, Gypsy musicians were very popular in Finland, with Hungarian and Russian Gypsy music proving particularly popular with Finnish people of all classes. The Folklore Archives of the Finnish Literary Society started to collect Gypsy songs in 1968 and now has over 1,000 titles. In 1972 the Folklore Archives and Love Records jointly produced an anthology called *Kaale dzambena* (Finnish Gypsies Sing). Singers and musicians include **Olli Palm**, the group **Hortto Kaalo, Anneli Sari** and the classical violinist Basil Borteanou.

There has been a revival of the Romani language, and textbooks have been prepared for the younger generation. The language of the Finnish Gypsies is a distinct dialect.

FLAG. In the years after 1945, a Romany flag appeared with green, red and blue horizontal stripes. By 1962 it had spread widely. It was said that green represented the grass, red the fire and blue the sky. Because of the alleged communist connection of the red stripe, some groups changed it to a fire-shaped emblem. The most commonly used flag nowadays is one with blue and green horizontal divisions and a superimposed wheel. This flag was decided at the first **World Romany Congress**. According to the congress decision, the wheel was to be identical with the ashoka symbol on the Indian flag.

FLAMENCO. A form of dance that emerged in the south of Spain in the 19th century. It is considered to be the result of a combination of Gypsy, Moorish and Andalusian dance and music. Gypsies are the prime performers of flamenco, which has spread from Andalusia to the rest of Spain. The word *flamenco* means "Flemish"—that is, "exotic." A number of 20th-century flamenco dancers and singers are given entries in this dictionary. The Presencia Gitana research team has listed 240 Gypsy singers in Spain from 1749 to the age of the flamenco.

FOLK LITERATURE. The Romanies' oral literature consisted of ballads, songs and tales as well as riddles and proverbs. These began to be collected and published in the 19th century by non-Gypsies. After 1945 several Gypsies have began to collect their oral literature in anthologies that are listed in the bibliography.

FONSECA, ISABEL. An American writer, now resident in England. After several visits to meet Gypsies in Eastern Europe, she wrote the controversial travel book *Bury Me Standing*.

FORTUNE-TELLING. Although comparatively few Gypsy women practice fortune-telling, it provides a useful first or second income for those families who pursue this profession. Many **Kalderash** families specialize in fortune-telling, with the daughters learning from their mothers. But **Sinti** also have traditionally told fortunes. In western Europe fortune-telling is usually done by **palmreading**, while in Eastern Europe coffee beans are often used. In England and Wales fortune-telling was controlled until recently by the Vagrancy Act of 1824. Any person professing to tell fortunes could be arrested without a warrant. In fact, prosecutions normally take place under section 15 of the Theft Act, where, for example, a fortune-teller takes money away to be blessed and does not return it. The Fraudulent Mediums Act of 1951 is rarely used against fortune-tellers.

FOUNDATION FOR THE RENEWAL AND DEVELOPMENT OF TRADITIONAL ROMANY VALUES. An organization in Prague run by Ivan Vesely. It is the Czech partner of the **Minority Rights Group**.

FRANCE. Estimated Gypsy population: 310,000. The first Gypsies came to France, to the town of Colmar in 1418. In 1419 more Gypsies arrived in Provence and Savoy. Nine years later the first Gypsies were recorded in Paris. In 1504 Louis XII issued the first of many decrees ordering the expulsion of the Gypsies. Further decrees followed in 1539, 1561 and 1682. In the latter year Louis XIV recognized that it had been impossible to expel the Gypsies because of the protection they had received from nobles and other landowners. During the 18th century, there are reports of armed Gypsies resisting arrest and expulsion. Others served in the French army as soldiers and musicians. Often this was the only alternative to imprisonment. Jean de la Fleur, born in Lorraine, served as a mercenary in several armies. In 1802 there was a determined campaign to clear Gypsies from the French Basque provinces. More than 500 were captured and imprisoned pending their planned deportation to the French colony of Louisiana. The colony was, however, sold in 1803 to the United States. It was 1806 before the last of the captives were released, four years during which many had died from disease and malnutrition.

Gypsies, such as **Liance**, were well known in France as dancers and are mentioned several times by the playwright Molière. In 1607 they danced before King Henri IV at Fontainebleau Castle, although legally they had no right to be in France. It was not until the 20th century that instrumentalists such as **Django Reinhardt** attained the fame of the Gypsy dancers.

The first Romanies to come to France appear to have merged over the years with indigenous nomads to form the community known today as *Voyageurs*. They no longer speak Romani but a variety of French with Romani words. In the south of France many families speak **Caló**. There have been two migrations from Germany—of families of the **Sinti** and **Manouche** clans. **Vlah** Gypsies arrived from the end of the 19th century onward, both from Romania directly and via Russia.

It was probably the newcomers that led the French government to introduce new measures to control the nomadic population. In 1898 a report gave the exaggerated figure of 25,000 nomads traveling in bands with caravans. As a result, in 1912 the authorities introduced a special identity card—the *carnet anthropométrique*—for nomads. This carried the photograph and fingerprints of the owner and other details such as the length of the right ear. It was not to be abolished until after World War II.

When Germany occupied most of France during World War II, nomadic Gypsies were interned in some 27 camps run by the French police. The camps at Jargeau, Les Alliers, Montreuil-Bellay, Rennes and St. Maurice held internees for most of the war. Other camps were closed as the conditions in them worsened, and the prisoners were transferred from camp to camp. In some places Gypsies were allowed out to work under supervision. Conditions in these camps were poor, and many prisoners died from disease and malnutrition. A small number were deported to concentration camps in Poland. Others, who had Belgian nationality, were released, only to be rearrested by the Germans in Belgium and northern France and sent to **Auschwitz**. House-dwelling Romanies were not affected by any special regulations.

The years following 1945 witnessed the arrival of large numbers of Gypsies from Eastern Europe, in particular Yugoslavia. They came as factory workers and settled in houses and flats in Paris and elsewhere. Meanwhile, nomadic Gypsies found that there were few official camp sites, and many districts prohibited the stationing of **caravans**. It was on French territory that **Vaida Voivod III** and **Vanko Rouda** founded the first international Gypsy organizations, while the **Etudes Tsiganes** association pioneered serious research into Romany history and culture. There are writers publishing in French, such as **Matéo Maximoff** and **Sandra Jayat**. In France, too, **Pentecostalism** first took hold among the Gypsies.

FRANKHAM, ELI. A contemporary poet and activist in England. He was the founder of the National Romany Rights Association.

FRANKHAM, JOHNNY. A contemporary English boxer.

FRANZ, PHILOMENA (1922–). A contemporary writer living near Cologne. She survived internment in **Auschwitz**, Ravensbrück and Oranienburg concentration camps. Franz has written her autobiography and tales in the folk idiom.

FRIENDS, FAMILIES AND TRAVELLERS' ADVICE AND INFORMATION UNIT. Based in Glastonbury and working mainly with **New Age Travellers.**

FUREY, EDDIE and FINBAR. Pipers of **Irish Traveller** origin. In 1967 they moved to Scotland as laborers but then developed a successful musical career. They have played at the Edinburgh Festival and toured widely in Britain. Apart from their recordings, the Furey brothers have appeared on both Scottish and English TV.

FUREY, MARTIN. An **Irish Traveller** currently residing in England and a musician in the folk rock group Bohinta.

G

GADES, ANTONIO. A Spanish **flamenco** dancer and choreographer. He has produced a stage version of *Carmen* as well as a film version in conjunction with Carlos Saura.

GADJO. See *GAJO.*

GAISFORD, PAUL (ca.1960–). An English painter and teacher of Romany descent.

GAJO. The Romani word for a non-Gypsy. The etymology is disputed, but it probably comes from a Greek word for "farmer." Another suggestion is from the Sanscrit *gramaja* (villager). In Romani the feminine is *Gaji* and the plural *Gaje*. It is also spelled *Gadjo* and, in English, Gorgio.

GAMMON. (i) An alternative name for **Irish Travellers' cant.** (ii) One of the sources of vocabulary for this cant. It is a secret vocabulary from the Middle Ages formed by reversing or changing the order of the letters in a word. An example is the word *gred* (money) from Irish *airgead*. The name Gammon itself is probably formed from the word *Ogam*, an ancient alphabet used in Britain and Ireland.

GANDHI SCHOOL. A school in Pécs, Hungary. It was set up to teach mainly children of the **Bayash** clan. There is a strong Romany cultural element in the timetable.

GARCIA LORCA, FEDERICO. A 20th-century Spanish poet and playwright, born in Granada. In 1922 he organized a festival in Granada that paid tribute to Gypsy traditions. His *Romancero Gitano* (*Gypsy Ballad Book*) was published in 1928 and demonstrates his empathy with the Romany community. He had already shown this sentiment two years earlier by opposing the brutal expulsion of Gypsies from Alpujarra. Speaking of this book, he said, "I gave it the name *Gypsy Romances* because the Gypsies are the highest, the deepest and the most aristocratic people of my land." The **Pralipe** Theater perform

Lorca's play *Blood Wedding* in their repertoire, and the Hungarian Romany poet **Jószef Choli Daroczi** has translated it into Romani.

GATLIF, TONY. A film producer, born in Algeria and resident in France, who has made several documentary films about Gypsies: *Corre Gitano, Les Princes* and *Latcho drom* (1993), in addition to two fiction films *Canto Gitano* (*Gypsy Song*)(1981) and *Dinilo Gadjo* (*Foolish non-Gypsy*)(1997).

GELEM, GELEM. The Romany national anthem, chosen at the first **World Romany Congress**. The title means "we went, we went" and the first lines are as follows:
Gelem gelem lungone dromensa,
Maladilem bahtale Romensa.
[We went, we went down long roads,
We met happy Gypsies.]
    The tune is traditional, and the lyrics were composed by **Žarko Jovanović.**

GEORGIEVDEN. See ST GEORGE'S DAY.

GERMAN, ALEKSANDER (1893–?). A cultural worker and a leader of the All-Russian Union of Gypsies in the 1920s. He translated Russian literature into Romani as well as writing original works.

GERMANY. Estimated Gypsy population: 120,000. Records state that in September 1407 wine was given to Gypsies while their papers were being checked at the town hall in Hildesheim. Another early description is of a group of acrobats in Magdeburg who danced on each others' shoulders and did "wonderful tricks." They were rewarded with food and drink. In 1416 we find the first anti-Gypsy action in Germany when the Margrave of Meissen ordered the expulsion of Gypsies from the territory under his authority. In September 1498 the Parliament of the Holy Roman Empire, as the German Empire was then called, meeting in Freiburg under Maximilian I, ordered them to leave the country by next Easter. Any who did not leave would be regarded as outlaws. It would then not be a crime to beat, rob or even kill them. In 1516 they were forbidden to enter Bavaria. By the 18th century, the laws were becoming more severe. Saxony ordered Gypsies to be executed if they reappeared in the state after once being expelled. In 1714 Mainz decreed the execution of any Gypsy men captured, while their wives and children would be flogged and branded. In Frankfurt am Main in 1722 it was stated that children would be taken away from their parents and placed in institutions while their parents would be branded and expelled from the district.

The harsh laws led to some emigration when some of the **Sinti** and all of the **Manouche** clans left for France, and other Sinti went east to Poland and Russia and down into Italy. The existing laws fell into disuse, and in the 19th century we find assimilation programs replacing expulsion. Schools for Gypsies were set up in a few places. When **Otto Bismarck** became chancellor of Germany in 1886, he sent a letter to all the individual states to unify, at least in theory, the various decrees in force against Gypsies. He recommended the expulsion of all foreign Gypsies "to free the territory of the country completely and permanently from this plague." In March 1899 an Information Service on Gypsies was set up at the Imperial Police Headquarters in Munich. There, the registration and surveillance of the entire Gypsy population group was organized. This included the Vlah Romanies who were immigrating from the east. Alfred Dillmann, an officer of the Munich police, published in 1905 his *Zigeunerbuch* (*Gypsy Book*), giving details of over 3,500 Gypsies and persons travelling as Gypsies. By 1925 the center already had 14,000 individual and family files for Gypsies from all over Germany.

Two years after the Nazi Party came to power, the **Nuremberg Laws** made Gypsies, alongside Jews, second-class citizens. Internment camps for nomadic Gypsies were established in the towns of Cologne and Gelsenkirchen in 1935. More camps followed, and settled Gypsies were removed from their houses and also interned. In 1936 the Race Hygiene and Population Biology Research Center was established under the direction of **Robert Ritter.** Its role was to search out, register and classify Gypsies as pure or mixed race. The first mass arrests came in the week of June 13–18, 1938, when many Gypsies were deported to concentration camps. In October of the same year the National Center for the Fight against the Gypsy Menace was set up. In 1940 a policy of making Germany Gypsy-free began when 2,800 Gypsies were deported to German-occupied Poland. Then, starting in March 1943, the mass deportation of some 10,000 Gypsies—both Romanies and Sinti—to the concentration camp of **Auschwitz** was organized. It is estimated that 15,000 died there and in other camps—three-quarters of the Gypsy population of Germany.

After the end of World War II, those who had survived found it difficult to get **reparations** as compensation for their suffering. In 1956 Oskar Rose founded an organization, Union and Society for racially persecuted German Citizens of non-Jewish Belief, the first organization for Sinti and Romanies. In 1979 the **Verband der deutschen** Sinti was recognized throughout the republic as the representative body for Sinti. It has some non-Sinti members.

Many Romanies have come to Germany since 1945 as guest workers, particularly from Yugoslavia. Others arrived from Poland and more recently, Romania as asylum seekers. This explains the high estimated Gypsy population. **Rudko Kawcinski** in Hamburg set up the **Romany National Congress,** which represents the interests of these recent arrivals.

Germany and Romania have now signed a formal agreement, whereby Germany will deport asylum-seekers back to Romania, which accepts them in exchange for monetary assistance to the Romanian government. Repatriation of Romanies to Macedonia and Bosnia is also taking place.

GESELLSCHAFT FÜR BEDROHTE VÖLKER (SOCIETY FOR ENDANGERED PEOPLES). A German organization that helped the German **Sinti** develop their own representative bodies. It supported the third **World Romany Congress** and its journal *Pogrom* often has articles on Gypsies.

GHEORGHE, NICOLAE. A contemporary sociologist from Romania and author of several reports on the current situation of Romanies in Eastern Europe. He is active on the international scene and has represented Romany interests at many international conferences. Gheorghe has organized the rebuilding of Romany communities that had suffered from pogroms in Romania.

GIESSEN. A town in Germany where a project to encourage the culture and educational prospects of Romanies and **Sinti** has been running. The program includes a publication called *Giessener Zigeunerhefte*.

GITANOS, GITANS. The Spanish and French (alongside *Tsigane*) names for Romany Gypsies, deriving from the term **Egyptian**. The terms are particularly used of Romanies in Spain and the South of France.

GILDEROY, (JACK) SCAMP (1812–1857). "KING" OF THE KENTISH GYPSIES. Born in Kent, England, Scamp had several brothers who worked in the scissors-grinding trade. His striking appearance in a top hat, given to him by Baron Rothschild in return for Scamp's vote in the Hythe Parliamentary elections, was well known to contemporaries. He was a prizefighter and took part in pony trap races.

GILLIAT-SMITH, BERNARD. A 20th-century diplomat and amateur scholar of the Romani language. A regular contributor to the journal of the **Gypsy Lore Society**. He also translated St. Luke's Gospel into Romani.

GINĂ, ANDREJ (1936–   ). A writer in the Czech Republic. He has written a play in Romani entitled *Biav* (*Wedding*).

GINĂ, ONDREJ. A contemporary musician and leader of the Romany community in **Rokycany**. He was a member of Parliament in the first postcommunist parliament in Czechoslovakia

GJUNLER, ABDULA. A poet originally from Macedonia but currently living in Holland. A book of poems in Dutch and Romani was published in 1995 under the title *Bizoagor/Eindeloos* (*Without End*).

GOLEMANOV, DIMITER (1938–1994). A poet and teacher in Sliven, Bulgaria. His father had been active in trade union politics as early as the 1930s and was honored as a fighter against fascism. Golemanov became known to the world of Gypsy studies through a version of the Balkan tale "Song of the Bridge" that **Lev Cherenkov** had published in the journal of the **Gypsy Lore Society**. He had a great love for the Russian language, which he had studied at Sofia University, and he wrote poetry and songs in Russian as well as Bulgarian and Romani. Golemanov attended the second **World Romany Congress** in Geneva. He died of a heart attack shortly after the political changes in Bulgaria.

GOMEZ, HELIOS (1906–   ). Born in Seville, he was one of the founders of the anarchist trade union but then joined the Communist party. Gomez was detained 72 times, faced 42 criminal charges and was expelled from Spain, France, Belgium and Germany. He then worked in the Kuznetsoy factory in Siberia. He returned to Spain in 1936 after the election victory of the left-wing government. He was in Barcelona when the civil war broke out, and he fought there and later in Aragon. He was the political commissar of the Balearic command. During the war, many Gypsies were members of the Catalan Nationalist party and fought for the government. Following Franco's victory, he sought refuge in the USSR again.

GORGIO. See *GAJO*.

GRANICA. A town in Kosovo, Yugoslavia. Since 1945 it has become a place of Gypsy pilgrimage on the Orthodox Feast of the Assumption (August 27–28).

GREAT BRITAIN. See ENGLAND, SCOTLAND and WALES.

GREECE. Estimated Gypsy population: 180,000. At an early date Gypsies were recorded on the islands of the eastern Mediterranean. By

1384 Gypsy shoemakers were established on the mainland of Greece in Modon (then a part of the Venetian Empire), and by the end of the 14th century a large number of Gypsies were living on the Peloponnese peninsula. As the Turks advanced into Europe, many Romanies fled to Italy and other countries of Western Europe. Under the **Ottoman Empire** those Gypsies who remained were given comparative freedom provided they paid their taxes to the Turkish rulers. In 1829 Greece gained its independence. There have been a number of population exchanges between Greece and Turkey, and some Muslim Gypsies have taken the opportunity to migrate eastwards, to Turkey.

Toward the end of World War II, the Germans began to arrest Gypsies to use them as hostages, but the majority survived unscathed.

In Greece today the Gypsies are largely settled and ignored, except by some educational authorities, and the majority live in poverty. As many of them are not registered as citizens, their children are refused entry by schools. There have also been reports of pressure on nomadic Muslim Romanies in the northeast to convert to Orthodoxy. A positive note is the establishment of a museum of basket making in Thrace. Gypsy musicians are popular. They include the singers Eleni Vitali, Kostas Pavlides and Vasilis Paiteris, together with the clarinettist Vasilis Saleas. At least four distinct dialects of Romani are spoken. See also BYZANTIUM.

GRELLMAN, HEINRICH. Author of a treatise in 1783 entitled *Die Zigeuner. Ein historischer Versuch.* This was translated into English as *A Dissertation on the History of the Gypsies* in 1787. The English edition was influential in affecting thinking on the treatment of Gypsies and inspiring the evangelical movement of persons such as John Hoyland and Samuel Roberts to start missions to the Gypsies in Britain in the 19th century.

GROTA BRIDGE. A bridge in Warsaw. In 1994 hundreds of Romany refugees from pogroms in Romania found shelter under this bridge. In 1995 the settlement was broken up by police.

GURBET. (i) A clan in Yugoslavia. Archaic features in their dialect suggest that they were one of the first clans to reach Europe. (ii) A name given to the Muslim Gypsies of Cyprus.

GYPSIES FOR CHRIST. Part of the current **Pentecostalism** movement in England and Wales. They are now independent of the international organization.

GYPSY. The term is derived from **Egyptian** because, when the Romanies first came to Western Europe, it was wrongly thought they had come from Egypt. Some authors suggest that the name may come from a place called Gyppe in Greece. Early English laws and authors such as **William Shakespeare** write "Egyptian" (e.g., in the play *Othello*). The Spanish word *gitano* and the French word *gitan* are of the same derivation.

Gypsy is not a Gypsy word, and there is no single word for Gypsy in all Romani dialects. *Rom* (plural *Rom* or *Roma*) is a noun meaning "Gypsy," but not all Gypsies call themselves Roma. The **Sinti**, **Manouche** and **Kaale** in Finland use the word *Rom* only in the meaning of "husband." There is ironically, a universal word for non-Gypsy, which is **Gajo**.

The primary unifying concepts of the Gypsy people are their awareness of a common history and destiny and of a language (even if no longer spoken). Gypsy culture preserves a spirit of nomadism, whether exercised or not, a preference for self-employment and laws of hygiene.

For the non-Gypsy in Western Europe the idea of nomadism is predominant, so we find, for example, a site on the World Wide Web proclaiming "We are Cyber Gypsies—we roam the Net." In Eastern Europe, on the other hand, we find a paradox, with the Gypsies considered at the same time as lazy but taking on the dirtiest work, and foolish and at the same time cunning. Nomadism is not seen as a fundamental meaning of the word *Gypsy* in Eastern Europe.

In British law (as defined by the judges) the term *Gypsy*, when used in planning law, does not apply to an ethnic group but anyone travelling in a caravan for an economic purpose. With regard to race relations legislation, however, *Gypsy* is considered to be a synonym for the ethnic term *Romany*.

GYPSY COUNCIL. United Kingdom. Founded in December 1966. The first secretary was **Grattan Puxon**. It carried out a campaign of passive resistance to the moving on of caravans by the police and local authorities. The campaign was a major factor in persuading the government to take some action over the problem of sites for Gypsies, culminating in the **Caravan Sites Act of 1968**. Realignments within the Gypsy civil rights movement led to the formation of the **Romany Guild** in 1972, the **National Gypsy Council** in 1974 and the **Association of Gypsy Organizations** in 1975.

GYPSY COUNCIL FOR EDUCATION, CULTURE, WELFARE AND CIVIL RIGHTS. This is the new name of the **National Gypsy Education Council.**

GYPSY CSARDAS. A poem written by the 19th-century Russian poet Appolon Grigoriev after his beloved Leonida married someone else.

Ivan Vasiliev, conductor of a Gypsy choir, composed the music and it became popular with Gypsies in both St. Petersburg and Moscow. The tune is often sung with different words, but in recent years the original lyrics have returned to popularity.

GYPSY EVANGELICAL MOVEMENT. See PENTECOSTALISM.

GYPSY KINGS. A band playing flamenco-rock. It was first formed under the name Los Reyes in 1972 by younger members of the Reyes and Balliardo families in the south of France, and in 1982 adopted the name Gypsy Kings. Their first record appeared in 1987, and they have toured widely since. An early hit was the song *Bamboleo,* which reached the Top 10 in the United Kingdom. Another well-known song is *Djobi, Djoba.* They sing in a number of languages, including **Calo**.

GYPSY LORE SOCIETY. The oldest society for the study of Gypsies founded in 1888 by David McRitchie. It ceased activities in 1892 and was revived in 1907. In the early days few meetings were held, but it published the *Journal of the Gypsy Lore Society* (*JGLS*). Members of the newly created American chapter of the society took over its running in the 1980s, and it has since had its headquarters in the United States. In adition to the journal, there is now a newsletter. Annual meetings are usually held in America, but two have taken place in Europe—in Leicester and Leiden.

GYPSYLORISTS. A term used for non-Gypsy amateur scholars in the 19th and early 20th centuries who saw the Gypsy life as romantic, at least for short periods in the summer. They used to travel in horse-drawn wagons and make campfires around which they sang their own translations into Romani of non-Romani songs. So, the student song *Gaudeamus igitur'* was translated as *Kesa paias kana 'men tarniben atchela* (*Let us make merry while we still have youth*). They have been criticized for ignoring the harassment suffered by the Romanies they studied.

GYPSY SCALE. Also known as the Hungarian scale. This is a scale with the notes c—d—e flat—f sharp—g—a flat—b—c', popular in Hungary in the 19th century.

GYPSY RONDO. The final movement of a piano trio by Haydn.

GYPSY STUDIES. Gypsy studies were largely amateur until the 1950s. Since then, departments for or courses in Gypsy studies have been set up at a number of academic institutions in Europe—for example,

St. Charles University in Prague (Romani language), Greenwich University in England and the pedagogical college in Košice in Slovakia.

H

HABSBURGS. The Habsburg family ruled much of Central Europe from 1438 to 1745. **Maria Theresa** and her son **Joseph II** inherited part of the Habsburg Empire.

HAGA, ANTONIA (1960–). A teacher in Debrecen. She was previously a member of the Hungarian Parliament and is currently president of the Ariadne Foundation, a cultural organization.

HALADITKO (Xaladytko). Haladitka is the name given to a large clan of Gypsies living in Russia and adjoining countries. Their dialect is called haladitko. Many members of the clan consider the term (which means "soldier") as being pejorative and prefer being called Russian Gypsies.

HALL, GEORGE. An English clergyman and supporter of the Romany way of life in the Midlands in the 19th century,

HANCOCK, IAN. A contemporary lecturer, writer and political activist. He was born in England but is now teaching in Texas. He is vice-president of the **Romany Union**.

HAVEL, VACLAV. The president of Czechoslovakia and later the Czech Republic. Addressing the international Romany festival, Romfest, in **Brno** in July 1990, he stressed the right of Romanies to their own ethnic consciousness and said that they should enjoy the same rights and duties as all citizens of the nation.

HEDMAN, HENRIK. Currently, the leader of the Lutheran Mission to Gypsies in Finland and a translator of the New Testament.

HELSINKI CITIZENS' ASSEMBLY (hCa). The Helsinki Citizens' Assembly, founded in 1990, is an international coalition of civic initiatives, East and West, working for the democratic integration of Europe. At its Ankara Assembly, several workshops were devoted to the problems of the Romanies, and an hCa Roma Committee with Romany and non-Romany members was established in March 1944. It was involved in a seminar in **Brno**, where it has its headquarters, in 1994. **Karel Holomek** is the contact (in Brno).

HELSINKI FOUNDATION FOR HUMAN RIGHTS. Located in Warsaw, this organization's aim is to produce a handbook that will enable activists and nongovernmental organizations to gain access to information about Romanies' rights and educational possibilities. It will cover international agreements, national legislation and individual case studies.

HEREDIA, JOSE. A contemporary professor of modern Spanish literature at Granada University.

HEREDIA, JUAN DE DIOS. See HEREDIA RAMÍREZ, JUAN DE DIOS.

HIDRELLEZ/HEDERLEZI. Turkish feast celebrated by Gypsies, corresponding to **St. George's Day** (May 6).

HIGGINS, LIZZIE. A contemporary **Scottish Traveller** singer and a member of the **Stewart family**.

HOLLAND (THE NETHERLANDS). Estimated Gypsy population: 37,500 (including Dutch **Travellers**, the **Woonwagenbewoners**). In 1420 the first Gypsies appeared in Deventer, in the shape of Andrew, duke of Little Egypt, with a company of 100 persons and 40 horses. In 1429 a similar group appeared in Nijmegen. In 1526 Gypsies were forbidden to travel through the country by the German emperor Charles V, who had authority at that time over much of Holland. The punishment would be a whipping, and their nose would be slit. In the 16th century placards begin to appear throughout Holland warning the Gypsies of punishments if they remained in the district.

In 1609 Holland became independent. With the emergence of a central government, it became more difficult for Gypsies to escape persecution in one province by fleeing to another. "Gypsy hunts" (*Heidenjachten*) at the start of the 18th century were to be the means by which the Gypsies were finally driven out of the country. Soldiers and police combined to scour the woods for Gypsies. An edict of 1714 forbade citizens to harbor them. Ten Gypsies were executed at Zattbommel in 1725. It is likely that all Gypsies left Holland by 1728, the year that saw the last of the hunts, and that there were none in the country for over a century until the 1830s when new **Sinti** Gypsy immigrants arrived from Germany.

From 1868 there are reports of the arrival of three groups of Gypsies: Hungarian coppersmiths (**Kalderash**), Bosnian bear leaders and Sinti with circuses from Piedmont. These immigrants had money and valid travel documents but were nevertheless put under strong control, which made it difficult for them to earn their living. At the beginning of the 20th century, **Lovari** horse dealers arrived from Germany. In 1918 the Caravan and Houseboat Law was instituted to control the indigenous Travellers and the newly arriving Gypsies. A few **caravan** sites were set up.

During World War II, the German-controlled government made all caravan dwellers live on fixed sites. Fearful of what might happen to them next, many of the Travellers and Gypsies abandoned their caravans to live in houses. The Germans deported all the Romanies they could lay their hands on to **Auschwitz.** The transport held 245 prisoners in all, of whom only 30 survived.

After the end of World War II, the Dutch government decided to tackle the problem of caravans. In 1957 local authorities were allowed to link up and build sites. The Government gave a grant per caravan and 50 percent of the running costs. Then in 1968 it was made compulsory for all local authorities to take part in the program. The aim was 50 large regional sites, on the scale of a village with a school, shop and church. Soon 7,000 Travellers were on the large sites, and a similar number on smaller sites. Recent policy has been to close the larger sites and move the Travellers to smaller ones so that there is less competition for work in a particular area.

After 1945 there was a steady immigration of Romanies from Yugoslavia in particular. The newcomers were made unwelcome by the authorities and their caravans were moved on by the police. Some were pushed over the border into neighboring countries. In 1978 the Dutch government decided to legalize those Gypsies who had come into the country from eastern Europe after World War II. This followed adverse publicity in the media on the situation of these largely stateless aliens and lobbying by the ROM Society. In 1977 Zeevalking, the minister of justice, legalized some 500 of these Gypsies. A separate civil servant with responsibility for Gypsies was appointed to the Department of Caravan Affairs, which had until then mainly been concerned with the indigenous Dutch caravan dwellers. In fact, the majority of the immigrants have been settled in houses. The late **Koka Petalo** was recognized as a leader by many of the **Vlah** Romany families.

The Sinti in Holland first organized themselves into an association, the Zigeunerorganisatie Sinti, in 1989. In 1991 the Stichting Sintiwerk was set up and currently the Landelijke Sinti Organisatie represents the Dutch Sinti. The **Lau Mazirel Association**, with its journal *Drom* (*Way*) and exhibitions, informs and fights against discrimination.

A feature of the Romany and Sinti community is the large number of musicians amongst them, such as the Gipsy Swing Quintet, Hot-club de Gipsys, Het Koniklijk Zigeunerorkest **Tata Mirando Jr.,** Zigeunerorkest **Tata Mirando Sr.,** the Rosenberg Trio and many others.

HOLOCAUST. The term used to describe the Nazi genocide of Jews, Gypsies and others, particularly in the period following 1941. When the Nazi party came to power in 1933, it inherited laws against nomadism already in operation. From the beginning, the National Socialists considered the Romanies and **Sinti**—whether nomads or sedentary—as non-Aryans. Together with the Jews, they were classed as alien and considered a danger to the German race. Already by 1935 they had been deprived of citizenship and given the second-class status of "nationals." In the same year the Law for the Protection of German Blood made marriages between Gypsies and Germans illegal. There was no place in the image of Germany under the New Order for a group of people who traveled around the country freely, worked as craftsmen and sold their wares from door to door. A quasi-scientific research program was set up, under the leadership of **Robert Ritter**, in Berlin. Later this program was carried out at the Race Hygiene and Population Biology Research Center. The researchers had to accept the historical and linguistic fact that the Romany and Sinti peoples came originally from India and therefore should count as Aryan, but they claimed that on the route to Europe they had intermarried with other races and as a "mixed race" had no place in Nazi Germany. Allegations were made against the whole race in pamphlets and articles.

Internment camps were set up on the outskirts of towns in Germany, and both **caravan** and house-dwelling Gypsies were sent there. Discipline was strict and the internees were only allowed out to work. In 1938 several hundred Gypsy men were deported to Buchenwald and Sachsenhausen concentration camps as "people who have shown that they do not wish to fit into society" under the Decree against Crime of the previous year.

Heinrich Himmler, who became police chief in 1936, was particularly interested in the Romanies and Sinti and led the campaign against them. In 1938 he signed the Decree for Fighting the Gypsy Menace under which Ritter's Research Center was linked with an established Gypsy Police Office and the new combined institution was put under the direct control of police headquarters in Berlin. The first task of this institution was to classify all nomads by their ethnic origin. To be classed as a "Gypsy of mixed race" it was sufficient to have two great-grandparents who were considered to have been Gypsies, which meant that part-Gypsies were considered to be a greater danger than part-Jews. In general, a person with one Jewish grandparent was not affected in the Nazi anti-Jewish legislation, whereas one-eighth "Gypsy blood" was considered strong enough to outweigh seven-eighths of German blood—so dangerous were the Gypsies considered. Alongside the program of registration and classification, new laws were imposed on the Romanies and Sinti. Any children who were foreign "nationals" were excluded from school; the German Gypsies could be excluded if they represented a "moral danger" to their classmates. The race scientists discussed what should happen next. Eva Justin proposed sterilization except for those "with pure Gypsy blood" while Ritter himself wanted to put an end to the whole race by sterilization of those with one-eighth or more Gypsy blood. In fact, a law of 1933 had already been used to carry out this operation on individual Sinti and Romanies.

In the end, the Nazi leaders decided in 1940 that deportation was the means to clear Germany of Gypsies. Adolf Eichmann was responsible for the transporting of Gypsies alongside the Jews. In a first operation, 2,800 were sent to Poland and housed in Jewish ghettos or hutted camps.

In 1941, however, the Nazi leaders had carried out an experiment with Zyklon B gas in **Auschwitz** where they had murdered 250 sick prisoners and 600 Russian POW's in underground cells. The discovery of this cheap and rapid method of mass murder led to a change in the treatment of the Jews. Deportation was replaced by death, and in 1942 Himmler decided that the same "final solution" should be applied to the Gypsies.

On December 16, 1942, he signed an order condemning all the German and Austrian Gypsies to imprisonment in Auschwitz, and in February of the following year the police began rounding up the Romanies and Sinti. Within the first few months 10,000 persons had been transported to the camp. Children were taken out of orphanages and Germans were asked to inform the police of any Gypsies living in houses that might have been missed. We are not yet in a position to say how many German Sinti remained outside the camps. They can be numbered in hundreds and lived under strict police control.

When Austria was annexed to Germany in 1938, it was announced that the Gypsies there would be treated as those in Germany. Two years later a camp was opened in Lackenbach just for the Austrian Romanies and Sinti. The western part of Czechoslovakia was also annexed, but many Romanies succeeded in escaping across the border to the puppet state of Slovakia. Two internment camps were opened in 1942 in the German-controlled provinces of Bohemia and Moravia. The majority of the nomads were immediately locked up in the new camps, and later several hundred were sent to Auschwitz from the camps when they were closed together with the sedentary Gypsies. Only a handful of the Czech Gypsies survived the occupation.

The Romany population in Eastern Europe was mainly sedentary and integrated into the life of town and village. Many had been to school and had regular work. They had cultural and sports clubs and had begun to develop Romani as a literary language. Nevertheless, the German troops carried out the same policies of murder against these populations as against the nomads. It is, of course, not a greater crime to kill an educated house dweller than an illiterate nomad, but it was economic and political folly to annihilate these sedentary Romanies. It illustrates the clearly racist nature of the Nazi actions—to eventually eliminate all non-Germanic peoples.

The Romanies who lived in Poland were crammed into the Jewish quarters of towns and villages. The Germans forced the Jews to give up their houses and move in with other families, and then the Romanies were allocated the empty houses. In addition, a transport of 5,000 Sinti and Romanies were brought from Germany and Austria and housed in the Jewish ghetto of Lodz. An epidemic of typhus broke out, but no medical help was provided. In the first two months, 600 died. When spring arrived, the survivors were taken to Chelmno and gassed.

The task of murdering the Romanies in the occupied areas of the Soviet Union was allocated to the Task Forces (*Einsatzgruppen*), who were given their orders soon after the invasion. Their orders were to eliminate "racially undesirable elements," and most reports of the Forces mention the killing of Gypsies. In all, they murdered over 30,000 Romanies.

After the rapid capture of Yugoslavia in 1941, Serbia came under German military rule, and the Romanies were compelled to wear a yellow armband with the word *Gypsy* on it. Trams and buses bore the notice "No Jews or Gypsies." A new tactic was used to kill the Romanies. They were shot as hostages for German soldiers who had been killed by the partisans. In Kragujevac soldiers with machine guns executed 200 Romanies, alongside 7,000 Serbians, in revenge for the death of 10 German soldiers. These executions were carried out by regular soldiers of the German army. After so many of the men had been shot, the occupying forces were faced with the problem of a large number of women and children with no breadwinners. A solution was easily found. Mobile gas vans were brought from Germany, women and children were loaded into these vans, taken to the forests, gassed and buried. Their possessions were sent to Germany to be distributed by charitable organizations to the civilian populations.

In most of the countries that came under German rule, the alternative was often between death on the spot and a journey without food or water to a concentration camp. Nearly all the larger camps had their section for Romanies: Bergen-Belsen, Buchenwald, Mauthausen, Natzweiler, Neuengamme, Ravensbrück, Sachsenhausen, Theresienstadt and others. From 1943 on, the camps were merely waiting rooms for the journey to death by gas or shooting. Chelmno, Sobibor and Treblinka were names that meant immediate death on arrival. From all the camps where Romanies and Sinti were held, the best records available are for Auschwitz where Jewish prisoners kept secret notes.

It is also known that Romanies and Sinti were used in the camps for experiments with typhus, salt water and smallpox, but perhaps the most horrifying were the attempts to find new quick methods of sterilization. These were to be used on all the races considered inferior so that they could be used as a workforce while preventing the birth of a new generation.

As Soviet and Allied troops advanced in 1944, the last tragic phase began in the life of the concentration camps. The remaining prisoners were evacuated on foot in the direction of Austria and Germany. Anyone who could not keep up during these marches was shot.

During the Hitler period, the Romanies and Sinti of Europe suffered a terrible blow from which they have not yet fully recovered. The accompanying table gives approximate numbers for those who died as a result of Nazi action. It should not be forgotten that these figures do not give the whole extent of the persecution of the many thousands more who suffered internment or other repressive measures.

Each country cited in the table refers to the country where the Gypsies were living in 1939, not the country where they were killed. It is likely that the total would be higher if a fuller documentation, particularly from eastern Europe, were available. See also REPARATIONS.

Country	Deaths
Austria	7,000
Belgium	340
Croatia	28,000
Czech lands	6,000
Estonia	1,000
France	100
Germany	15,000
Greece	100
Holland	200
Hungary	20,000
Italy	1,000

Latvia	2,000
Lithuania	1,000
Luxemburg	200
Macedonia	100
Poland	13,000
Romania	9,000
Serbia	60,000
Slovakia	3,000
Slovenia	1,000
USSR	30,000

HOLOMEK, KAREL. Karel is currently the Romany contact, based in Brno, for the **Helsinki Citizens' Assembly**. He was a member of the national Parliament before the breakup of Czechoslovakia.

HOLOMEK, MIROSLAV (1925–1989). A sociologist in Czechoslovakia who was one of the founders of the Romany civil rights and cultural movement in the Republic in the 1970s.

HOLOMEK, TOMAS (1911–1988). A lawyer and writer in Czechoslovakia. He was one of the founders of the Romany civil rights and cultural movement in Slovakia in the 1970s.

HOLY ROMAN EMPIRE. For centuries (962–1806), this term was applied to the German Empire, and from 1438 it can be considered for practical purposes the same as the Habsburg Empire. Its boundaries varied. For the policy of the Empire toward Gypsies, see GERMANY; JOSEPH II; MARIA THERESA.

HOME MISSIONARY SOCIETY. This group in England carried out some reform work with Gypsies in the 1820s with the aim of encouraging them to settle and take up regular employment.

HORSMONDEN. The Horse Fair at Horsmonden in Kent in October, together with the Barnet Fair, is one of the last events in the English Gypsies' calendar before the winter sets in. Unlike some of the other fairs, Horsmonden is an all-Gypsy event. Attempts have been made to stop the fair or move it to another location, but it still survives.

HORTTO KAALO. Finnish Gypsy music group, playing traditional music, founded in 1970 by the two brothers Feija Akerlund and Taisto Lundberg together with Marko Putkonen. Their first record was a protest song against discrimination *Miksi ovet ei aukene meille? (Why are the Doors Not Open for Us?)*, which reached the Top 10 in Finland. Their repertoire is varied: Russian-style Gypsy songs, folk songs from various countries and their own compositions. They have toured in Scandinavia and appeared regularly on television.

HORVATH ALADAR (1964–). Formerly a teacher, now a cultural activist, Horvath was formerly president of the **Roma Parliament** in Hungary and, standing for the Free Democrat Party, he was one of the first two Romany MPs in the Hungarian Parliament (1990–1994). From 1995 he has run the Foundation for Romany Civil Rights in Budapest and set up the Roma Press Center.

HOSKINS, BOB. A contemporary British actor and producer. His films include *The Raggedy Rawnie* in which a deserter disguises himself as a Gypsy girl.

HOST (Hnuti Občanske Solidarity a Tolerance—Citizens' Solidarity and Tolerance Movement). The movement was founded in Prague late in 1993 after four people, including two Romanies, were killed in violent attacks in one month. Its aims include monitoring ethnic violence and opposing discrimination. Gypsies are only part of HOST's work.

HÜBSCHMANNOVÁ, MILENA. A contemporary Czech scholar and cultural activist. She helped to keep Romany culture alive during the period 1973–1989 when it was discouraged by the government in Czechoslovakia. She was instrumental in small-scale publishing during this period, including *Romane Gil'a*, a book of songs in Romani, and teaching the language. Hübschmannová has writtten many articles and books in and on the language. She is the editor of the learned journal *Romano Džaniben* (*Romany Knowledge*).

HUMAN RIGHTS PROJECT. Under director Dimiter Georgiev, this Bulgarian group documents human rights abuses against Romanies and provides free legal services to combat discrimination. It has published a newsletter called *Focus* as well as a number of reports and organizes training meetings for activists. It is based in Sofia with branches in Montana, Pleven, Shumen and Stara Zagora.

HUNGARIAN GYPSY MUSIC. Apart from the groups playing what is popularly regarded as Gypsy music in Hungary, such as waltzes and polkas by Strauss, there is also a strong singing tradition amongst the **Vlah** clans in the country. This includes slow songs for listening to and fast songs for dancing. The slow song (*loki gili*) is often sung in harmony when others join in with the soloist, often improvising the words. The dance song (*khelimaski gili*) is used for the Gypsy **csardas,** and much of the text consists of nonsense syllables (mouth music). They are accompanied by other singers imitating various instruments such as the double bass and percussion (snapping fingers, spoons etc.). Finally there are the "stick songs" which usually have short verses and accompany stick and other solo dances (*csapás*). Groups such as **Kalyi Jag**, playing a kind of folk rock, have become popular among both Gypsies and Hungarians.

HUNGARY. Estimated Gypsy population: 700,000. Gypsies may have reached Hungary by 1316, but the first certain reference to Gypsies refers to musicians who played on the island of Czepel for Queen Beatrice in 1489. However, others certainly passed through the country earlier in the 15th century. Sigismund, the king of Hungary and of the Holy Roman Empire, attended the empire's Great Council in 1417 at Constance on the lake of the same name. While he was spending some free days in the neighboring town of Lindau, some Gypsies arrived from Hungary and asked him for a letter of safe conduct. In 1423 Sigismund gave a safe conduct letter to another Gypsy leader, Ladislaus and his company, in Slovakia (then part of the Hungarian Empire). These Gypsies then traveled to Germany where they used Sigismund's letters to get food and lodging from the authorities. Later in 1476 Gypsies were sent to work by King Matthias Corvinus as smiths in Sibiu in Transylvania (also part of Hungary at that time). In these early years, Gypsies in Hungary were under the jurisdiction of their own leaders. Things were to change with the rule of **Maria Theresa.**

From 1758 Empress Maria Theresa legislated to assimilate the Gypsies, or New Hungarians (*Ujmagyar*) as they were thenceforth to be called. They were to settle and farm the land. Her son **Joseph II** continued his mother's policies. The 1893 census recorded 275,000 Gypsies, of whom over 80,000 spoke Romani. The vast majority were sedentary, as a result of Maria Theresa's intervention.

Apart from the musicians, Gypsies have been viewed with mistrust. From the mid-1930s calls were made in the Hungarian Parliament for the internment of Gypsies in labor camps. However, although Hungary was allied to Germany in World War II, it was not until German troops occupied Hungary in March 1944 that mass deportations of Romanies to concentration camps began. One postwar report suggests that 28,000 died in the camps, but this figure may be too high. The accession to power of the fascist Arrow Cross party in October 1944 gave a new impetus to the persecution, and, with the Soviet army approaching Budapest, killing increased. Over 100 were shot in a wood near the town of Varpalota in February 1945.

After the liberation of Hungary in 1945, the policy was that the Romanies had the same rights and responsibilities as other Hungarians. This policy was meaningless because it did nothing to remedy the neglect of years and the general prejudice against the Rom. They continued to live in settlements, and many children were not accepted into schools.

On coming to power the following year, the Hungarian Workers Party adopted a policy of assimilation. Prime Minister Matyas Rákosi referred to them as New Hungarian Citizens, a similar term to that of Maria Theresa. Nomadism was prohibited. The Kadar regime (after the 1956 counterrevolution) took more interest in the Romany population and in 1958 the Politburo of the Hungarian Socialist Workers Party (MSZMP) adopted a policy of active support for minority culture and education. Part of this policy included the creation of the Cigányszövetség (Gypsy Union), the first Romany organization officially operating in Hungary (1958–1961). A report revealed that two-thirds of the Gypsies still lived in substandard housing, mainly in rural Gypsy settlements or Gypsy quarters in towns. A rehousing program began in 1964 with low-interest, long-term loans. A debate in 1961 concerning whether the Romanies were an ethnic minority resulted in the conclusion that they were not and that Romani should not be taught in schools. The Gypsy Union was closed in the same year.

Rom Som (*I Am a Romany*), a bilingual journal in Hungary, published its first issue in January 1975. It was produced with stencils by the Romany cultural club in District 15 of Budapest but circulated outside the capital. By 1982 it had disappeared, although the title has now been revived in a printed format.

In 1976 the government ordered measures to ensure full employment for men and preschool nursery education for children in an attempt to integrate the Gypsy population. By 1986, the need to support a political organization for the Romanies was acknowledged, and the Orzsagos Cigánytanacs (National Gypsy Council) came into being. The head of the new body was **József Choli Daróczi,** who was formerly a Presidium member of the **Romany Union**. The establishment of the national body was soon followed by the creation of councils in each county, who dealt with individual cases of discrimination. A further body, the Ungro-themeske Romane Kulturake Ekipe (Romany Cultural Association), was created in 1986 to encourage and sponsor Gypsy artists and support Romany culture. It received a large grant to assist over 200 cultural groups and 40 dance troupes. The president was **Menyhért Lakatos**. In 1979 the Gypsies in Hungary were finally recognized as an ethnic group.

In 1989 multiparty democracy came to Hungary and Dr. Gyula

Naday formed the Magyar Cigányok Demokrata Szövetség (Democratic Union of Hungarian Gypsies), and Pal Farkas became chairman of the Social Democratic Party of Gypsies of Hungary. The Hungarian **Roma Parliament** was set up in the same year, as was the organization **Phralipe** under Bela Osztojkan. The Minorities Law, passed in July 1993, defined the rights of minorities in Hungary and led to the creation of the short-lived Minorities Round Table, a body that negotiated with the government Office of National and Ethnic Minorities. In 1994 the Romanies were able for the first time to elect local Romany councils, and in April 1995 a Hungarian National Council of Romany Representatives was formed with Florian Farkas as its president.

Independent Romany political parties have been able to put up candidates at the recent general elections: Magyarorszagi Cigányok Békepartja (Hungarian Gypsies' Peace party), led by Albert Horvath, Magyar Cigányok Antifasiszta Orszagos Szervezet (National Organization of Gypsy Antifascists) and Roma Parliament Választási Szövetség (Romanies' Parliament Electoral Alliance). Magyar Cigányok Szolidaritás Partja (Hungarian Gypsies Solidarity Party) presented three candidates, including Bela Osztojkan.

Democracy has also meant freedom for right-wing nationalists and skinheads to organize and racist attacks against Romanies have occurred in Eger and other towns. Three Romanies were killed in 1992, but the government denied any racist motivation. In September 1992 there was an arson attack on Romany homes in Ketegyhaza. Heavy-handed police raids have taken place in Arantyosapoti, Orkeny and elsewhere. In 1995 two assaults took place in Kalocsa. Joszef Sarkozi was shot after an argument in a bar in Pilisvorosvar in July 1996 and a Romany man was beaten up in a police car near Nyíregháza in February 1997. A petition signed by 827 residents in Szentetornya in 1994 called for the expulsion of all Gypsies in the area. A poll taken earlier by Helsinki Watch found that one third of the Hungarian population supported the idea of compulsory repatriation of the Romanies to India. In another poll by the Median agency, three-quarters of those asked rejected the Gypsies.

Music has always been a popular profession for the Gypsies of Hungary. In 1683 it was said that every nobleman in Transylvania had either his own Gypsy violinist or locksmith. In 1839 the first Hungarian Gypsy orchestra visited Western Europe, and in 1847 **Barba Lautari** met the composer **Franz Liszt**. In 1938 the Federation of Hungarian Gypsy Musicians arranged a Gypsy music festival to commemorate the 500th anniversary of the Gypsies' first appearance in Magyar territory. Apart from the polkas and waltzes that they play in restaurants, there is **Hungarian Gypsy music.** The **Vlah** Romanies have a lively culture of their own, with ballads and songs to accompany dancing.

Three main groups of Gypsies live in Hungary: the Hungarian Romanies, who form some 70 percent of the population, very few of whom speak (the Carpathian dialect of) Romani; the Vlah, some 20 percent, and the **Bayash**, who speak a dialect of Romanian.

Weekly radio and television programs are aimed at Gypsies but also have a Hungarian audience. **Agnes Daróczi** is on the teams that produce these programs.

I

ICELAND. Apart from short visits early this century by horsedealers from Scandinavia (and one woman and her child on their way to America in 1933), there has been no migration of Gypsies to Iceland.

ILIJAZ, ŠABAN. A contemporary poet from **Shuto (Šuto) Orizari** in Macedonia.

INDIAN ORIGIN. Some references to Indian origin are made in the early accounts of Gypsies in Europe. This was then forgotten both by Gypsies and non-Gypsies and replaced by the theory that they came from Egypt. However, investigations into the **Romani language** showed that it originated in North India and had been brought to Europe by the Gypsies. A small number of writers have recently denied the Indian origin and claim that the Gypsies are Europeans who acquired the language through contact with Indian merchants.

Many Gypsies are actively aware of the Indian connection. They like to watch Indian films, and play the music of these films, and some even have statuettes of Indian gods in their houses. The **Teatr Romen** in Moscow includes translations of Indian plays in its repertoire. Some contemporary writers, in particular, poets, have introduced Hindi words into their works. In India itself the connection was recognized by the Prime Minister Indira Gandhi, the two **Chandigarh Festivals** and the activities of the Indian Institute of Romany Studies in Chandigarh.

INDORAMA. An association founded in Bulgaria in 1991. The president was Vasil Danev, and the vice-president was the businessman and sometime poet Georgi Parushev.

INFOROMA. Bratislava, Slovakia. Inforoma collects documentation and runs training courses. It is supported partly by the **Open Society.**

INSTITUTO ROMANÓ. (i) A cultural and welfare organization in Barcelona affiliated with the **Union Romani**. The secretary is Juan Reyes Reyes. (ii) The Romani title of the **Romany Institute** of Britain.

INTERFACE. (i) The newsletter of the **Centre de Recherches Tsiganes**. It is currently published in several Western European languages. (ii) The Interface Collection, a publication program of educational books by the Centre.

INTERNATIONAL MEETINGS. The first meeting mentioned in some books is the **Cannstadt Conference** of 1871. Recent research has discovered that this was a *Zeitungsente* (a story made up by a newspaper). Some books also mention an international **Sofia Congress** of 1905. However, it seems that this gathering was just for Gypsies living in Bulgaria. In 1934 the Romanian Gypsy Union organized what can be considered the first international meeting, the **Bucharest Conference**, although very few foreigners participated. A number of resolutions were passed but little was done. After World War II, four international congresses have been held as well as a **European Congress** in Seville. Both Catholic and Protestant organizations arrange international conferences and meetings. See WORLD ROMANY CONGRESS.

INTERNATIONAL ROMANY UNION. See ROMANI UNION.

IRELAND. See IRISH REPUBLIC and NORTHERN IRELAND.

IRISH REPUBLIC. Estimated Traveller population: 25,000. Only a few Romany families live in the Irish Republic, but there is a large population of indigenous Travellers. No one knows exactly how far back the origin of the Travellers goes. They form a separate social group and are distinguished by mainstream Irish society even when the Travellers are settled in houses. About a third live in **caravan** camps run by local councils, while the others nomadize or settle on unofficial sites. Their main occupation is recycling waste material. There is considerable discrimination against the Travellers, for example, in entry to hotels and bars. Several hundred Irish Travellers emigrated to mainland Britain from 1880 onward.

In 1960 the Irish government established a Commission on Itinerancy whose report was published three years later. This report was the basis for a later assimilation program. Around this time a civil rights movement emerged amongst the Travellers. In 1963 a school for Travellers, St. Christopher's School, was built by Johnny Mac-

Donald and was opened on an unofficial site at the Ring Road, Bally-fermot, Dublin.

On January 6, 1964, it was burned down by Dublin Corporation employees and later rebuilt on Cherry Orchard, Dallyford. In 1964 the Itinerant Action Group was set up to fight for better living conditions and access to education. In 1981 Travellers took a test case to the Court of Human Rights in Strasbourg. They claimed that their constitutional right to educate their children was denied by their being moved constantly without caravan sites being available. Families sought the ruling that they could not be evicted unless an alternative site was provided. The court ruled favorably. So, in that same year, a new report was requested, and the Travelling People Review Body was set up by the minister of health. It consisted of 24 members, including representatives of the National Council for Travelling People (a network of settlement committees) and three Travellers. Its remit was to review current policies and services for the Travelling people and to improve the then-current situation. The group reported in 1983. The thrust of this report, as that of 1963, was the need to provide official stopping places for the Travellers' caravans and to help with education and employment.

Task Force on the Travelling People was set up in 1993 and published yet another report two years later. In March 1996 a National Strategy for Traveller Accommodation was announced to provide 3,100 units of accommodation. This would consist of 1,200 permanent caravan pitches, 1,000 transit pitches and 900 houses. A Traveller Accommodation Unit has been established at the Department of the Environment to oversee the strategy. It is intended to initiate legislation that will require local authorities to draw up five-year plans for Traveller accommodation. See also IRISH TRAVELLERS.

IRISH TRAVELLERS. Some writers would trace the Irish Travellers back in history to A.D. 200 or even as early as 600 B.C. when metalworkers traveled the country with their families. These families were joined by traveling musicians and later by Druid priests displaced from their villages after Christianity defeated Druidism, forming the core of the Traveller population. Others may have joined them when tenants were dispossessed of their lands in 1585 after the introduction of rents to be paid in money by tenant farmers, and again in 1652 when lands were confiscated under the Act of Settlement. By 1834 the traveling community was clearly distinguished from other poor who wandered the land in the report of the Royal Commission on the Poor Laws in that year.

Nomadism of Irish Travellers to England probably started soon after the English first landed in the country in 1172, and this movement may be connected with the first appearance of "**tinker**" as a trade or surname in England three years later. In 1214 a law was passed for the expulsion of Irish beggars from England, and in 1413 all Irish (with a few exceptions) were to be expelled. Emigration on a large scale to England and Scotland came much later, in the 19th century. There are currently several hundred Irish Traveller families living in **caravans** in Great Britain, including children who were born there. In spite of some intermarriage with the English **Romany Chal** Gypsies, they form a separate ethnic group, partly because of their strong Catholicism. It is estimated that there are also 10,000 people of Irish Traveller descent in the United States, whose ancestors left Ireland even before the 19th-century famine.

The main organizations are the **Irish Travellers Movement** and **Pavee Point** (previously known as the Dublin Traveller Education and Development Group). There is also a national organizer appointed by the Catholic Church whose main role is educational. In Ireland itself the Travellers number some 25,000. They used to speak Irish with a special vocabulary known as **cant, Gammon** or **Shelta**, but by this century the vast majority speak English, again with a special vocabulary. A strong musical tradition thrives among the Travellers.

IRISH TRAVELLERS MOVEMENT. A national association in the Irish Republic, linking a number of local groups.

ISLE OF MAN. Circa 1950 a Gypsy caravan stopped on Douglas Head, then disappeared because of the banning of camping on the island. In 1975 a fortune teller operated in Douglas. There were also a few families—some dealing with scrap metal—living in houses, also in Douglas.

ITALY. Estimated Gypsy population: 100,000. In 1422 the first Gypsies came from the north into Italy, to the town of Bologna, in the shape of Duke Andrew of Little Egypt with a party some 100 strong. They had a letter of safe conduct from King Sigismund of Hungary and said they were on their way to Rome to see the pope. The local priests in Bologna threatened to excommunicate anyone who had their fortune told by the Gypsies. There is no record of them being received by the pope at that time. We later find a series of edicts from different parts of Italy that, on the one hand, enable us to follow the travels of the Gypsies but, on the other, reveal the antipathy toward these nomadic groups. The first edict was in 1493 in Milan where the duke ordered all the Gypsies in the area to leave under the threat of execution. Similar decrees followed in Modena (1524), the Papal states (1535), Venice (1540), Tuscany (1547) and Naples (1555). These decrees did not succeed in banishing the Gypsies from Italy, however.

We find them depicted in paintings by Leonardo da Vinci and Cara-vaggio, amongst others. In Lombardy and Piedmont, Gypsies nomad-ized with their crafts without attracting the same attention of lawmakers as had the companies led by the dukes.

Following a different route, across the sea from the Balkans, Gyp-sies came to central and southern Italy—Abruzzi and Calabria—in the period 1448–1532, along with Greeks and Albanian immigrants, fleeing from the advancing Turks. They settled here and only traveled in limited areas, up to and including Rome. Later, **Sinti** Gypsies came from Germany into northern Italy and toward the end of the 19th century, **Vlah** Gypsies from Romania. Some Yugoslav Gypsies no-madized in Italy between the two world wars.

During the reign of Mussolini, racist attitudes were extended from Jews to Gypsies. Many were expelled from the mainland and de-ported to coastal islands and Sicily. A number of internment camps were set up, in particular for "foreign" Gypsies. Toward the end of World War II when Italy changed sides and the Germans took over the north of the country, they began to send Gypsies to the concentra-tion camps in Poland.

The years after 1945 have witnessed a great influx of Romanies from Yugoslavia. Most of these live in shantytowns on the outskirts of the cities. There have been a number of anti-Gypsy actions by right-wingers. In March 1995 a bomb was thrown at two children who were begging by the roadside near Pisa. Local authorities have evicted nomadic families from sites in Florence, Milan, Turin and Verona. The right-wing National Alliance (AN) has organized dem-onstrations against Gypsy camps in Rome and elsewhere. The North-ern League in Verona has distributed a pamphlet alleging that "Gypsies are parasites." In Genoa in June 1996 two demonstrations against Romany immigrants were held. Heavy-handed police action against new immigrants has been alleged, and at least one death in police custody has occurred, that of Zoran Ahmetovic in 1996.

On the other hand, the voluntary **Opera Nomadi** organization has worked to get education to the children of nomadic families and those in the shantytowns while the **Centro Studi Zingari** publishes the informative journal *Lacio Drom*. Vittorio Pasquale Mayer and Zlato Levak are amongst the Romanies who have contributed to the journal. **Santino Spinelli** established the magazine *Romano Them* as well as annual competitions for writing and art that draw entries from all over Europe.

ITINERANTS. A term sometimes used in Ireland for **Travellers.**

J

JAKOWICZ, WLADYSLAW (1915–   ). Born in Krakow, Poland. From 1939 to 1945 he lived in Russia. On his return to Poland he was a dancer and then emigrated to Sweden where he worked as a teacher. Jakowicz wrote *O Tari thaj e Zerfi*, the ballad of two lovers, in the Romani language in 1981.

JASENOVAC. A concentration camp set up by the puppet Croatian government in 1941. Some 28,000 Gypsies were killed there, alongside Jews, Serbs and left-wingers, by the Ustashe guards. The majority were killed on arrival. Men and women were separated and then taken across the river Sava to extermination units at Gradina and Uštice. A few men were set to forced labor in a brick factory where they soon perished through the poor conditions. A few Gypsy survivors escaped while being led to execution.

JAYAT, SANDRA. A **Manouche** Gypsy and self-taught poet and painter who describes herself as "a daughter of the wind." Born in Italy, she is a cousin of the renowned guitarist, **Django Reinhardt**. She left Italy, where her parents lived, as a teenager and worked as a commercial artist in Paris. Small exhibitions culminated in having her work shown in the Grand Palais Salon. In 1985 she organized an international exhibition of Gypsy art in Paris and in 1992 exhibited at the Musée Bourdelle. The French government then commissioned her to create a postage stamp depicting "travelling people" in the same year.

Among her collections of poems are *Herbes Manouches* (1961), illustrated by the writer Jean Cocteau, and the 1963 publication *Lunes nomades* (*Nomad Moons*), translated into English by Ruth Partington in 1995. She has also written a novel, *El Romanes*. Her many honors include the 1972 Children's Literature Prize (Paris), the Poetry Book Prize (Stockholm) in 1978 and an international prize for painting, also in 1978.

JENISCH (Yéniche). A clan of **Travellers** established in Germany, some of whom later migrated to Switzerland, Belgium and France. They may well number 10,000. They speak a variety of German with loan words from Romani as well as Yiddish. Traditionally they were basketmakers and peddlers. Some scholars say they originated with a group of basketmakers and broommakers in the Eifel region of Germany from where they spread out. During the Nazi period in Germany, many of the Jenisch were sent to concentration camps as "antisocial" and perished. In occupied France they were kept alongside Romanies in internment camps for nomads during the period of World War II. For many years a Swiss mission took Jenisch children away from their parents and sent them to be brought up in children's homes. In both France and Germany, small numbers continue to survive as seminomads.

JEWS. The destiny of the Gypsies and the Jews has been intertwined since the former arrived in Europe. For example, in Spain the deportation of the Moors and the Jews and the attempted deportation of the Gypsies happened at about the same time. In the Russian Empire some Gypsies were converted to Judaism. They survived the Nazi occupation because they were thought not to be ethnically Jewish or Gypsy. See HOLOCAUST.

JOHN, AUGUSTUS. A 20th-century English painter who painted Gypsy themes. He learned many Romani words that he used in correspondence to his closest friends.

JONES, NELLA (née Saunders) (1932–   ). A Romany Gypsy who was brought up at Belvedere marshes in Kent. As a recognized psychic and healer, she reputedly assisted in solving many cases for Scotland Yard, including the famous Yorkshire Ripper case—that of Peter Sutcliffe who was sentenced at the Old Bailey in 1981 for the murder of 13 women. She also helped to locate Stephanie Slater, a kidnap victim.

JORDACHE, TONI. A **cimbalom** player in Romania in the years after World War II.

JOSEPH, CHARLES LOUIS. The archduke of Austria who published a number of works at the end of the 19th century on the Romani language in Hungary.

JOSEPH II. The Habsburg emperor of Austria and Hungary (part of the Holy Roman Empire) from 1765. He was the son of **Maria Theresa** and continued her assimilationist policies towards Gypsies. The Romani language and dress were banned, and music was only allowed on feast days. Schooling and church attendance were made compulsory. Resistance by the Gypsies led to Joseph modifying some of his decrees.

JOVANOVIĆ, ŽARKO. A mandolin player and singer from Yugoslavia in the years after 1945 who made many recordings. He wrote the lyrics of the Romany national anthem *Gelem, Gelem*.

JOYCE, NAN. Irish civil rights worker. She stood unsuccessfully in Dublin for election to the Irish Dáil (Parliament) to draw attention to Travellers' needs.

JUSTIN, EVA. Working with **Robert Ritter** in the Race Hygiene Research Center in Nazi Germany. She saw sterilization as the way to solve the "Gypsy problem." See HOLOCAUST.

JUSUF, SHAIP (ŠAIP). A contemporary Romani writer, living in Skopje, Macedonia. He was active in the early days of the **Romany Union**. Jusuf has written a normative grammar of Macedonian Romani and translated Tito's official biography into Romani.

K

KAALO. The term used for self-ascription by Finnish Gypsies. It is from the Romani word meaning "black." See also *KALO.*

KALBELIA. The Kalbelia are nomads in Rajasthan, also known as Sapera, one of whose occupations is snake charming. They are considered by many scholars to be close cousins of the European Romanies. Kalbelia dancers from Rajasthan have appeared several times in Western Europe with folk dance groups from India. Gulab and Mera, who danced with the Surnai company in Rajasthan, came to London and performed at the Albert Hall in March 1986. They also appear in the documentary film *Latcho drom* (*Good Road*).

KALDERASH. (i) Name of a clan derived from the Romanian word *calderar* (coppersmith). Many emigrated from Romania after the end of slavery in the 19th century. They are probably the largest Romany clan, numbering nearly one million, spread throughout the world. Many still work in the traditional trade of repairing copper utensils. (ii) A dialect of Romani.

KALI. An incarnation of God in the Hindu religion. When the Gypsies came to Europe, they transferred their adoration of Kali to the many black statues of the Virgin Mary in Poland and elsewhere, as well as St. Sara at **Saintes Maries de la Mer**. There is a report from 1471 of Duke Paul of Egypt making a pilgrimage to Compostela to see the **Black Virgin** of Guadalupe.

KALININ, VALDEMAR. A contemporary teacher and writer in Belarus. He has translated the New Testament into Romani. Matthew's gospel has already been published.

KALO. The Romani word for "black." The north Welsh and Finnish Gypsies use Kalo/Kaalo as a self-ascription rather than "Rom." It is likely that many of the Finnish Gypsies came there via Britain, and there are some similarities in the dialect. The connection with the use of **Caló** for the language spoken by the Spanish Gypsies or with the **Koli** clan in Iran is unclear.

KALYI JAG (Black fire). A contemporary folk-rock group, originally from northeast Hungary. Their music has developed from traditional **Vlah** dance tunes with the accompaniment of mouth music and improvised percussion instruments. They have made several recordings and have toured abroad.

KALYI JAG ROMA SCHOOL. A vocational comprehensive school in Budapest, Hungary.

KANTEA, GEORGI. A contemporary poet and collector of folklore in **Moldava**. He is a member of the **Ursari** clan. A small booklet of material he collected was one of the very few publications in Romani permitted in the Soviet Union in the period 1945–1991.

KARSAI, ERVIN. A contemporary teacher and poet in Hungary.

KARWAY, RUDOLF. A Polish **Lovari** who emigrated to Germany. Karway was president of the Zigeunermission, a civil rights movement based in Hamburg that was active in the 1960s. In 1968 the mission organized a delegation to the **European Commission on Human Rights** in Strasbourg protesting against discrimination. Karway visited England in 1970.

KATITZI. Character, largely autobiographical, in a series of books for children written by **Katerina Taikon**. There was also, for a short period, a children's magazine with that title featuring the young girl in many of the stories. **Hans Caldaras** recorded the song *Katitzi* in Katerina Taikon's honor.

KAVALEVSKY, SONYA. In 1884 Kavalevsky, whose mother was a Gypsy, became the first woman professor in Swede, teaching mathematics at Stockholm University.

KAWCZYNSKI, RUDKO. Contemporary activist. Born in Poland, he came to Germany as a refugee in the 1970s. He was a singer in the **Duo Z**. Later, Kawczynski entered the Gypsy civil rights movement and set up the Romany National Congress in Hamburg. He was also active in setting up **Eurom.** Kawczynski has organized many demonstrations such as the Bettlermarsch, a march across Germany to the

Swiss frontier, and the occupation of the Neuengamme concentration camp site.

KEENAN, PADDY. Contemporary **Irish Traveller** piper in the style of **Johnny Doran**. He was part of the band called **the Pavees** and has recorded as a soloist.

KERIM, USIN (1928–   ). A poet in post-1945 Bulgaria. He has written in Bulgarian and, later, Romani. His first book of poems was entitled *Songs from the Tent* (1955).

KETAMA. A contemporary folk rock group in Spain founded by Ray Heredia, Jose Soto and Juan Carmona. The Carmona family of Madrid have been musicians for three generations, starting with Tio Habichuela, the grandfather of Juan. Later they were joined by Antonio Carmona. Their first recording was issued in 1985. Heredia left the group to be a solo act but died shortly afterward. The second recording was *La pipa de Kif* (1987). Josemi Carmona—a cousin of Jose and Juan—then joined the group before their third recording *Songhai 1*, which incorporated a fusion of flamenco and Mali music. In 1992 the sixth recording was *Pa gente con Alma* in collaboration with the Dominican jazz pianist Michel Camilo. Soto has now left the group, and Ketama consists of the three Carmonas. In their first disk as a family trio *El arte de lo invisible*, salsa predominated over flamenco. They have also played in films such as Saura's *Flamenco*. Their latest record, *Aki a Ketama*, is a mixture of flamenco jazz and funk.

KIEFFER, JANE. A contemporary poet writing in French. The collection *Cette sauvage lumière* (*This savage Light*) appeared in 1961, followed by the collection *Pour ceux de la nuit* (For Those of the Night) in 1964.

KINGS. When the Romanies first came to Europe, their leaders adopted European titles, and we find in the records references to dukes in particular. The use of the titles king and queen started perhaps in the 19th century. In some cases, the person designated king is not the real leader—a device to deceive the authorities. Most kings and queens only have authority over their own extended family.

KISFALU CONFERENCE. A meeting of Gypsies held in Hungary in 1879. The participants were from Hungary only.

KLIMT, ERNST. A post-1945 political leader of the **Sinti** in Hildesheim and Lower Saxony. Klimt's family lived in the Sudetenland where his father was a miner. The family was arrested and taken to **Auschwitz**, where Klimt arrived still wearing his Hitler Youth uniform. He was transferred, as being fit for work, to Buchenwald, where he took part in the internal camp resistance movement and helped to free the camp just as the American army arrived. In 1965 he gave up his business activities and devoted himself to civil rights. His life story was turned into a musical play by the Fahrenheit Theater of Germany.

KOCHANOWSKI, VANYA DE GILYA. A linguist, originally from Latvia, he is now living in France. Kochanowski has written *Gypsy Studies* (1963), a novel *Romano atmo* (*L'Ame Tsigane*); and *Parlons Tsigane*.

KODALY, ZOLTAN. A 20th-century Hungarian composer who has used Gypsy themes in his orchestral works.

KOGALNICEANU, MIHAEL. A Romanian politician who strove for the emancipation of the Gypsy slaves in the 19th century.

KOIVISTO, VILJO. A contemporary Finnish writer and translator in Finland who attended the first **World Romany Congress**. He writes for the religious bilingual periodical *Romano Boodos* (*Romany Information*) and has translated parts of the New Testament as well as producing an ABC primer.

KOLI. A clan of Indian origin in Iran. In recent years some members have visited Italy, mainly trading in gold.

KOPTOVÁ, ANNA. A writer in Slovakia and founder of the **Romathan** theater in **Kosice**.

KOŠICE. A town in Slovakia that is home to the **Romathan** theater and a college that has a faculty for training Romany teachers.

KOSOVO. Estimated Gypsy population: 40,000. Kosovo is a province in the Balkans, currently part of Serbia and Yugoslavia. During World War II, it was garrisoned by Albanian fascists. Gypsies were made to wear distinctive armbands and recruited for forced labor. **Ljatif Sucuri** is regarded as having saved the Gypsies of Kosovo from massacre. Many Romanies joined the partisans. Kosovo has been a strong center for Romany culture since 1945. The 1971 census showed 14,493 Romanies. There was a regular TV program from Tetovo as well as a locally produced magazine called *Amaro Lav* (*Our Word*).

In 1990, following the example of some Romanies in Macedonia, an **Egyptians** Association was set up in Kosovo. It claimed that several thousand "descendants of the Pharaohs" lived in the province.

KRASNICI, ALI (1952–   ). A writer in Pristina, Yugoslavia, he has written two dramas in Romani as well as short stories.

KRIS. The legal system of some clans of the Romany people. Some writers thinks this policy goes back to the village courts of India. The Kris is an assembly of the elders of a group of extended families or, in the case of a serious problem, the whole clan.

KWIEK DYNASTY. One of several families named Kwiek emigrated to Poland from Romania, via Hungary, at the beginning of the 20th century. They established a royal dynasty, which continued until shortly after the end of the World War II. These kings were not recognized by the long-settled Polish Romanies, who had their own chief called **Shero Rom.** In the period between the two world wars, there was sometimes more than one claimant for the title of king.

King Michal II (elected in 1930) took part in the **Bucharest Conference** in 1934 and addressed a meeting in London's Hyde Park later that year, putting the case for a Gypsy state in Africa. Janusz Kwiek was crowned king in 1937 by the Archbishop of Warsaw. He, too, was influenced by Zionism and asked Mussolini to grant the Gypsies an area of land in recently conquered Abyssinia (present-day Ethiopia). He disappeared during the Nazi occupation of Poland. In 1946 Rudolf Kwiek was declared king but, living in a communist state, he changed the title to that of president of the Gypsies. He died in 1964.

KYUCHUKOV, CHRISTO. A contemporary educationalist in Bulgaria. He compiled the first Romani ABC primer for children there and has produced teaching material on Romany culture for schools.

L

LABOUR CAMPAIGN FOR TRAVELLERS' RIGHTS. United Kingdom. This is a recognized Labour party group set up in 1986 and open to members of the British Labour Party. Its aims include sensitizing members of the Labour party to the needs of Gypsies and New Age Travellers.

LACIO DROM. (i) An academic journal founded in Italy in 1964 and, since 1966, published by the **Centro Studi Zingari.** The editor is Mirella Karpati. (ii) The Lacio Drom schools were established to further the education of Gypsy children in Italy. In Romani *lacio drom* means "Good road."

LACKOVÁ, ELENA. A contemporary writer from Slovakia. Her first work was a play in the Slovak language, *Horiaci cigansky tabor* (*The Gypsy Camp Is Burning*), in 1947. Later, however, she has worked in Romani. She is currently President of the Kulturny Zvaz Občanov Romskej Narodnosti na Slovensku (The Cultural Association of Citizens of Romany Nationality in Slovakia).

LAFERTIN, FAPY (ca.1950–). A **Manouche** jazz guitarist and violinist renowned for his performances in the Belgian-based Gypsy group **Waso** and for his forays into British jazz. Lafertin has been fascinated from childhood with the 12-stringed Portuguese guitar and mastered the "fado," a Portuguese love song style. He plays regularly with the British band Le Jazz and his own group, the Hot Club Quintet.

LAGRÈNE, BIRELI (1966–). A **Sinto** Gypsy jazz guitarist born in Alsace. Taught by his father, Fiso, from the age of four, he began touring at an early age. He started recording at the age of 11, with *Routes de Django* (1981) and later, *Acoustic Moments* and *Bireli Swing*. Switching to the electric guitar, he developed a style of fiery speed and versatility, moving away from mere imitation of **Django Reinhardt.**

LAGRÈNE, JEAN (PÈRE). An artist's model in Paris in the 19th century. Manet painted him in 1862.

LAGUILLER, ARLETTE. A **New Age Traveller** who was an unsuccessful candidate for the European Parliament in southern France in 1995.

LAKATOS, ANKA. The daughter of **Menyhért Lakatos** and a poetess writing in Hungarian.

LAKATOS, MENYHÉRT. (1926–) A contemporary novelist in Hungary who writes in Hungarian. His first novel *Füstös képek* has been translated into German as *Bitterer Rauch* (*Bitter Smoke*).

LALORE SINTI. Literally "dumb Gypsies." The name given by the **Sinti** Gypsies of Germany to all those in the country who did not speak their dialect. During the Nazi period, the Lalore Sinti were classed as German Gypsies because it was said they had lived among

Germans in Bohemia and Moravia. This did not save them from the concentration camps.

LAMBRINO, ZIZI. The first wife of King Carol II of Romania. She was Jewish rather than Gypsy, as some books suggest.

LATVIA. Estimated Gypsy population: 14,000. Latvia was an independent country in the period 1919–1940 and from 1991. By this century the majority of Romanies living in the country had been sedentarized during the years of Russian rule. In 1933 **Janis Leimanis** translated St. John's gospel into Romani. Soon after the German occupation in 1941, the ***Einsatzgruppen*** began killing Gypsies. At Ludza Gypsies were locked up in a synagogue, then taken to the nearby forest and shot. Only in Talsen and Daugawpils were local Latvian officials able to protect the Gypsies. It is thought that about 2,000 were killed in all, a third of the population.

Since 1944 when Soviet troops reoccupied the country, there has been immigration by Gypsies. The official population according to the 1989 census recorded 7,044, with 84 percent speaking Romani as their mother tongue. Some anti-Gypsy activity perists today. Joachim Siegerist, leader of the People's Movement for Latvia, was convicted in Germany for incitement to racial hatred as a result of distributing more than 17,000 circulars in which he said "Gypsies produce children like rabbits" and they are "a seedy criminal pack who should be driven out of the country." His party gained 15 percent of the vote in the general election of October 1995 in Latvia.

Janis Neilands is the leader of a small educational movement that has opened two Romany schools and produced an ABC primer in the local **Chuhni** dialect.

LAU MAZIREL ASSOCIATION. An organization in the Netherlands that has been working since 1981 for the interests of the Romanies. It published the journal *Drom* and also gives help to individual Gypsies and organizations in the Netherlands. The association is named after Lau Mazirel (who died in 1974), a lawyer, who supported the rights of minorities.

LAUTARI. A clan of violin players in Romania.

LAUTARI, BARBA. A Gypsy violinist in Moldavia in the 19th century. He was an acquaintance of the composer **Franz Liszt**.

LĂZURICĂ, LĂZĂRESCU. A civil rights activist in Romania between the world wars. At first he worked with **Popp Serboianu,** but then in

1933 he set up his own organization, Uniunea Generala a Romilor din Romania (the General Union of the Gypsies of Romania). A year later he handed over the presidency to **Gheorghe Niculescu.**

LE COSSEC, CLEMENT. A Breton lay pastor in the years after World War II. He was the initiator of **Pentecostalism** among Gypsies in 1952. Le Cossec was preaching in Lisieux when a **Manouche** couple—Mandz Duvil and his wife (by Romany custom)—came to his prayer meetings and were converted. They spread the message among their relatives and friends. The number of converts grew and in 1958 Le Cossec decided to devote himself to work among the Gypsies.

LEIMANIS, JANIS. The translator of St. John's Gospel into Latvian Romani (**Chuhni** dialect) in 1933. Together with **Vanya de Gilya Kochanowski,** he tried, with very little success, to persuade the German occupiers during World War II to stop the killing of Gypsies in Latvia.

LESHAKI. A subdialect of Polish Romani.

LIANCE. A famous dancer in France in the 17th century. She was feted by poets and nobles and had her portrait painted by Beaubrun. Her husband was arrested for highway robbery and executed. After this incident Liance wore mourning clothes for the rest of her life and never danced again.

LIÉGEOIS, JEAN-PIERRE. A contemporary French sociologist and author of many books on Gypsies. He is director of the **Centre de Recherches Tsiganes** in Paris.

LIOZNA. A collective farm in the Soviet Union, near Vitebsk, in the years between the world wars. Originally a Jewish collective farm, the authorities moved the Jewish farmers out and replaced them by Romanies. Later, the Gypsies in their turn were displaced, as Stalin decided that Gypsy nationalism was dangerous.

LISZT, FRANZ. A 19th-century Hungarian composer. He was fond of Gypsy music as a child. Between 1840 and 1847 he published 20 pieces based on **Hungarian Gypsy music**. These became the basis for his *Hungarian Rhapsodies* (1851–1853).

LITERATURE, GYPSY. Until the 20th century, Romani literature was almost entirely oral—songs and folktales. The temporary encouragement of the Romani language in the newly founded **Soviet Union** led to a flourishing of literature in the period between the world wars. Since 1945 there much poetry, short stories and drama has been written. Many Gypsy writers, such as **Matéo Maximoff** and **Veijo Baltzar**, have written novels in the majority languages of the country where they live. See DRAMA; FOLK LITERATURE; POETRY.

LITERATURE, GYPSIES IN. Many famous authors have put Gypsy characters into their novels and plays or written poems on Gypsy themes. Amongst them are Guillaume Apollinaire, Louis Aragon, Matthew Arnold, Charles Baudelaire, Vicente Blasco Ibanez, Charlotte Brontë, Robert Browning, Miguel de Cervantes, Arthur Conan Doyle, the Greek writer Drossinis, George Eliot, Ralph Waldo Emerson, Henry Fielding, Wolfgang von Goethe, Oliver Goldsmith, Ernest Hemingway, Ben Jonson, John Keats, Jack Kerouac, Blaze Koneski, D. H. Lawrence, **Federico Garcia Lorca,** Antonio Machado, Osip Mandelstam, Boris Pasternak, Ezra Pound, **Aleksandr Pushkin**, Walter Scott, Jules Verne, Tennessee Williams and Virginia Woolf. It might almost be easier to list famous authors who have never created a Gypsy character.

LITHUANIA. Estimated Gypsy population: 5,500. The earliest reference to Gypsies on the territory of present-day Lithuania dates from 1501, but it is likely that they had been there for some years before. In that year Earl Alexander granted the right to Vasil to govern the Gypsy clans in Lithuania, Poland and Belarus, the Gypsies being permitted to nomadize under the authority of their own leader. In 1564, however, Gypsies were invited to settle or leave the country. In 1569 Poland and Lithuania became one country. A new decree was issued, confirming the existing policy of expelling nomads, in 1586. Some Gypsies left, some settled down, and a third group continued to nomadize in spite of the prohibition. In 1795 the Russian czar became ruler of the country. From 1919 to 1940 Lithuania was independent, then it was taken over by the USSR for one year until Nazi Germany invaded.

During the German occupation (1941–1944) about half of the Gypsies were killed, with the collaboration of Lithuanian nationalists. One transport of 20 persons was sent to **Auschwitz**; the others were killed in Lithuania itself.

In 1944 the Soviet Union once more occupied Lithuania. The country finally became independent again in 1991.

Nationalist feelings against the Russians spread to incorporate the Gypsy minority. In 1992 there was a pogrom in Kaunas. Some Gypsies were killed, cars were set on fire, and homes were ransacked.

The official population, according to the last Soviet census (in

1989), was recorded as 2,700 with 81 percent speaking Romani as their mother tongue. The majority of the present population are Catholics, the rest Orthodox. Three dialects of Romani are spoken: Litovski, Lotfitka and **Chuhni**. A Gypsy organization has been set up, and a project to develop Romani as a written language is under way.

LITTLE EGYPT. When the Gypsies moved west again in the 15th century, many came in groups of sometimes over 100 persons, led by a duke of Little Egypt. It is thought that Little Egypt referred to a part of Greece.

LIULI. One-time nomadic Gypsies in the Asian Republics that were part of the USSR. Many of them have come into Russia in search of better conditions.

LODZ GHETTO. In October 1941 the German ordered the Jews imprisoned in the ghetto at Lodz to evacuate several streets that were then wired off and used to house 5,000 Gypsies, mainly from Austria. An epidemic of typhus broke out, and several Jewish doctors volunteered to treat the sick. Apart from those who died of typhus, many Gypsies were beaten to death in the first weeks. The fate of 120 adults who were apparently sent to work in a factory in Germany is not known. Early in 1942 the remaining Gypsy prisoners were taken to the Chelmno extermination camp and gassed.

LOLI PHABAI (Red Apple). The first international journal all in Romani was published in Greece in the 1970s under the editorship of **Grattan Puxon**. Three numbers appeared. The contents included articles by **Shaip Jusuf**, **Lázló Szegö** and others, as well as folktales and reprints from Soviet literature of the interwar period.

LONGTHORNE, JOE. A contemporary singer living in England in concerts and on television in the country-and-western idiom.

LORCA, FEDERICO GARCIA. See GARCIA LORCA, FEDERICO.

LOVARI. A clan living mainly in Hungary (many thousands) and in Poland. In the past many were horse dealers, and some still carry on this trade. From 1870 onward, small numbers nomadized in Western Europe, though they were never as numerous as the **Kalderash**. The Romani spoken by the Lovari belongs to the **Vlah** dialect cluster. The Lovari rarely play music for the public, though they have a strong tradition of singing and dancing.

LOVERIDGE, SAMUEL. Supposed author of *Being the Autobiography of a Gipsy* published in 1890. Although allegedly written by Loveridge, it was edited by F. W. Carew, the pseudonym of A. E. C. Way.

LOYKO. A partly Gypsy trio of musicians from Russia, including Sergei Edenko and Oleg Ponomarev, now resident in Ireland. They have toured widely in Europe and made several recordings. The name comes from a legendary Russian Gypsy musician.

LUBBOCK, ERIC. A liberal member of Parliament in the United Kingdom who added a section on Gypsy sites to a bill he was introducing in Parliament to champion the rights of non-Gypsies living in mobile homes. This became the **Caravan Sites Act of 1968**. As a result, he became to some extent the guardian of Gypsy rights, a role that he continued to a lesser degree as Lord Avebury in the House of Lords.

LUNIK IX. A housing project on the edge of the town of **Košice** in Slovakia. The population of Lunik IX is already 70 percent Romany, and the city council of Košice has proposed moving the remaining Gypsy population of the city there.

LUTE. It is thought that some of the Gypsies of Europe are descended from lute players brought from India to Persia by the Shah Bahram Gur. There are early records of a Gypsy lutanist in Dubrovnik. With the dying out of the lute as a popular instrument, lute players adopted the violin and other stringed instruments.

LUTHER, MARTIN. The 16th-century Protestant reformer Luther was no friend of the Gypsies or the Jews, condemning both in his sermons.

LUXEMBURG. Estimated Gypsy population: 150. The first Gypsies appeared during the 16th century. They struggled against newcomers from Germany and France to preserve their trading area. In 1603 a mercenary, Jean de la Fleur, was put on trial for entering the country contrary to a decree forbidding Gypsies to enter the Grand Duchy. During World War II, the Germans deported the small number of Gypsies in the country to camps in Poland.

M

MACE, JEM. Nicknamed "The Gypsy," Jem was the bare-knuckle English boxing champion in 1861.

MACEDONIA, REPUBLIC OF. Estimated Gypsy population: 100,000. This entry deals with Macedonia from 1941 onward. Previously it was part of the **Ottoman Empire** and the kingdom of **Yugoslavi**a.

During World War II, Macedonia was handed over by the Germans to the Bulgarians and Italians. Most of the Romanies managed to persuade the occupiers that they were Turks or Muslim Albanians. Those who were identified as Romanies had to wear yellow armbands. Some were taken as forced laborers to Bulgaria and a small number to camps in Poland. Many joined the partisans, and it was said that Tito promised them their own state after the war. This promise—if it had been made—was not carried out as the Yugoslav government would have seen a smaller Macedonia as a prey for Greek and Bulgarian expansionist ambitions.

The largest Gypsy community in Europe developed in **Shuto (Šuto) Orizari** on the outskirts of Skopje in the aftermath of the earthquake of 1963. About 90 percent of the inhabitants are Gypsies.

In May 1980 Naša Kniga, a publishing house in Skopje, produced the first Romani grammar to be written in the Romani language. The author was **Shaip Jusuf.** The **Pralipe** theater operated until 1990 when the Communist party forced the company to vacate its premises and the actors emigrated to Germany.

In 1990, too, the Egyptian Association of Citizens was founded in Ohrid by Nazim Arifi, consisting of some 4,000 residents of Ohrid and neighboring Struga, who—although many scholars consider them to be of Romani origin—claim to be descendants of **Egyptians** brought to the Balkans during the Ottoman rule. The Association claimed 20,000–30,000 adherents, and Egyptian was included as a separate identity in the 1994 census in Macedonia.

On September 1, 1990, the leaders of the Macedonian Romany community called on all Romanies to stop identifying themselves as Albanians simply on the basis of a common religion, Islam, and declared October 11, 1990—already a public holiday—to be a day of celebration of the cultural achievements of Romanies in Macedonia. Nevertheless, the census in 1994 recorded only 43,000 "Roma," as many declared themselves to be Macedonians or, if they were Muslims, Albanians or Turks.

In 1991 Macedonia became de facto independent. President Kiro Gligorov publicly acknowledged the Romanies as "full and equal citizens of the Republic of Macedonia." They were recognized as a nationality in the new constitution. Romani language radio and television programs from Skopje joined those already being broadcast from Tetovo. A few bilingual (Macedonian and Romani) magazines are published.

A Romany educational program in schools began in principle in

September 1993 consisting of language classes for grades 1–8. A 40,000-word Macedonian-Romany dictionary and other teaching material are still being prepared. The main dialects are Arlia (**Erlia**), the most widely spoken and the mother tongue of an estimated 80 percent of Macedonia's Romanies, Burgudji, Djambazi and **Gurbet**. It has been agreed to use Arlia as the basis for a standard language using the Latin alphabet for educational purposes. In addition to the planned introduction of the Romani language in primary education classes from the 1993–1994 academic year, there are proposals for Skopje University to inaugurate a Department of Romany Studies for the study of, and research into, language, history and culture. Some hundred potential teachers of Romani attended a seminar convened by the Ministry of Education at Skopje University in October 1993. The full implementation of the Romani language program has been slowed down by the lack of materials and qualified teachers. There are over 50 Romany students attending various full-time courses at the university.

The main political party for the Gypsies in Macedonia is PSERM (Party for the Complete Emancipation of Romanies in Macedonia), claiming a membership of 36,000. Its president, **Faik Abdi,** is also a member of the Macedonian parliament representing Shuto Orizari. PSERM has been the prime mover in securing Romany rights.

Many Romanies from all over the country took part in the festivities on April 8, 1993, marking the de jure creation of the new state. Some inter-ethnic conflict, mainly between Albanians and Romanies, has been reported.

McALISKEY, BERNADETTE (née DEVLIN). McAliskey is from an **Irish Traveller** family and is a nationalist politician in Northern Ireland. She was for a time a member of the British Parliament.

MacCOLL, EWAN. The stage name of a 20th-century Scottish singer, born as Jimmie Miller. He recorded the Gypsies' own stories of their life and composed the music for a popular documentary—a radio ballad, as it was called by the BBC—*The Travelling People*. Many of his songs have become part of the traditional repertoire of Gypsy singers such as *The Moving on Song* and *A Freeborn Man.*

MACFIE, ROBERT ANDREW SCOTT. Twentieth-century scholar and contributor to the *Journal of the Gypsy Lore Society*. He sometimes wrote under the Romani pseudonym Andreas Mui Shuko (Dry Face). His collection of books was donated to the Liverpool University Library.

MACPHEE, WILLIE (1910–   ). A **Scottish Traveller** musician, tin-smith, basket-maker, piper and singer. He has been a regular performer at folk clubs and festivals.

MAGERIPEN. A term for the hygienic rules of the Romany community. Romani names in other dialects for the same concept are *mockerdi* and *mahrime.* There is a broad set of concepts of cleanliness and a system of taboos maintaining the opposition of the socially or spiritually clean to persons or objects seen as unclean or dirty. Traditionally Gypsies have placed much emphasis on the uncleanness of women at the time of their menses and after childbirth. Dogs are considered as having the potential to make things dirty and are excluded from the caravan or home. To preserve cleanliness, a strict separation is observed when washing clothes, food and the human body. Many Gypsies consider non-Gypsies to be dirty by definition and reserve special cups for visitors.

MAGNETEN. A company of Gypsy dancers, musicians and singers from many countries, formed by Andre Heller, that toured Germany and elsewhere with great success in 1993. The ensemble included **Kalyi Jag, Kálmán Balogh, Loyko** and **Esma Redjepova**

MAGYARI, IMRE. A violinist in Hungary in the 1930s.

MAHRIME. See *MAGERIPEN.*

MALIKOV, JASHAR (1922–1994). A composer of songs and collector of folk music and tales in Bulgaria. Already while at school he played the trumpet and accordion in a band at weddings. He learned to write music and took up light music, including the so-called town songs. In 1949 he was in charge of music at the Roma Theater in Sofia. He was one of the first Gypsy musicians to be recorded by the company Balkanton. He is also the author of the first Romani-Bulgarian dictionary.

MALTA. There are no Gypsies currently on the island and no historical record of their presence in the past.

MANISCH. See JENISCH.

MANITAS DE PLATA (Little Hands of Silver). The stage name of a contemporary Flamenco guitarist from the Ballardo family. He was born in a caravan in the south of France where he still lives. He learned to play from his father, who was a horse dealer. Manitas has made many recordings and has toured widely.

MANOUCHE. A clan of Gypsies living mainly in France and Belgium but whose ancestors spent many years in Germany. The word *manouche* means "man" in Romani. Their dialect has many German loan words and is close to that of the **Sinti**.

MANUSH, ROMANOV. The director of the Roma Theater in Sofia, Bulgaria, until 1951 when the theater was closed and he was exiled to the country. He wrote many plays, some of which were confiscated by secret police after he was allowed to return to the capital. Manush became an MP on the list of the Union of Democratic Forces in the first post-Communist parliament. However, at the next election he was not reelected. A book has been published containing some of the songs he collected.

MANUŠ, LEKSA. See BELUGINS, ALEKSANDR.

MARIA THERESA. She was Empress of Austria-Hungary from 1740 to 1780. From 1758 she brought in a series of decrees with the intention of turning the Gypsies into *Ujmagyar* (New Hungarians). Government-built huts replaced tents while travel and horse-dealing were forbidden. Gypsy children were taken away, often by force, to be fostered by Hungarians. Her son **Joseph II** continued her policies.

MARCINKIEWICZ, JAN. In 1778 he set up a school for bear trainers in Russia and held the title of Gypsy king. After the failure of the so-called Katyushka Revolt against the Czar, he fled to Turkey.

MARSHALL, BILLY. A **Scottish Traveller** who in 1724 led an alliance of extreme Protestants and peasants against land enclosures and the imposition of the Presbyterian church. They were defeated after an initial success.

MAXIMOFF, MATÉO (1917–). A writer, translator and preacher who was born in Barcelona but moved to France with his family as a child. As a young man he was involved in an interfamily dispute concerning an abducted girl and was sent to prison, where he met the lawyer Jacques Isorni. The latter suggested that Maximoff write about his life and thus he began his writing career. Maximoff has written many novels, including *The Ursitory* (1946). This is one of the few books that gives an account of Gypsy life from a Gypsy perspective. He then wrote several more novels including *Le Prix de la liberté*

(1955), about the revolt of Romany slaves in Romania, and *Savina* (1969). He has published ghost stories related to him by his mother and also translated the Bible into Romani after becoming a convert to **Pentecostalism**. Maximoff worked on his Old Testament translation for over nine years, finishing in 1981. So far, only two parts have been published. His New Testament was finally published in 1995.

MAYA, PEPE HEREDIA. A contemporary flamenco teacher and dancer. He founded a flamenco company whose first production was the history of the Gypsies in Spain portrayed through flamenco. This was made into the film *Let Us Be Heard.*

MERIMÉE, PROSPER. A French writer born in Paris who worked in the civil service and under Napoleon III was employed on unofficial missions. Among his works he wrote ***Carmen*** in 1846 after a visit to a tobacco factory in Spain. After his death, the novel served as the basis of the romantic scenario for Bizet's opera, first performed in 1855.

MÉSZÁROS, GYÖRGY. A 20th-century Hungarian expert on Gypsies, living in Eger. He wrote numerous articles and a dictionary. At one time he worked at the Eger Museum. The eyewitness accounts he collected from victims of the Nazi period are an invaluable record.

MG-S-ROM. See SPECIALIST GROUP ON ROMA/GYPSIES.

MICHALCZUK, KAZIMIERZ. The vice president of the Roma Organization of Poland. He was killed by an unknown assassin on September 1, 1996.

MINORITY RIGHTS GROUP, SLOVAKIA. Partners in a project with the **Minority Rights Group, United Kingdom.** The group is concerned with offering training to young Romanies in central and eastern Slovakia.

MINORITY RIGHTS GROUP, UNITED KINGDOM. Amongst its manifold activities, the group runs a project for Romany rights and education with partners in Bulgaria, Poland and Slovakia. These are the **Committee for the Defense of Minority Rights** (Bulgaria), the Helsinki Foundation for Human Rights (Poland) and the **Minority Rights Group, Slovakia**. It has also published two editions of a report on Romanies by **Grattan Puxon** and a new report by **Jean-Pierre Liégeois** and **Nicolae Gheorghe**.

MINORITY STUDIES SOCIETY. The society was founded in 1992 as a center for studying the minorities in Bulgaria. As the situation of the Gypsies is the most complicated, this topic has been the main focus of the group's work. Its aims include popularizing Gypsy culture, stopping discrimination and researching the history and culture of the Gypsies of Bulgaria. The society publishes the journal *Studii Romani*. Members are taking part in a number of international projects such as the History Group based at the **Centre de Recherches Tsiganes** in Paris.

MIRANDO, TATA JR and SR. The stage names of the brothers Kokalo Weiss and Meisel Weiss who are the leaders of two contemporary bands playing Balkan style music in Holland.

MIRGA, ANDRZEJ. A contemporary ethnologist, writer and civil rights activist in Poland and a member of the **Specialist Group on Roma/Gypsies**. His writings include *Dissimilarity and Intolerance* (1994), coauthored with **Lech Mroz**. He ran for office in the Polish Sejm (Parliament) in 1994, although he was not elected. He is active in Gypsy politics on the international scene and attends many conferences to report on the situation of Gypsies in eastern Europe.

MITTEILUNGEN ZUR ZIGEUNERKUNDE. At least two publications have had this title.

(i) *Organ der Gesellschaft für Zigeunerforschung*. volume 1, January 1891. This is identical with volume 7 of the journal *Ethnologische Mitteilungen aus Ungarn* and contains a German translation of Archduke Joseph's Romani grammar.

(ii) Several numbers of a journal with this title were published in Mainz, Germany, in the 1970s.

MLAWA. A town in Poland that was the scene of an anti-Gypsy pogrom at the end of the communist period in 1991 during which many houses were burned down. Many of the Romanies fled to Sweden but were refused residence and returned to Poland.

MOCKERDI. The term used by English Gypsies for "ritually unclean." See *MAGERIPEN*.

MODON. A town in Greece with a Gypsy settlement of 300 huts in 1483–1486, 200 in 1495, and dropping to 100 in 1497. By the time the Turks took Modon in 1500, most of the inhabitants had fled to escape their advance and in 1519 only 30 occupied huts remained. The Gypsies living there were shoemakers. Their fate is unknown.

There is no trace of the arrival of any Gypsy shoemakers in the West, and the trade is generally considered unclean by today's Gypsies, as it involves working with the skin of dead animals.

MOLDAVIA. A province of Romania.

MOLDAVIAN SOVIET SOCIALIST REPUBLIC (1945–1991). See MOLDOVA.

MOLDOVA. Estimated Gypsy population: 22,500. It occupies part of **Bessarabia**, which belonged to Russia from 1812 to 1917 and to Romania from 1917 to 1940. From 1945 to 1991 the territory was the Moldavian SSR.

Aleksandr Pushkin's epic poem *The Gypsies* is set among the nomads of Bessarabia, while Kishinev had a large settled Gypsy population. During the Nazi occupation of the western Soviet Union during World War II, there are reports of a thousand nomadic Bessarabian Gypsies being driven to the death camp at Treblinka. A collection of oral literature from the region made by **Georgi Kantea** was one of the few publications in Romani permitted in the Soviet Union between 1945 and 1991. The official Gypsy population (based on the Soviet 1989 census) was 11,517, of whom 85 percent had Romani as their mother tongue.

MONDIALE OF GYPSY ART. The first Mondiale was held in Paris in 1985 and the second in Budapest from August 31 to October 31, 1995. Alongside the exhibition of paintings, the second Mondiale had a program of music and dance.

MONTENEGRO. Estimated Gypsy population: 2,000. Montenegro was independent or semi-independent from 1389 to 1918, when it became part of Yugoslavia. Up to 1940 the Gypsies in Montenegro were almost entirely nomadic, unlike elsewhere in the Balkans. During the 1930s police prevented them from entering the then capital Cetinje. During World War II Montenegro was occupied by the Italians. Some Gypsies organized an independent partisan unit in the mountains but eventually succumbed to the Italian army. The 1971 census recorded 396 Romanies. Many Romanies from Montenegro emigrated as workers to Western Europe in the 1970s. For the period 1918 onward, See YUGOSLAVIA.

MORELLI, BRUNO (1958–) A painter in Italy. As a self-educated painter, Morelli specializes in graphics and realistic portraiture and has had many exhibitions since his first in Avezzano in 1981. He exhibited at the first and second **Mondiale of Gypsy Art.**

MOVEABLE DWELLINGS BILLS. These Bills were proposed as legislation in the British Parliament between 1885 to 1908, under the instigation of **George Smith**. In 1891, for the first time, English Gypsies went on delegations to Parliament. To delegations—one led by George Smith and the other led by a Gypsy, George Lazzy Smith—opposed the bill. The bills were never passed because the opposition of the owners of circuses and fairs persuaded members of Parliament to vote against them.

MRÓZ, LECH. A contemporary Polish ethnologist and writer, teaching at the University of Warsaw. With **Andrzej Mirga** he wrote *Gypsies. Differentness and Intolerance.*

MUSEUMS. Museums devoted to Gypsy culture operate in **Brno**, Czech Republic; Pécs, Hungary; and a private museum run by **Gordon Boswell** in Leicestershire, England. Sections are devoted to Gypsy history and culture in the district museum in **Tarnów**, Poland and the Lapp provincial museum in Rovaniemi, Finland. The Museum für Völkerkunde in Hamburg owns the Max Haferkorn Gypsy collection, but this is not on permanent display. Gypsy handicrafts and wagons are exhibited in a number of museums, including a small display as far afield as the National Museum of Ethnology in Osaka, Japan.

A museum illustrating Romany basketmaking was opened in 1995 in Komotini in Thrace (Greece). Two applications for planning permission for further museums in Essex, England, were refused by the Planning Inspectorate.

MUSIC. There is probably no such thing as Gypsy music—that is, relics of the music brought from India—except, some would say, in Albania. But there is a Gypsy style of playing that is often improvised and always dramatic. A small selection of the many professional Gypsy musicians have individual entries in the dictionary. See also FLA-MENCO.

MUSTAFOV, FERUS. A musician from Strumica in Macedonia. He plays the clarinet, saxophone and most other instruments and currently leads a band in Skopje. He has toured widely and has recorded.

N

NA CHMELNICI. A theater in Prague that has a Romany company attached to it.

NĂFTĂNĂILĂ, LAZĂR. A farmer in Calbor in Transylvania who was the first to fight for Gypsy civil rights in Romania. In the 1920s he set up the society Infrăţirea Neorustica, The Brotherhood of New Farmers, which organized lectures and theater events to raise the cultural level of the Romanies. In 1933 he founded the journal *Neamul Ţiganesc*.

NATIONAL ANTHEM. The internationally recognized anthem for the Gypsies is **Gelem, Gelem**. In Hungary a second song is popular, sung to words by **Károly Bari**.

NATIONAL DAY. April 8 was chosen by the first **World Romany Congress**—the day it opened—to be celebrated by all Gypsy communities as a national day. It is sporadically honored. For example, in 1993 the Cidinipe Roma (Gypsy Association) of Zagreb held a formal meeting in the Hotel Intercontinental.

NATIONAL EMBLEM. See FLAG.

NATIONAL GYPSY COUNCIL. Located in Britain, the de facto successor to the **Gypsy Council**. The president is Hughie Smith. It was formed in 1973 after a merger of the Gypsy Council and the **Romany Guild**. The Romany Guild later withdrew and again became an independent body.

NATIONAL GYPSY EDUCATION COUNCIL. Located in Britain and founded in 1970 with a committee of Gypsy activists and educationalists. Lady Plowden, author of the **Plowden Report**, was invited to head this body, and it was able to obtain substantial grants from charitable funds. A program of education by volunteers was set up that continued for several years until local authorities gradually took over the work of teaching Gypsy children, whether they were living on official sites or still travelling. In 1988 the council split, with some members forming the **Advisory Committee for the Education of Romanies and Other Travellers** (ACERT). The National Gypsy Education Council changed its name recently to the **Gypsy Council for Education, Culture, Welfare and Civil Rights**.

NATIONAL ROMANY RIGHTS ASSOCIATION. A civil rights organization in the United Kingdom led by the activist and poet **Eli Frankham**.

NAWKIN. A name the **Scottish Travellers** use for themselves. Also spelled *noggin*. The word is possibly from Gaelic *an fheadhainn*—pronounced "an nyogin"—meaning "the people."

NAWWAR, NURI. A clan of Gypsies living in Lebanon, Syria and elsewhere in the Middle East. They speak a language of Indian origin, related to Romani. The name may have originally meant "blacksmith"—from the Arabic word *nar* (fire). In 1912 two Nuri women from Jaffa traveled through Germany with a circus troupe. Since about 1970 a number of Nawwar individuals and families have come to Western Europe as traders.

NEILANDS, JANIS. A contemporary writer and cultural worker in Latvia. He founded the first Romani school in the post-1945 period.

NETHERLANDS, THE. See HOLLAND.

NETOTSI. The name given to a group of Romanies who, according to one account, escaped from slavery in Romania and lived in the forests, resisting all attempts to recapture them. An alternative explanation of their origin is that they fled from **Maria Theresa**'s efforts to sedentarize them.

NETWORK OF CITIES. The Network of Cities interested in Roma/Gypsy issues was set up by the **Standing Conference Of Local And Regional Authorities** Of Europe following its resolution 249 of 1993. It has held a series of hearings on human rights and legal issues. The second hearing took place in Košice (Slovakia) and the third in 1996 in Ploeşti (Romania).

NEVIPENS ROMANI. A periodical in Barcelona published in Spanish by the **Instituto Romanó**. About once a year there is a special number in **Romanó-kaló**, which the Instituto supports.

NEW AGE TRAVELLERS. From around 1960 a number of housedwellers in the United Kingdom started living in **caravans** and buses. Some did this for economic reasons, others because of frustration at town life. By 1986 the numbers had grown to several hundred, and they are mentioned in a report on Gypsies prepared in that year for the secretary of state for the environment by Professor Gerald Wibberley of London University. The government brought in the concept of trespassing on private property as being a crime, to deal with what it saw as a new problem. This was introduced into the Criminal Justice Act of that year and strengthened in the 1994 **Criminal Justice Act**. New Age Travellers are classed as "Gypsies" in English law if they travel for an economic purpose. The term is sometimes loosely applied to people who do not travel at all but live in tents and grow food on organic principles.

NICOLAE GHEORGHE (ca.1940–). A sociologist and civil rights worker in Romania who has traveled extensively in Europe investigating the situation of the Romanies and has made reports to major international organizations.

NICULESCU, GHEORGHE. A civil rights activist. A flower dealer from Bucharest, in 1934 he took over the presidency of the Uniunea Generala a Romilor din Romania (General Union of the Gypsies of Romania) from **Lăzărescu Lăzurică.** This organization continued its activities until 1940.

NIKOLIĆ, JOVAN (1955–). A poet from Belgrade, Yugoslavia.

NICOLESCU, GRIGORAS. One of the organizers of the 1934 **Bucharest Congress**.

NOMADISM. The Romanies were never cattle-raising nomads who moved from place to place with their flocks. Many of them were, however, industrial nomads (sometimes termed peripatetics) who traveled from place to place practicing their crafts, whether they were smiths, acrobats or fortune-tellers. The word *Gypsy* has become a synonym for *nomad*. However, it is not sure that all Gypsies were nomadic by choice in the past. The Gypsies of Modon, for example, lived in a settlement and worked as shoemakers for several generations until the Turkish occupation of the town. Often Gypsies moved because they were forced to do so. Nomadism was almost impossible during World War II, and afterwards many countries in Eastern Europe banned nomadism. In Western Europe it became more difficult to travel as land became scarce. At present it is doubtful whether more than 10 percent of European Romanies are nomads.

NORDISKA ZIGENARRÅDET. Founded in 1973 to link Gypsy organizations in the Nordic countries.

NORTHERN GYPSY COUNCIL. A regional association formed in the north of England in 1992. The chairman is William Nicholson.

NORTHERN IRELAND. **Traveller** population: 1,100. Northern Ireland is currently ruled directly from London. The first legislation concerning sites was contained in the Local Government (Miscellaneous Provisions) Order of 1985. This gave 100 percent grants for site provision and councils the power (but not the duty) of providing sites. In 1986 an Advisory Committee on Travellers was set up to advise the Department of the Environment for Northern Ireland. About 7 families out of 10 live on authorized sites, including 10 run by local authorities. Four districts have been "designated" under the Order as areas where Travellers cannot stop except on official sites. In 1997 the Race Relations (Northern Ireland) Order was passed. The outlawing of discrimination on racial grounds in this order also applies to discrimination against **Irish Travellers.** As a result, it was proposed to repeal the designation paragraphs of the 1985 order. The Travellers in Northern Ireland have the same lifestyle as those in the Irish Republic. The Traveller Support Movement is a network of local groups that works for the civil rights of Travellers, in addition to the Belfast Travellers Education Development Group.

NORWAY. Estimated nomadic or seminomadic population: 400 Romanies and some 5,000 **Travellers**. Norway had become part of Denmark in 1380, and Danish laws applied. So, when the Danish King Christian III expelled Gypsies from his kingdom in 1536, this action applied to Norway as well. It is thought that, because he and his people became Protestant in that year, his tolerance waned for immigrants claiming to be pilgrims. There may well have been no Romanies in Norway at the time. One group was deported from England to Norway in 1544, and others entered from Germany. In 1554 the king again ordered their banishment from his territories. If they then returned, the magistrates were to set them in irons to work for up to a year, following which they were to be expelled again. A further order from King Frederick II in 1589 became valid for Norway on August 1, when Gypsies were to be imprisoned, their possessions confiscated, and the leaders executed without mercy. The followers would be killed if they did not leave. Mayors of towns would forfeit their property if they did not denounce Gypsies, and anyone protecting or sheltering them for the night would be punished, as were ferrymen and captains of ships that brought Gypsies into the country.

Some Romanies then left—for Finland probably—and others went underground in the country, mixing and intermarrying with Norwegian nomads to form the group known as Reisende (**Norwegian Travellers).**

In 1814 Norway set up its own Parliament. In 1860 the immigration of Romanies from Romania and Hungary was helped by the relaxation of the Passport Law in 1860, and in 1884 the first Romany birth in the country for many years was recorded. In 1888 a new law stating that citizenship depended on descent, not birth, was introduced. That meant that Romanies born in Norway did not get Norwegian citizenship until 1914 when the law was changed, and between 30 and 40 Romanies acquired Norwegian citizenship. However, between 1918 and 1939 the Norwegian government tried hard to keep Romanies out, specifically invoking the Foreigners Law of 1901, which meant they could not get permission to enter the country to work as nomadic craftspeople. A few who had relatives already in the country were allowed to come. In 1924 the Justice Department accused the Catholic Church of issuing false baptism certificates to Romanies. The following year the Justice Department said that all Norwegian passports held by Romanies were false and should be withdrawn. In 1927 all the Romanies left the country, precipitated by the Aliens Law, which said that "Gypsies or other Travellers who cannot prove they have Norwegian citizenship shall be forbidden access to Norway."

An international incident occurred in 1933 when a group of Romanies, some with Norwegian passports, wanting to go to Norway were stopped on the frontier between Germany and Denmark. The Danish government would not allow them transit until the Norwegian government agreed to take them which it refused to do. These Gypsies were held in an internment camp in Germany for some months and then pushed over unmanned border crossings into Belgium. During the Nazi occupation of Belgium, some of these Gypsies with Norwegian nationality were to be arrested and sent to **Auschwitz.**

Between 1927 and 1954 there were no Romanies in Norway. After 1954 a number of Gypsy families came into the country from France, but there has never been a large population. Some families were able to regain Norwegian citizenship. In 1955 Oslo social workers ordered a Romany family to move from their two tents to the workhouse at Svanvike. The parents refused because they had heard about the place from Travellers. Their six children were then taken away by force, the press took up the story and the authorities then agreed to return the children to the parents. In 1956 a new Law on Foreigners left out an earlier provision about Gypsies (Sigøiner) seen as racist and replaced it by a section on nomads: "foreigners shall be refused admittance at the border if it is thought that they will try and support themselves as nomads."

In 1956 some Romany families regained their Norwegian citizenship and permission to live in the country. Temporary camps were set up around Oslo.

In 1961 the authorities in Oslo discussed the problem of Romany children not going to school. The Mission for the Homeless, set up for the Norwegian Travellers, was still involved and suggested sending families to work in a kind of labor camp. A Gypsy committee was set up by the Social Services Department in 1962 for a Romany population of about 40 persons. A new Gypsy committee was set up in 1969, excluding the Mission for the Homeless. In fact, no Romanies were in Norway at this time. In 1970 and again in 1973 the government published reports and proposals for the Romanies. By this time some families had returned and in 1973 Parliament passed a decree on support for Gypsies. In 1975 all immigration was stopped, affecting newcomers but not the existing population of about 100.

Several initiatives of 1978 were aimed at Romanies in Oslo: the opening of the first nursery school, an agreement that all Romany children were to have mother tongue tuition and the appointment of a special employment adviser. Romanies were not, however, considered as immigrants but had a special status. In 1979 an ABC book in Romani was printed, *Me ginavav Romanes* (*I Read Romani*), and two years later a reader for primary-age children appeared. In the last years there has been renewed immigration from Eastern Europe.

NORWEGIAN TRAVELLERS. The indigenous **Travellers** in Norway have many names but they prefer to be known by the nonpejorative name of *Reisende* (Travellers). They are traditionally divided into two groups by both themselves and outside experts—the *storvandringer* and the *småvandringer* (long- and short-distance Travellers). The long-distance Travellers are generally considered to be the descendants of Romanies who went underground to avoid deportation in the 15th and 16th centuries and intermarried with local nomads. On the other hand, the short-distance Travellers are thought to be of Norwegian origin, with some intermarriage with German **Jenisch**, who came to Norway to trade.

By the 19th century the existence of the Travellers was worrying the government, and in 1841 a Commission of Enquiry was set up. Three years later the discussion of the "problem of the *Fanter*" (another name for the Travellers) in the Norwegian Parliament resulted in a new Poor Law. Aimed specifically at the Travellers, it imposed a punishment of two years' imprisonment for any of them who nomadized in bands. The government voted in 1855 an annual sum of money to educate Travellers. This budget was later used for placing them in workhouses, where they were forced to labor. The policy failed due to a lack of suitable institutions. In 1893 the Church Department, which had responsibility for Travellers, estimated that there were some 4,000 of them. In 1896 a law was passed permitting the state to remove children from parents to state institutions. In some cases the child could be detained until the age of 21. This law was also invoked against some Romany families in the 20th century.

In 1897 pastor Jacob Walnum followed **Eilert Sundt** as the official expert on Travellers. He became general secretary of the Association for the Fight against Nomadism, which, under the new name of Norwegian Mission for the Homeless, operated until 1986. In 1934 about 1,800 Travellers were said to still be living as nomads. Articles written by J. Scharffenberg appeared in the press recommending their sterilization, and many Traveller women were operated on from 1935 until 1950 or even later. During World War II and the German occupation moves were made to intern the Travellers in work camps. A story is told that some Traveller families painted swastikas on their caravans to convince the Germans that they too were of Aryan origin, but this has not been substantiated. The proposal of the puppet Norwegian government was to submit the Travellers to tests to see to what extent they were of Romany origin and sterilize those who were. The government minister Jonas Lie compared the Traveller question with the Jewish question, while the Norwegian Mission for the Homeless offered its card index of Travellers to the police and recommended more stringent laws. Fortunately, the German occupation of Norway ended before these plans could be put into effect.

Two varieties of Norwegian are spoken by the Travellers, known as *romani* and *rodi* (or *rotipa*). The grammar is Norwegian, but there are many loans of vocabulary from Romani as well as from Jenisch. Many Travellers played the violin and contributed to Norwegian folk music, including in the 19th century Karl Frederiksen and his pupil Fredrik Fredriksen. Another Traveller musician was Nils Gulbrand Frederiksen. The songs and melodies of the Travellers have been collected and form part of the repertoire of contemporary folk singers.

NOVITCH, MIRIAM. A Jewish writer. Novitch escaped death during World War II because she was arrested as a resistance worker—not as a Jew—and therefore held in a prison, rather than a camp. She was among the first to become interested in the fate of the Gypsies during the **Holocaust**. In 1961 she wrote her first article on the subject—*"Le second génocide"* (*"The Second Genocide"*)—and followed this up in 1965 with a 31-page report on the killing of the Gypsies and a pamphlet supporting a campaign to get a monument erected for the Gypsies killed in **Auschwitz**. She attended the second **World Romany Congress**. After emigrating to Israel, she established a section on Gypsies in the Museum of the Kibbutz Lohamei ha-Ghettaoth.

NUREMBERG LAWS. From 1933 to 1938 the German Nazi party held rallies in the town of Nuremberg. During the 1935 rally three decrees were announced, including two on nationality and marriage. They made "non-Aryans" second-class citizens and forbade marriage between the Aryan Germans and persons of "foreign blood" (i.e., Jews, Gypsies, Blacks).

NUREMBERG TRIBUNAL. After the end of World War II, a series of trials of war criminals was held at Nuremberg from 1945. Former SS General Otto Ohlendorf told the court that in the campaigns of killing in the East "there was no difference between Gypsies and Jews." The accused at the first trial (1945–1946) included Ernst Kaltenbrunner, who had been involved in the murder of Jews and Gypsies. He was sentenced to death and executed.

NUSSBAUMER-MOSER, JEANETTE (1947–). A **Jenisch** nomad living in Switzerland. She has published an autobiography, *Die Kellerkinder von Nivagl*, describing the life of her family, with a winter base in a small village and travelling in the summer with her grandfather.

O

OCCUPATIONS. Certain occupations are associated with Gypsies such as fortune telling, music, metal work and trading with horses, but Gypsies are to be found in many fields. There are surgeons, lawyers and other professionals, especially in Eastern Europe, where most Gypsies are sedentary and educational opportunities better. It is not always easy to identify professionals who are Gypsies (Romanies), as they may hide their origin because of real or imagined prejudice.

OFFICE FOR DEMOCRATIC INSTITUTIONS AND HUMAN RIGHTS (ODIHR). An institution of the **Organization for Security and Cooperation in Europe** (OSCE). Founded in 1992, its aim is to promote human rights by assisting participating states to build democratic societies. Its field of work includes the Romanies, and it organized the Human Dimension Seminar on Roma in the OSCE region held in Warsaw in 1994. It also publishes the newsletter of the **Contact Point on Roma and Sinti Issues** (CPRSI), which works within ODIHR.

OLAH, DEZIDER. A contemporary activist in Slovakia. President of the Demokraticky zvaz Romov na Slovensku (Democratic Union of Romanies in Slovakia) and the Strana Socialnej Demokracie Romov (Romany Social Democratic Party).

OLAH, VLADO (1947–). A teacher and writer, born in Slovakia and now living in the Czech Republic. Teacher and writer. A collection of his poetry was published in 1996 under the title *Khamori lulud'i* (*Sunflower*). He is a founder of Matice Romska a Christian-oriented educational organization, and coauthor of a children's Bible in Romani. Olah is now translating the New Testament.

OPEN MEDIA RESEARCH INSTITUTE (OMRI). A **Soros Foundation**-supported organization in Prague whose field of interest includes Gypsies.

OPEN SOCIETY. A **Soros Foundation**-funded organisation which includes Gypsies in its activities.

OPERA NOMADI. An organization in Italy concerned to promote the education of Gypsy children. It was founded at Bolzano in 1963 by Bruno Nicolini.

OPRE. Music producers whose aim is to preserve the authenticity of Romany music and further its development. Based in Zurich, Switzerland, they have issued two CDs to date. *Opre* in Romani means "upwards."

ORGANIZATION FOR SECURITY AND CO-OPERATION IN EUROPE (OSCE). The OSCE was set up at a meeting of the Great Powers in 1975 as the **Conference on Security and Cooperation in Europe**. Its present name and structure date from 1994. It has included Gypsy affairs in its meetings and other activities. In September 1995 it organized a hearing of 23 Gypsy women from all over Europe. During the meeting of the OSCE in Warsaw in October 1995, a workshop on networking was run for Romany associations. See also CONTACT POINT ON ROMA AND SINTI ISSUES and OFFICE FOR DEMOCRATIC INSTITUTIONS AND HUMAN RIGHTS.

ORHAN, GALYUS. A contemporary journalist. Born in Yugoslavia, he is currently living in Slovakia and is editor of *Patrin*, a bilingual Romani-English journal.

ORS. The Romani National News Service in Hungary.

OSTIA CONFERENCE. Under the title "East and West" the **Centro Studi Zingari** organized a conference for Gypsies and non-Gypsy experts at New Ostia near Rome in 1991. The arrangement of workshops by topics gave an opportunity for the members of the working parties elected at the Fourth **World Romany Congress** to meet. The results of the conference were published in the journal *Lacio Drom*.

OTTOMAN EMPIRE. The Ottoman Turks conquered Constantinople (present-day Istanbul) in 1453. They were to expand and rule parts of Eastern Europe for many hundred years beginning in the 16th century. The Gypsies were generally treated like other ethnic groups and organized with their leaders being responsible for, for example, tax collection. During this time, many Gypsies became converted to Islam, while Gypsies who were already Muslims came into Europe with the Turkish conquerors as soldiers, musicians and courtiers of various kinds. From time to time the Ottomans banned nomadism, probably because of the difficulty of collecting taxes from nomads rather than any special ill will toward nomads as such. In Serbia, Gypsies paid higher taxes than the Serbs but were exempt from other obligations to the state.

P

PAINTING. Since 1945 there have been a number of Gypsy painters and artists. In Austria **Karl Stojka** and afterward his sister, **Ceija Stojka,** have become well known. Karl's paintings have been exhibited outside Austria. In the Czech Republic Rudolf Djurko paints on glass. Another painter in the Czech Republic is Mirka Preussova. Naive artists have emerged particularly in Hungary, where there have been two national exhibitions of work by self-taught Gypsy artists.

The first exhibition in Hungary was held in 1979 and the second in 1989. Seventeen artists showed their works at the second exhibition, including **János Balázs.** See also MONDIALE OF GYPSY ART.

PALM, KAI and PERTTI. Two contemporary singers, brothers, in Finland who play rock music. They have lately begun to introduce songs in Romani into their repertoire.

PALM, OLLI. A contemporary singer in Finland who combines the tradition of the Finnish tango with the American folk-rock style. Among his repertoire are jailhouse blues.

PALMROTH, ARVO VALTE (1916–). A Finnish born songwriter and singer who began his music career in 1962 after his wife's death. He had been involved in music on a casual level for many years but was then inspired to record an eponymous record in 1973 that included both Gypsy songs, romances and airs and some original compositions. Some of his family accompanied him. This long-playing record launched Arvo on his singing career.

PALMREADING. Palmistry was one of the trades mentioned in the early reports of Gypsies—for example, in 1422 in Belgium and in the same year in Italy. The first record of palmistry in England is in 1530.

The art probably originated in India. Many clans have continued the tradition. It is predominantly women who read palms.

PANKOK, OTTO. A 20th-century German artist who drew many Gypsy subjects. His *Passion* was based on visits to a Gypsy camp in Heinefeld near Düsseldorf in 1933–1934. In July 1937 came the opening of the National Socialist propaganda exhibition Degenerate Art (*Entartete Kunst*). Amongst the works on display was Otto Pankok's lithography *Hoto II*, the portrait of a **Sinto**.

PANKOV, NIKOLAI (1895–1959). Born in St. Petersburg, Pankov received only a primary education. He translated **Prosper Merimée**'s *Carmen* and works by **Aleksandr Pushkin** into Romani. He worked as a journalist, first on a Russian newspaper and then on the Romani magazine *Romani Zorya*. He strove from 1924 on to persuade the Romanies to settle down and have an education. His writings include *Buti i džinaiben* (*Work and Knowledge*) (1929) and *Džidi buti* (*Living Work*)(1930). Pankov taught in the Gypsy technical school in Moscow from 1933 to 1938. In 1942 he suffered from an illness brought on from working as a night-watchman, after which he wrote little. He was elected a member of the Union of Soviet Writers in 1944.

PANNA, CZINKA (1711–1772). A musician born in the Austro-Hungarian Empire in a district that is now part of Slovakia. Coming from a musical family, she was encouraged to study music and later played the violin in her own band with her husband and brothers-in-law. Her repertoire included folk songs and her own compositions. Panna was honored both during her life and after her death as a great musician. Since 1970 musical festivals in her honor have been organized in the Gemer, the county of her birth. She is one of the very few Gypsies to appear on an official postage stamp.

PAPUSZA. See WAJS, BRONISLAWA.

PARA-ROMANI. A name given by some linguists to varieties of non-Romani languages that have been influenced by Romani.
    See also CANT.

PARIS CONFERENCE. The Paris Conference—which some books wrongly call the fourth **World Romany Congress**—took place on February 22–23, 1986. It has been called variously an open meeting of the Presidium of the **International Romani Union** or a meeting of the **Comité International Tsigane**. The main purpose of the meeting was to consider the campaign to get reparations from the German government for victims of the Nazi period. This meeting saw one of the last public appearances of **Vaida Voevod III**, the founder of the modern Gypsy civil rights movement. Some delegates regarded it as a prelude to holding the fourth Congress in Paris, but efforts to obtain financial backing failed, and that congress was eventually held in Poland.

PASHOV, SHAKIR. A cultural activist in Bulgaria. As early as 1923 he was editor of the Romany journal *Istikbal* (*Future*) and in 1929 head of the organization of the same name. In 1934 the right-wing government banned all the Gypsy magazines and organizations. Following the establishment of a Communist government in 1945, he became head of the new Gypsy Organization for the Fight against Fascism and Racism and editor of a new magazine for Gypsies. He became a member of Parliament but was interned at Belen prison camp during the later Communist clampdown on Romany nationalism.

PATRIN. An international periodical in Romani and English. Two issues have so far appeared. The current editorial office is in Prešov, Slovakia. The editor is **Galjus Orhan** and assistant editor, Erika Godlová.

PAVEE. A word used by **Irish Travellers** for self-ascription.

PAVEE POINT. (i) The name given to the headquarters of the Dublin Travellers' Education and Development Group. (ii) The new name of the group. Its membership consists of settled people (non-Travellers) and **Travellers** who are committed to the right of Travellers to equality in Irish society. It runs training courses, has publications and tries to influence local and national policy.

PAVEES, THE. A folk band in Ireland in the 1980s with mixed membership, **Travellers** and non-Travellers.

PELE, EL (Ceferino Jiménez Malla) (1861–1936). A cattle dealer in Spain who in 1926 became a brother in the Third Order of the Holy Friars. At the outbreak of the Civil War, he defended an imprisoned priest and was thrown into prison. He refused the offer of freedom and was shot in August with other brothers of the order. His beatification took place in 1997.

PEN. See ROMANI PEN.

PENTECOSTALISM. The start of a Pentecostal revival among Gypsies came in 1952 when a French **Manouche**, Mandz Duvil, asked the

Breton pastor **Clement Le Cossec** to baptize him and his partner. Mandz spread the news of his new faith among his family and friends. Two years later, the hundred or so converted Gypsies chose four of their number to be elders. In the same year the first large convention was held in Brest. From 1960 the movement spread outside France, to Germany, Spain and most countries in Europe, as well as the United States. Along with the Manouche who were the original converts, members of other Gypsy groups (**Kalderash** and **Gitanos**) also became converted. By 1982 it was estimated that 70,000 Gypsies had already been converted and baptized.

The first contact with England came when an English Gypsy visited a convention of the Pentecostals in Montpellier in 1954. The first convention in England was held in 1983 at Fox Hall Farm, Nottinghamshire, and the second—also in the Midlands—in 1984. *Vie et Lumière* is the organ of the movement. In 1995 the Romani speakers (**Kalderash** and others) decided to form their own organization known as **Centre Missionaire Évangelique Rom Internationale (CMERI).**

PERIPATETICS. A term used by some authors to describe industrial or commercial nomads, as opposed to traditional nomads who move around with cattle.

PERUMOS. A popular music troupe in the Czech Republic.

PETALO, KOKA (?–1996). A spokesman for Gypsies in Holland in the first years after World War II.

PETROV, MIHAIL (1968–). A poet in Bulgaria. A collection of his poems *Mo Vogi* (*My Soul*) was published in 1996.

PETROVA, DIMITRINA. The former director of the **Human Rights Project** (Bulgaria), she is now director of the **European Roma Rights Center** in Budapest.

PETROVIČ, ALEXANDER (ca.1900–1942). A Gypsy medical practitioner. Petrovic aided victims of the dysentery epidemic in Smolensk, USSR. He was a military doctor in Corfu during the World War I and in Yugoslavia. Between 1920 and 1931 he was a medical assistant at the University of Odessa, after which he returned to Yugoslavia to the Central Institute of Hygiene. He was murdered by unknown assailants in September 1942.

PETULENGRO. The Romani word for a blacksmith and used by several authors named Smith as a penname. One of these, Xavier Petulengro, wrote *A Romany Life* (1935).

PHRALIPE (Brotherhood). The name given to a number of Gypsy organizations, particularly in Yugoslavia after 1945. See also PRALIPE.

PHRALIPE. A national organization founded in Hungary in 1988.

PISTA, DANKA (1858–1903). A composer of urban folk songs in Hungary.

PITO, JOZKO (1800–1896). A musician born in southwest Slovakia, he was a popular violinist in the town of Liptovský Mikuláš. Pitko collected and played folk songs. His sons and grandsons have followed in his musical footsteps.

PLOWDEN REPORT. Under the chairmanship of Lady Plowden, a report was published in the United Kingdom entitled *Children and Their Primary Schools*. (1967). It found that Gypsies were "probably the most severely deprived children in the country." Lady Plowden was later to become President of the **National Gypsy Education Council**, set up to help Gypsy children get schooling.

POETRY. Romani poetry has developed from song. Some poetry was written during the early years of the Soviet Union before the use of the Romani language was discouraged. **Aleksandr German** and O. Pankova were the outstanding names in a repertoire that followed the state policy in seeing nomadism as romantic but outdated. Poetry has only really become a common literary form since 1945. Well-known poets include **Rajko Djurić**, **Leksa Manuš** and **Bronislawa Wajs.** A number of anthologies are listed in the bibliography.

Increased settlement and educational opportunity have also produced writers who use the language of the country where they live. They include **Dezider Banga** (Czechoslovakia), **Károly Bari** (Hungary), **Slobodan Berberski** (Yugoslavia), **Luminiţa Mihai Cioabá** (Romania), **Sandra Jayat** (France) and Jozsef Kovacs (Hungary), together with many in the USSR. Their themes often mirror those of non-Gypsy poets. In Yugoslavia, where radio and periodicals have fostered the language, a circle of poets developed in Skopje and its satellite town of **Shuto (Šuto) Orizari**, alongside a flourishing theater in Romani.

Nowadays, however, the lyric writers of **Kosovo** are better known. Characteristic of this school is the creation of neologisms from

Romani roots rather than using loan words from Serbo-Croat or Albanian. From the score of writers in Yugoslavia we can mention only three: Dževad Găsi (1958–), Iliaz Šaban and Ismet Jasarević (1951–). The latter in his rhymed autobiographical poem *Te dzanel thaarako ternipe* (*That Tomorrow's Youth Might Know*), tells of his hard struggle against poverty and illness. On a smaller scale than in the 1920s and 1930s, the Soviet Union has seen a small revival with Satkevič and **Leksa Manuš**. Gypsy poets in Hungary have seen their work appear in a number of anthologies and in magazines such as *Rom som* (*I Am a Romany*). **Jószef Choli Daróczi** takes his inspiration from Brecht and the Hungarian poet Joszef Attila. **Ervin Karsai,** on the other hand, is best known for his children's poems. Characteristic of Czech and Slovak writers was that have often been manual workers with little formal schooling. Worthy of mention are **Bartolomej Daniel**, **Tera Fabianová**, František Demeter (ca.1947–), **Elena Lacková**, Vojtech Fabian and Ondrej Pesta (ca.1922–).

Vitorio Pasquale writes in the less used **Sinti** dialect and, together with Rasim Sejdic, has been published in Italy. There are other occasional poets such as **Matéo Maximoff** (better known for his novels), **Dimiter Golemanov** (primarily a composer of songs), and **Rosa Taikon** (an artist in metal).

An outstanding achievement of post-1945 Romani poetry is the full-length verse ballad *Tari thaj Zerfi* (*Tari and Zerfi*) by the **Lovari** dialect writer **Wladyslaw Jakowicz** (1915–), recounting the story of two lovers. It has been published in Sweden with a glossary in **Kalderash**, thus making it accessible to a wider circle of readers. The poets writing in Romani are part of the wider European tradition and important instruments in the development of the Gypsies' own culture.

POGADI CHIB/JIB. Literally "broken language." The name given to the variety of English spoken by Gypsies in England and south Wales that has a large vocabulary borrowed from Romani but with the grammar and syntax largely based on English. This form of speech spread during the 19th century, replacing the Romani language proper. There are conflicting theories about its origin.

An example of a sentence in Pogadi Chib is: *The rakli jelled to lel some pani* (The girl went to fetch some water). Similar varieties of the majority language have been developed in Ireland, Norway, Scotland, Spain (**Caló**) and Sweden.

POLAND. Estimated Gypsy population: 55,000. Romanies first arrived on the territory of present-day Poland during the 15th century. By the end of that century several places were named after the Gypsies (such as Cyhanowa Luka) where Gypsies had presumably settled. Following harassment in Germany and other countries, more Gypsies followed. In 1501 a Gypsy, Vasil, was appointed by Earl Alexander of Lithuania to govern the Romany clans in Poland, as well as Lithuania and Belarus. However, in 1557 the Polish Parliament ordered the expulsion of Gypsies from the country. This was not carried out, as is shown by the passing of similar laws five times between 1565 and 1618. From around 1650 Polish kings began to appoint Gypsies as heads of their own community. Even when this role was given to non-Gypsies, the Romanies continued to have their own recognized leaders. The Polish Lowland Gypsies still acknowledge the *shero Rom* (Gypsy chief) as their leader. In the 18th century, Gypsy families immigrated from Slovakia and settled in the Carpathians. These Gypsies settled in permanent communities and formed the group now known as *Bergitka Roma* (Mountain Gypsies) as opposed to the longer established Lowland or Polish Romanies. In 1791 the Settlement Law was passed, abolishing the previous decrees on expulsion but—again unsuccessfully—banning nomadism. By 1793 Poland ceased to exist as a separate nation, being partitioned between Russia and Prussia (Germany).

The first writings on the Gypsies in Polish were by Tadeusz Czacki at the end of the 18th century and, in 1824, by Ignacy Danilowicz. In the 19th century **Kalderash** and **Lovari** Gypsies from Romania arrived on Polish territory. Poland regained its independence in 1918. After the end of World War I, the Kalderash elected their own kings, forming the **Kwiek dynasty**. These kings were recognized by the Polish government.

In 1939 Germany occupied part of Poland in 1939 and already in 1940 began to deport Gypsies and Jews there from Germany. These Gypsies were put in ghettos and workcamps. In 1941 Germany occupied the rest of Poland, and the following year massacres began. At Karczew 200 Gypsies were killed, 104 at Zahroczyma, 115 in Lohaczy and smaller numbers throughout the country. Hundreds were deported to the extermination camps at Belzec, Chelmno, Sobibor and Treblinka. These camps, as well as **Auschwitz** (Oświęcim), also witnessed the death of Romanies brought from outside Poland. Probably some 13,000 Polish Romanies were killed during the Nazi occupation.

In the first years after 1945, the Polish authorities did not regard the Romanies as a problem, in contrast to the other countries of Eastern Europe. Romanies make up only 1 percent of the population, and many have been sedentary for generations. There was also little fear that the Polish Catholics would be outstripped in births by the Romanies, and any racist feeling was directed toward the small Jewish population. After the election of a Communist government in 1947, Romanies were required to take up employment in factories and farms alongside the rest of the population, and private trading was restricted. Many Lovari and Kalderash were allowed to leave for Sweden or West Germany and were provided exit visas.

A Government resolution of 1952 aimed at integrating the Gypsy population, the Resolution on Assistance to the Gypsy Population in Moving Toward a Settled Style of Life, but this had little effect at local level. Then in 1964 nomadism was stopped by strict interpretation of laws on schooling, camping and so on. Many young Gypsies moved into towns to work in factories. Until 1989 national minorities were supervised by the Ministry of Internal Affairs, and Romanies were de facto classed as an ethnic minority. A census in 1983, deriving from this ministry's registers, counted 21,000 Romanies in Poland.

In 1963 the first Romany cultural organization in Poland was founded in Andrychów, and it still functions. However, all cultural associations were in those years controlled by the government.

The only publishing in Romani in that period were the poems of **Bronislawa Wajs** (Papusza). There were also a small number of books in Polish about the Romanies, by Ficowski, Mroz and others. Some musical ensembles were formed, including the **Roma Ensemble** in Kraków founded in 1948 which toured in Poland and abroad. A cultural club was established and a Gypsy exhibition put on permanent display in **Tarnów**.

In the late Communist period there were pogroms in Oświęcim (1981) Konin, (1981) and Kety. Houses were broken into, plundered and set on fire.

As Poland moved toward democratic government, an annual Gypsy music festival was started in Gorzow Wielkopolski, and the bilingual newspaper *Rrom p-o Drom (Romanies on the Road)* began to appear in 1990 under the editorship of **Stanislaw Stankiewicz**.

After the end of the Communist regime, surplus unskilled laborers were sacked from their work. These were mainly Gypsies. On the other hand, many Gypsies have established small businesses and attracted the envy of their poorer Polish neighbors.

Since the breakup of the Communist state there has been one big pogrom in Mlawa where the houses of Gypsies were set on fire, following an incident in which a car driven by a Gypsy hit three pedestrians. Many Gypsies from Mlawa tried to flee to Sweden. This was in 1991. In the same year three Gypsies were killed in a second incident elsewhere. In 1992 there was an attack on the house belonging to one of the only seven remaining Gypsies in Oświęcim, the majority having left after the 1981 pogrom. Windows were smashed, and anti-

Gypsy slogans were painted on nearby walls. The political party Narodowy Front Polski (Polish National Front) circulated leaflets during 1993 complaining about an exaggerated figure of 90,000 Gypsies and campaigning for them all to be expelled from the country. In March 1995 a Romany couple was killed in Pabianice, and in October of the same year a mob attacked a house in the Warsaw suburb of Marki. The problem of harassment is widespread.

Several hundred Romanian Gypsies have immigrated to Poland. At the same time large numbers of Polish Romanies have sought to establish themselves in Western Europe—some as asylum seekers on the grounds of racial persecution

The Gypsy population consists of a number of different groups speaking different dialects. Apart from those already mentioned (Lowland Gypsies, Bergitka, Kalderash and Lovari), there also Russian Gypsies who have immigrated since (and even in some cases before) 1945 and **Sinti** Gypsies.

Current organizations include the Central Council of Polish Roma (Chairman: Stanislaw Stankiewicz), which has representatives of the five largest associations: the Fundacia Mniejszosci Roma w Polsce (Association of the Roma Minority in Poland), the Romanies Social and Cultural Association in Tarnów, the Friends of Romany Culture in Gorzow Wielkopolski, the Kraków/Nowa Huta Romany Association and the Solidarity Association for the Romany Minority in Kielce. There is also the independent Romany Association in Poland (chairman: **Andrzej Mirga**), with headquarters in Oświęcim. The association publishes a number of books under the title of the Polish Library of Gypsy Studies (Biblioteczka Cyganologii Polskiej). There is also a monthly television program aimed at the Romany population. Reverend Edward Wesolek, a Jesuit, has been appointed the National Catholic Minister to the Romany community.

PONOMAREVA, VALENTINA. A contemporary Gypsy vocalist and musician in Russia who blends her vocals with electronic orchestral accompaniment. She has toured internationally in the late 1990s with the Volgograd (Stalingrad) band Orkestrion, which incorporates made-up instruments recycled from rubbish tips and give a unique performance of poetry and music.

POPES. Over the years a number of popes have interacted with the Gypsies—in a positive or negative way.

Martin: In 1423 Pope Martin possibly gave a safe conduct letter to Duke Andrew of Little Egypt. A copy of the presumed document has survived, and there is a record of Andrew and his followers setting off for Rome, but no record of a meeting.

Between 1550 and 1557 several edicts were passed in the papal states. Gypsies had to leave the territory, or the men would be sent to the galleys and the women whipped.

Pius XII: In his Christmas message of 1942 he spoke of the "hundreds of thousands of people who, solely because of their nation or their race, have been condemned to death or progressive extinction." He has been criticized for not opposing the Hitler regime more actively.

Paul VI: In September 1965 Paul VI addressed 2,000 Gypsies at Pomezia. He talked of his "dearest nomads—perpetual pilgrims who have found a home in the heart of the Catholic church" and named Mary as queen of the Gypsies. This was followed by a mass and a concert in St Peter's Square, Rome.

John Paul II: He attended the **Ostia conference** organized by the **Centro Studi Zingari** in 1991 and addressed the delegates. He stressed the Gypsies' love of the family and the fact that they were not using weapons in their fight for their rights. Later, in 1993, he wrote a letter of solidarity to the Gypsy memorial gathering at **Auschwitz**. John Paul includes Romani as one of the languages of his regular greetings.

POPULATION. See table in Appendix A.

PORTUGAL. Estimated Gypsy population: 60,000. Although there are no reports of the first Gypsies to arrive in Portugal, references to them appear in literature in 1516 and 1521. The number in the country must have been significant since in 1525 a law on Gypsies was passed, followed by 26 subsequent edicts. A law of 1573 ordered Gypsies to be arrested and used as galley slaves. In 1579 the wearing of Gypsy dress was banned. Deportation to the colonies in Africa and South America was a common way of dealing with Gypsies in Portugal from 1538.

In 1920 a law defining the role of the National Guard contained special provisions concerning Gypsies. The members of this police force were told to "exercise strict vigilance over the Gypsy population to suppress their habitual stealing" and "to detain immediately any Gypsy accused of any crime." In 1980 after the political changes in the country, the provisions of the law of 1920 were declared unconstitutional because they conflicted with paragraph 13 (against racial discrimination) of the new Portuguese Constitution.

The majority of Portugal's Gypsies live in the poorer areas of towns or on the outskirts. There has been some migration to Spain this century. There is no active national Gypsy organization in Portugal though the Catholic Church has a body working with Gypsies.

Marcellino Cabeca is a leader within the community, and his son Inocencio has attended international meetings.

POVERTY 3. The third European antipoverty program from 1990 to 94. This was a **European Community** program to support experimental projects to eradicate local poverty. A number of Gypsy projects received funding through Poverty 3, as either Model Actions or Innovatory Measures.

PRALIPE. A theater company originally from Skopje. It moved to Mulheim in Germany after the Yugoslav Communist party evicted it from its theater building and its grants were stopped. It tours widely using the buildings of the Theater a.d. Ruhr in Mulheim as a base. Pralipe's repertoire includes **William Shakespeare**'s (*Othello* and *Romeo and Juliet*) and **Federico Garcia Lorca**'s *Blood Wedding*. The name of the group comes from the Romani word for "brotherhood," generally spelled *Phralipe*.

PREMIO HIDALGO. A prize established in 1979 by the Asociación Nacional Presencia Gitana in Madrid. It is awarded each year to two personalities, one Spanish and one international, who have contributed to the development of Gypsy culture or rights. Laureates include Günther Grass.

PRESS. Before 1939 a small number of journals for the Gypsy community were published.
Bulgaria: *Istikbal* (*Future*.) (1923).
        Terbie (*Education*) (1933–1934)—in Turkish, banned by the government.
Romania: *Glasul Romilor* (*Voice of the Romanies*)—bilingual.
        Neamul Ţigănesc (*Gypsy News*) (1933-?)—bilingual.
        Timpul (*The Time*) (1933-?)—bilingual.
Soviet Union: *Nevo Drom*(*New Way*)(1928–?)—in Romani.
        Romani Zorya (*Romany Dawn*)—in Romani
Yugoslavia: *Romano Lil* (*Romany Paper*)(1935–?)—edited by Svetozar Simic, three issues only, in Romani and Serbian.
    The rise of fascism put a stop to these periodicals and it was not until around 1970 that new periodicals began to appear. Since 1989 there has been a stream of publications in Eastern Europe, some short-lived and some that have lasted longer. Yet others have closed and then revived as money again became available. A selection is listed alphabetically at the end of the bibliography.

PRO JUVENTUTE A Swiss charitable organization that in the period 1926–1973 took many Gypsy and **Traveller** children away from their parents and sent them for adoption.

PROJECT ON ETHNIC RELATIONS (PER). A U.S. non-governmental organization founded in 1991 to encouraged the peaceful resolution of ethnic conflicts in the new democracies of Central and Eastern Europe and the ex-USSR. It has organized a number of conferences in Europe on the position of Romanies. There is a council composed of Gypsies who advise PER, known as PERRAC (PER Romany Advisory Council).

PUSHKIN, ALEKSANDR. A Russian writer whose lyric poem *The Gypsies* took three years to write and was completed in 1827, depicting the Romanies of **Bessarabia** as ideal representatives of a natural state of human society. While celebrating the freedom of the Gypsy way of life, the poem also describes a fateful union between a Gypsy and non-Gypsy. This poem inspired Mikhail Lermontov's 1829 poem *The Gypsies* and was later turned into a play—with moderate success—by the Moscow **Teatr Romen**.

PUXON, GRATTAN. An English journalist. Puxon went to Ireland and there became involved with the campaign of the **Travellers** to get caravan sites. He returned to England and helped set up the **Gypsy Council,** of which he was the first secretary, in 1966. In 1971 he organized the first **World Romany Congress** and became secretary of the **Romany Union**. He served as its secretary until the third congress.

Q

QUINQUILLEROS, QUINQUIS. From the term *quincallero*, meaning "**tinker**" in Spanish. They were seminomadic in Spain until this century, trading from village to village. Some think the Quinquilleros are of German origin, as many are blond and blue-eyed. Another theory traces their origin to landless Castillian peasants. Until the 1950s they were completely nomadic, but punitive laws barring nomadism—with the penalty of from six months to five years prison or forced settlement—have caused them to setttle. Some 85 percent now live in urban slums. They prefer to be called *Mercheros* (Traders).

R

RACZ, ALADAR (JASZBARENY, ALADAR). A 20th-century **cimbalom** player in Hungary of international standing. Racz was well known for his interpretation of Bach, Beethoven and other classical composers by playing the technical equivalent on a reconstructed sounding board. He played in Budapest in a Gypsy band for 16 years. His recitals in Europe included a 1910 performance in Paris, a 1926 recital at the Concert Hall, in Lausanne and a 1938 concert in Rome, after which he was invited to join the Academy of Music in Budapest.

RADIO. No broadcasts for Gypsies were aired until after 1945. Now a number of stations regularly broadcast programs in Romani or aimed at Gypsy audiences. The earliest was perhaps in 1973 when a radio program started at Tetovo (Yugoslavia/Macedonia)

Stations currently broadcasting such programs include the following:

- Radio Belgrade
- Radio Budapest. Once a week. In Romani and Hungarian.
- Romano Krlo in Brescia, Italy
- Radio Libertaire. Paris. Once a week in Romani, Serbo-Croat and French.
- Radio Romania. One hour a week in Romanian and Romani from about 1992.
- Radio Skopje. In Romani

Two programs also are aired in Prague, mainly in the Czech language. In addition, there are some religious radio programs broadcast from various stations, such as Trans World Radio, transmitting from Tirana. The proposed broadcasts from Peterborough, England (which are mentioned in some books and articles) were never started.

RADUCANU, GHEORGHE. A contemporary civil rights activist in Romania. As a member of the political party Partida Romilor (Romany party) he was the first Romany to be elected to the Romanian Parliament.

RADULESCU, IULIAN. A **Kalderash** head of family. He was crowned Emperor of All the Gypsies in August 1993 in Romania. His son is married to Lucia, the daughter of his one time rival, the late **Ion Cioabă**.

RAHIM, BURHAN. Currently the director of the **Pralipe** theater.

RAJKO. A Children's orchestra in Hungary. The Romani word *rajko* means "boy."

RAJKO SCHOOL. A school for gifted Romany children in Hungary where they specialize in music.

RAJKO DJURIĆ FOUNDATION. This Prague foundation, named after the writer **Rajko Djurić**, carries out a number of charitable and civil rights activities. It organizes a national festival, Romfest, each year in Moravia, and has produced a number of TV programs for Czech television.

RAMÍREZ HEREDIA, JUAN DE DIOS. Former teacher and community worker in Barcelona, now a politician. He was elected to the Spanish Parliament and then became a member of the European Parliament in Brussels. He is active in the Union Romani, based in Barcelona, and the journal *Nevipens Romani* (*Romany News*). He helped to organize the **European Congress** in Madrid.

RANJIČIĆ, GINA (1830–1891). A singer in Serbia whose songs were recorded by Heinrich von Wlislocki and published in a book called *Vom wandernden Zigeunervolke* (*Of the Wandering Gypsy People*) in 1890.

RAOUL WALLENBERG FOUNDATION. Budapest. A civil rights organization in Budapest named after the World War II hero, it has investigated cases of discrimination or harassment against Gypsies in Hungary.

RASUMNY, MIKHAIL "KING." A Gypsy actor who played the Gypsy grandfather, Nino Koshetz, opposite Jane Russell and Cornel Wilde in the film *Hot Blood* (1955). The writer was Jean Evans.

RAYA. A contemporary Russian Gypsy singer. It is recounted how when the Moscow **Teatr Romen** came to play in her town, she jumped on the stage and joined in the singing. The director was so impressed he hired her on the spot. Later she married a Norwegian journalist, and since then Raya has lived in Norway and Paris. She has made several records of traditional songs.

RAZVAN, STEFAN (?–1595). The son of a slave and a free woman in Romania. He became ruler of Moldavia in April 1595. He was deposed four months later and murdered in December of the same year.

REDJEPOVA, ESMA. A singer from **Skopje**. who has her own ensemble, originally set up with her late husband. They have made many recordings and have toured widely in Europe and North America. She sang the Romanies' **national anthem**, *Gelem Gelem*, to open the fourth **World Romany Congress** and performed at the grand concert during that conference.

REINHARDT, BABIK. Guitarist son of **Jean-Baptiste "Django" Reinhardt**. He also organizes the annual Django Festival in Samois-sur-Seine, France.

REINHARDT, JEAN-BAPTISTE "DJANGO." (1910–1953). Reinhardt was his mother's surname, while his father was, in fact, called Weiss. As a young Gypsy musician, Reinhardt began his career busking in Paris. In 1920, a French accordionist heard him playing his guitar and offered him a professional engagement in a dance hall, from where he earned his first real money. Jack Hylton, the famous British bandleader, traveled to Paris twice to find him to offer him a contract. The night of their meeting, tragedy struck when a candle set fire to Reinhardt's caravan and his left hand was burned. It was a year before he could play in public again. Yet because of this disability, he spent hours working out how to play with the three usable fingers on his left hand, whereby his technique was said to reinvent guitar playing. At this stage he discovered jazz and formed a quartet with his brother Joseph and two non-Gypsies, Louis Vola and Stefan Grappelli. A fifth player was added, and they formed the quintet, which gained fame as the Hot Club de France.

By September 1939 the quintet was playing in London, on the eve of the World War II, which prompted Reinhardt to return to France. Unfortunately, France was soon conquered by the Germans, and jazz was condemned as "Negro music." Concerts were no longer advertised as "jazz." While playing later in occupied Belgium at the Club Rythmique de Belgique, Reinhardt was asked to tour Germany. He knew Gypsies were being arrested there and sent to the death camps so he avoided this danger by requesting 120,000 francs per concert, knowing the Germans would not pay such an amount. Toward the end of the war, he sensed danger again and moved from Paris to near Thonon-les-Bains at the Swiss border, where he once dared to play the *Marseillaise* in front of German officers. From there he tried to slip across the border but was arrested and found to have a membership card of the British Society of Composers. The German officer who interrogated him was a jazz fan and let Reinhardt go free.

Being cut off from the international world of jazz in occupied France led to a lukewarm reception in New York when Reinhardt did play there in 1946. Café society there no longer felt jazz was an art with mass appeal, and Reinhardt's name was not enough to make up for his lack of professionalism. On his return to France, he began to learn the electric guitar but died after refusing to call a doctor when suffering from a fatal brain hemorrhage in Samois.

REINHARDT, SCHUCKENACK (1921–). Born in Weinsberg, Germany. A violinist playing jazz and swing, he leads a quintet. His recordings include *Musik deutscher Zigeuner* in four volumes.

REISENDE. See NORWEGIAN TRAVELLERS.

REIZNEROVÁ, MARGITA. Writer from Slovakia and president of the Organization of Romany Authors. She translated Chekhov into Romani. Her work includes poetry, and her most recent publication is *Kali*, a collection of stories about the goddess, in Romani with an introduction in Czech.

RELIGION. Gypsies have tended to adopt the religion of the country where they live or travel. So, we find Protestant, Catholic and Orthodox Christians, as well as Muslims. Recently there has been a move among many persons to adopt **Pentecostalism**.

REPARATIONS. This entry deals with reparations for victims of the Nazi period. After the end of World War II, the Bonn Convention said that persons who were persecuted because of their race should be compensated. However, in 1950 the Interior Ministry in the German state of Wurtemberg told judges to remember that Gypsies were persecuted not because of their race but because they were antisocial. In 1953 a law on reparations (Bundesergänzungs Erlass zur Entschädigung für Opfer des NS) made reparations available but only to Gypsies who were of German nationality, stateless or refugees. The arrangement (from 1959) was that West Germany would pay global reparations to Western European countries which they would then use to pay their nationals who had suffered. In the case of Eastern European countries, a number of Gypsies who had been used for medical experiments have received reparations, but otherwise very few others have been compensated for their sufferings in this period.

In 1956 there was an important decision of the Higher Court (Bundesgerichthof) that a Gypsy woman should not be compensated for the 1940 deportations to Poland as these, the Court said, were not for racial reasons but because of the fear of espionage. In 1962, however, the Higher Court accepted that persecution had started as early as 1939 (the Blum case). In 1965 a new law (Bundesentschädigungsschlussgesetz) confirmed that Gypsies did not have to prove that persecution from 1938 was racial. This was assumed. Finally, a new law provided for reparations to be paid for those victims who had not yet been compensated.

Requests have been made for block reparations to be paid to international Gypsy organizations, in particular for families where all the members perished and noone survived to claim reparations. Following the third **World Romany Congress,** the **Romany Union** has been pursuing a claim for block reparations against first the West German and then the Federal German Government. The Indian government informally offered to be the trustee for such payments. The German government has given money to German **Sinti** organizations for cultural and educational purposes but these payments have not been seen by the government as being a form of global reparations. Since the fourth World Romany Congress, no progress has been made on this question, though two international funds have now been set up to provide pensions for survivors. See also HOLOCAUST.

REPUBLIKA SRPSKA. Part of Bosnia-Herzegovina under Serb rule. The current Gypsy population is unknown, but there are 200 living in the area of Banja Luka and a similar number in Bijeljina. When Bosnia was partitioned, the political entity known as Republika Sprska was set up. It is thought that the Gypsy population is small because during the 1992–95 fighting, many Muslims were expelled from this area and the majority of the Gypsy population was Muslim. Gypsies expelled from Bratunac, for example, now live in Virovitica in Croatia. Almost the entire prewar populations of Banja Luka and Bijeljina (both numbered in thousands) have left. The Gypsy settlements of Jasenje and Staro Selo have been destroyed. Several thousand Gypsies who formerly lived in the area now under Serb control are living as refugees in Western Europe, in particular Germany, Italy and the United Kingdom.

RESANDE. See SWEDISH TRAVELLERS.

REYES, LOS. See GYPSY KINGS.

REYES, ANTONIO. El Mono. Flamenco singer in Spain and grandfather of **Joaquín Cortes.**

REYES, JOSÉ (1930–   ). Cousin of **Manitas de Plata**. A metalworker and carpetseller who sings largely for his own pleasure.

RISHI, W. R. A contemporary Indian scholar from the Punjab who spent some time during his diplomatic service in Europe studying the Romanies. He has attended several congresses and conferences and been a strong link between the Romanies in Europe and their motherland India. After returning to the Punjab, he set up the Indian Institute of Romani Studies, edited the journal *Roma*, as well as organizing the two **Chandigarh Festivals**.

RITTER, ROBERT. A German race scientist during the Nazi regime who in 1936 founded an institute that later became the Race Hygiene and Population Biology Research Center of the Ministry of Health in Berlin. He took over existing records on Gypsies. His aim was to track down every Gypsy in the country and claasify them as pure or part-Gypsy. By 1942 he claimed to have files on 30,000 persons living in Germany and Austria. The policy he proposed was to intern part-Gypsies in work camps and sterilize them. Pure Gypsies should be allowed to travel but kept apart from mixing with Germans.

ROBERTSON, JEANNIE (1908–1975). A **Scottish Traveller** folk singer. Jeannie's parents traveled principally in the northeast of Scotland, and she first came to prominence in folk-song circles in 1953 when she was recorded by Peter Kennedy. Acknowledging her mother as the main source of her musical knowledge, she gained a reputation as one of the finest ballad singers in Western Europe. She made several records and videos and was honored by Queen Elizabeth II with the Medal of the British Empire. Her daughter Lizzie Higgins is also a singer and can be found on several recordings.

ROBERTSON, STANLEY. (1940–   ). A **Scottish Traveller** and the nephew of **Jeannie Robertson**. A traditional piper, singer and storyteller, he joined the Mormon Church and with its encouragement became a public entertainer. Stanley has toured in the United States and Europe.

ROKYCANY. A small town in Bohemia (Czech Republic) with a large Romany population who emigrated soon after 1945 from Slovakia. The community has a strong musical tradition, and the players include the Gina family, which first formed a folk band called Ginovci and later, playing more modern music, Rytmus 84.

ROM, ROMA. The majority of Gypsies call themselves *Rom* in their own language. The etymology is unclear, but the term may come from an old Indian word *dom*, the original meaning of which was "man." Derivation from the God Rama is unlikely. The plural is *Rom* or *Roma* according to the dialect. Other Gypsy groups—for example the **Sinti** and **Manouche**—have the word *rom* in their dialect but only in the sense of "husband." Some organizations and citations in this handbook use the word *Roma* in particular, rather than *Gypsy* or its equivalent.

ROMA CULTURAL SOCIETY. Founded in Poland in 1966 and still active.

ROMA ENSEMBLE. Poland. This Romany song and dance ensemble was originally formed in Kraków in 1946 by ex-members of the Moscow **Teatr Romen**. The first director of the ensemble was Michael Madziarowicz, followed by Wladyslaw Iszkiewicz in 1967. It toured abroad frequently and in 1970 came under the management of the state-owned Estrada Agency in Poznan. It made two recordings in Poland before some of the ensemble left for Sweden to form the group **Svarta Pärlor.**

ROMA PARLIAMENT. This Hungarian institution has been very dynamic in Romany politics after 1989, perhaps as it was built up by local organizations. It protects and promotes the interests of Roma through negotiations with the government during the development of new legislation for minorities. It has links with **Eurom**.

ROMAITSYA. A name used for self-ascription by the **Drindari** of Kotel.

ROMAN. The name given by its speakers to the **Romani** dialect of **Burgenland**, spoken by some 2,000 persons. It is close to the Carpathian dialects.

ROMANE DYVESA (Romany Days). An annual international meeting of Gypsy musician groups held in Gorzow, Poland, and organized by a local committee. The first gathering was in 1989.

ROMANES. An adverb in the Romani language meaning "in the Romany manner." So we find the usage "to speak Romanes."

ROMANESTAN (The Land of the Romanies). The name given to a planned Gypsy homeland on the lines of the Zionist idea of creating a Jewish state. The idea was first proposed by the kings of the **Kwiek Dynasty** in Poland in the 1930s. World War II put an end to these dreams. The idea of a Gypsy state was revived after 1945 by **Vaida Voevod III,** but nowadays most Gypsies would follow the thoughts of the Canadian Gypsy writer Ronald Lee who has said, "Romanestan is where my two feet stand."

ROMANI LANGUAGE. The Romani (Romany) language is a member of the north Indian group and is close to Punjabi and Hindi. It was brought to Europe by the Gypsies and has retained more of its earlier structure than the modern Indian languages. The sound system includes up to four aspirated consonants. There are five or six cases, and the verb has a number of tenses. Words are inflected to show changes of tense, person, gender and case. There is a masculine and feminine gender.

The discovery of the Indian origin of Romani. During the 1700s, a Hungarian pastor called Vályi, when at the University of Leiden in Holland, met some fellow students from west India's Malabar coast. They made a list of over a thousand Sanskrit words for him that Vályi took back to Hungary. Comparing them with words Romanies used in his region, he found some similarities. An article about this study was published in Vienna in 1776 and was noticed by the German linguists **Heinrich Grellmann** and Jakob Rüdiger, who each compiled a list of Romani words and compared these with a number of languages. Rüdiger saw the similarities between Romani and Hindustani (Urdu) and in 1781 first recorded his discovery. A further publication of his, a year later, demonstrating a scientific comparison between the two languages, aroused more attention. Another student of languages, Büttner, then found similarities between Romani and the Pashto language. Grellman saw Büttner's work and went on to publish in 1783 his book *Die Zigeuner. Ein historischer Versuch* (translated into English as *A Dissertation on the History of the Gypsies)* which included a section on the Indian origin of Romani.

Meanwhile, independently of all this, in England Jacob Bryant, an amateur coin collector and historian, compared a list of Romani words with a printed vocabulary of Hindustani around 1780. He revealed the similarities between words such as Romani *rup* (silver) and Hindustani *rupee*, but he also identified Greek words that Gypsies had borrowed on their journey across Europe to England. However, some of his links were unlikely and more important discoveries were made by William Marsden. Marsden, who was famous for his work on the Malay language, made the Romani/Hindustani link in 1783, compiling a paper that was presented to the London Society of Antiquaries on February 3, 1785. The society then published his findings.

Between 1763 and 1785 the news of the relationship between the two languages (Romani and Hindustani) spread from Russia to England and with it the forgotten truth as to the North Indian origin of Europe's Gypsies.

Dialects of Romani: At the time of their arrival in Europe, there were perhaps two main dialects (Romani and **Sinti**), but since then different clans have developed separate features that may have been present in the speech of some speakers of the two original dialects. Sedentary Gypsies have also been affected by the language of the majority population where they live. Now there are many dialects of which the main living ones can be grouped in the following clusters (the number of speakers represents a conservative estimate).

- **Vlah** dialects of Romania and throughout Europe (**Kalderash, Lovari** and others)—710,000
- **Erlia** (settled) Romani of the Balkans (Bulgarian, Yugoslavia, Greece)—570,000
- Balto-Slavic/"Northern"—the dialects of the Baltic states, Belarus, Poland and Russia, 500,000
- Slovak—in the Slovak and Czech Republics, 400,000
- "Nomadic" non-Vlah dialects of the Balkans—spoken by clans who have become settled during this century such as the **Sepedji** (Basket-makers) of Shumen in Bulgaria, 110,000
- Carpathian or Romungro—Poland (Bergitka dialect), Hungary, south Slovakia, Burgenland, Transylvania, Ukraine, 40,000
- South Russian—30,000
- Sinti and **Manouche**—Germany, France, Belgium, Holland, 30,000
- The language of the **Kaalo**—Finland and Sweden, 7,000
- The Romani of Calabria and Abruzzese—Italy, 2,000

With recent migration, speakers of the Balkan dialects can now be found in most countries of western Europe.

Romani is taught at INALCO (Paris University V), Charles University in Prague, Bucharest University and some other colleges and schools. It remained largely a spoken language until this century when it began to be written. See LITERATURE.

ROMANI PEN ZENTRUM. The center is a member of international PEN and has its official base in Berlin. Membership is open to writers in Romani and to those writing about Romanies. A newsletter *Stimme des Romani PEN* first appeared in 1996.

ROMANI UNION. See ROMANY UNION.

ROMANI ZORYA (*Romany Dawn*). A Russian Romani free journal published first in 1927 with a print run of 1,500 thirty-page copies. According to the editor, it was "written in Russian characters so that it could be read by Russians to illiterate Gypsies." The second issue appeared in 1929.

ROMANIA. Estimated Gypsy population: 2,100,000. Gypsies may have arrived with the invading **Tartars** in the 13th century. By the end of the next century, they were already treated as slaves. They had even fewer rights than the native serfs, as families could be split up and the members sold or given away as gifts. The first recorded transfer of Romany slaves took place in 1385. The Gypsies may have been brought to Romania as slaves by the Tartars and remained in the country with this status when the Tartars were driven out. Alternatively they may have been forced to sell themselves into slavery through debt. As the slaves in North America, they had no rights and could be beaten by their masters. The slaves included both farm workers and craftspeople.

The Gypsy slaves have a place in Romanian literature. Bogdan Hasdeu wrote the play *Razvan şi Vidra* (*Razvan and Vidra*) in which he tells the true story of a slave (**Stefan Razvan**) who was liberated in the 16th century and became a leader in Moldavia. *Istoria unui galbăn* (*The Story of a Gold Coin*) was written by Vasile Alecsandri in the 19th century. The heroine is Zamfria who is brought by a cruel owner. A Gypsy kills him and saves her, but he is executed while Zamfria is gripped by insanity. The ruler of the **Wallachia** region of Romania, Vlad IV (Dracula), is said to have brought back 11,000–12,000 Gypsies to his capital to be tortured or executed for his entertainment.

In Transylvania slavery was not widespread. In Moldavia it was, however, not to be abolished until 1855 and in Wallachia (Muntenia) one year later. Liberty did not mean equality. A trickle of emigration then became a flood and hundreds, if not thousands, of liberated slaves left Romania for other countries. Many of these **Vlah** Gypsies went as far as Australia and America.

A census in 1930, which counted only sedentary Gypsies, recorded 262,000, but this figure was recognized as too low. In the period between the wars, Gypsies began to organize themselves and demand social equality. In 1933 the journal *Glasul Romilor* (*The Voice of the Romanies*) was started and continued to appear until 1939. It was followed by other newspapers, such as *Neamul Ţigănesc* (*The Gypsy Nation*), and associations were set up in different parts of the country. In 1926 the first local Gypsy organization was founded in Calbor. In 1933 the Asociaţia Generală a Ţiganilor din Romania (General Association of Gypsies in Romania) was formed. It soon split into two organizations but later was reunited. **Lăzărescu Lăzurică**, **Gheorghe Niculescu** and **Popp Serboianu** were amongst the leaders at this time.

In 1934 the General Union arranged an international conference in Bucharest although there were few, if any, foreign participants. A number of resolutions were passed on education, employment and civil rights, but little was done to put these into practice.

At the same time, as fascist ideas spread through the country, racist commentators such as Ioan Făcăoru put forward a policy of preventing contact between the Gypsy and the Romanian peoples to avoid contaminating Romanian blood. This meant in theory that the nomadic clans who did not intermarry should be allowed to continue their traditional life.

Romania allied itself with Germany during World War II. It began a policy of deporting Gypsies to land in the east captured from the Soviet Union. During 1942, the government removed 25,000 Romanies to this land, known as **Transdniestria**, where some 19,000 died.

When the Communists came to power after World War II, the lot of the Gypsies changed again. The nomads were forced to settle down and abandon the nomadic life. The sedentary Gypsies found themselves placed in high-rise flats in the minitowns created later by Communist leader Nicolae Ceausescu's policy of destroying villages and resettling the population. At an official level, the Romanies did not exist during this period. There were no books about them and in contrast to, say, Bulgaria, Romany musicians were not advertised as such even for the tourist trade. Only one scholar, Olga Nagy, was able to publish work on Romany culture. For an idea of the treasures that were being lost through neglect, consider the fact that she alone produced eight volumes of tales and folk tales, all gleaned from Romanies.

During the Communist period, Gypsies were given jobs on state farms and in state factories. Prejudice against Gypsies continued, however. It was alleged that often police would raid their houses and steal their gold jewelry, claiming that it was the result of black market dealing. Visits from Romani leaders from the West were not made easy by the law that imposed a heavy fine on anyone allowing a nonmember of the household to stay in their accommodation after darkness. Leaving Romania was also difficult and costly. Only two Romanian Gypsies were able to attend the third World Romany Congress. Pentecostal missionaries worked underground and in 1979 St. John's gospel was translated into Romani, and printed in Holland by Open Doors for smuggling into Romania. During this period, the late **Ioan Cioabă** was an intermediary between his people and the government. The census of 1956 showed only 104,216 Gypsies, rising in 1979 to 225,000 because many Gypsies registered themselves as Romanian or Hungarian.

The fall of Communism in 1989 brought both good and bad results for the Gypsies. In the first place, they were free again to form associations and publish magazines. On the other hand, the new governments and many Romanians often blamed the Gypsies for the economic difficulties that the change to a free market brought. There were to be many pogroms in the following years. The worst attack was in Bucharest in 1990 when the then Prime Minister Petre Roman brought in miners to help him to retain power. After beating up opposition students and others in the center of Bucharest, the miners, together with secret police, then attacked the Gypsy quarter, causing much damage and injuries. In March 1993 a report in a Bucharest newspaper concerned the Ion Antonescu Command, a vigilante organization with a national network and considerable financial capital whose proclaimed aim was to "kill Gypsies who commit crimes against society." A representative of the Command stated that its members were not concerned about European public opinion and that the Gypsies were not a minority but a "curse on the Romanian nation." Romanies have formed paramilitary self-defense groups in response to the authorities' failure to protect them.

Since 1990, some 50 villages in Romania have experienced ethnic conflict where Romanians and/or Hungarians have come together to burn Gypsies out of their homes. More than 300 houses belonging to Romanies have been burned down and ten persons killed by mobs. No one has yet been convicted of arson or murder. In January 1995 houses were set on fire in Bacu and Botosani. In the same year there were heavy-handed police raids in Akos Bontida, Sectorul Agricol Ilfov and Tandarei. In the Curtea de Arges suburb of Bucharest, 21 houses were burned down in June 1996. The majority of those who lost their homes have been unable to return to them. Many now live in very poor circumstances as "illegal residents" in other towns. In 1997 three persons were finally arrested for trial in connection with events in 1993 in Hadareni where three Romany men were killed. These are the first arrests of anyone for this series of attacks. The attacks led to a second exodus, and Romanian Gypsies can be found in Poland as well as many Western countries, where they are usually tolerated for a short time and then sent back to their birthplace.

The situation today is that, while in some parts of Romania Gypsies live in fear of attack by their neighbors, elsewhere the community has been able to develop associations and magazines. The Bible is being translated and published legally, and the Romani language is taught in several schools and colleges. There was a move to replace the pejorative term *Ţigan* by the word *Rom* but in 1995 the government changed it back officially to *Ţigan* on the grounds that there was confusion with the word *Roman* (a Romanian). Romanian organizations operating in 1997 include the Ethnic Federation of Roma, the United Association of Rroma, **Aven Amentza Foundation** and **Rromani CRISS** (Romany Tribunal). There is a national body linking Gypsy associations, and one Gypsy is in the Upper House of Parliament.

ROMANICHEL. See ROMANY CHAL.

ROMANO CENTRO, VIENNA. This cultural and welfare center was founded in 1991. The president is Dragan Jevremovic.

ROMANO CHAVO (Romany youth). A term used by some groups in Eastern Europe as a self-denomination.

ROMANO DROM SCHOOLS. The Romano Drom (Romany Way) schools were established in England and Wales by the **Gypsy Council** around 1970 to provide education in caravans for nomadic Gypsies.

ROMANÓ-KALÓ. A development of **Caló** in Spain. Its aim is to reintroduce the lost grammar of Romani with the preserved vocabulary of Kaló (Caló). The magazine *Nevipens Romani* (*Romany News*) sometimes publishes in this form of speech. **Juan de Dios Ramírez Heredia** is one of the leading proponents of this program.

ROMANO ROM. A clan of **Vlah** Gypsies in Hungary.

ROMANY, ROMANI. Originally the feminine adjective formed from *Rom*.

ROMANY CHAL (Romany Youth). The name of a clan and sometimes used as self-ascription by Gypsies in England and Scandinavia. In France—in the form *romanichel*—it has become a pejorative term.

ROMANY CIVIC INITIATIVE (ROI). Czech Republic. A political party that fields candidates in local and national elections in the Czech Republic. Dr. **Emil Ščuka**, a former MP, is the chairperson.

ROMANY DEMOCRATIC CONGRESS. A nationwide forum in the Czech Republic to which many leading Romany figures contribute. It has no activities as such.

ROMANY GUILD. Founded in United Kingdom in 1972 by Travellers, this group was led by Tom Lee, who felt the non-Gypsy members of the **Gypsy Council** were too influential. Later it reunited for a short time with the Gypsy Council under the name **National Gypsy Council**.

ROMANY INSTITUTE. Set up in Britain after the first **World Romany Congress** with the support of **Slobodan Berberski**. It carried on the work of the Cultural Commission of the Congress until the third Congress.

ROMANY NATIONAL CONGRESS. An organization based in Hamburg and largely supported by Romanies from Eastern Europe. It has links in other countries and publishes the bulletin *Romnews*.

ROMANY (ROMANI) UNION. After the 2nd **World Romany Congress,** the Romany Union (International Romany Union) operated between congresses as the official body representing Gypsies, replacing the role of the **Comité International Tzigane.** The Romany Union was recognized with roster status by the Economic and Social Council of the United Nations in 1979 and later by UNICEF.

ROMATHAN. A theater using the Romani language founded in 1992, at **Košice** in Slovakia.

ROMEN THEATER, MOSCOW. See TEATR ROMEN.

ROMERIA. The name given to Gypsy festivals in Spain.

ROMINTERPRESS. RomInterpress is a cultural organization in Yugoslavia with the main aim of publishing films, books and periodicals. It wishes to coordinate the activities of the Gypsy elite in Yugoslavia, and other plans include establishing a Gypsy news agency and arranging cultural events, including film shows, of Romany interest. One of the initiators is **Dragoljub Acković.**

ROM-LEBEDEV, I. Writer in the Soviet Union in the 1930s. Some of his songs have been recorded by artists of the **Teatr Romen**.

ROMNET. A news group on the Internet.

ROMNEWS. A fax and e-mail news bulletin from the **Romany National Congress** in Hamburg.

ROSE, ROMANI. A **Sinti** activist in Germany and secretary of the **Verband der Deutschen Sinti.** He has written extensively on Gypsy rights, in particular, those of the Sinti as a long-standing minority living in Germany.

ROSTÁS-FARKAS, GYÖRGY. A contemporary writer and cultural activist in Hungary. He is president of the cultural association Cigány Tudományos és Müvészeti Társaság (Gypsy Scientific and Art Society) and organizer of the International Gypsy Conferences held in Budapest since 1993.

ROTARU, IONEL. See VAIDA VOEVOD III.

ROTWELSCH. A variety of German and the speech of the **Jenisch**, non-Romany nomads in Germany. It was used before the arrival of the Gypsies but has since borrowed words from Romani.

ROUDA, LEULEA. The brother of **Vanko Rouda**. He was active in the early days of the **Comité International Tzigane.**

ROUDA, VANKO. A civil rights activist in post-1945 Europe. He was living in North Africa in the early 1950s and read a newspaper report of a speech by **Vaida Voevod III**. He then worked with Vaida in the **Communauté Mondiale Gitane** and later set up the **Comité International Tzigane.**

For names beginning with RR, try also looking under entries for Romani and Romano.

RROM. In the standard alphabet, *Rom* is spelt *Rrom*. There are two *r* sounds in most Romani dialects. The one that is retroflex or guttural (depending on the dialect) is written *rr* in the standard alphabet and the trilled *r* is written with a single *r*.

RROMANI BAXT. A contemporary cultural organization with branches in Albania, France and Poland. Operating in cooperation with the International **Romany Union,** it publishes the periodical *Informaciaqo Lil.*

RROMANI CEXRAIN. A contemporary cultural and social action organization in Spain.

RROMANI CRISS. The Rroma Center for Social Intervention and Studies in Bucharest. The center is currently engaged in human rights activities including local social action—mainly in Romania—the documentation of violence and training for mediators

RUMANIA. See ROMANIA.

RUSSIA. Estimated Gypsy population (Russian Republic): 400,000. The first record of Gypsies in Russia dates from 1500, with a second report a year later. They entered from Wallachia. On the whole there was less persecution under the czars, compared with Western Europe. In 1759 a law promulgated by Empress Elizabeth prohibited Gypsies from entering St. Petersburg. The prohibition was not repealed until 1917, although musicians were exempted in practice and played in many cafes and restaurants. Passports were imposed in an attempt to stop nomadism in 1775. In 1783 they were invited to "settle." In 1800 Czar Nicolas I exempted sedentary Romany farmers from military service, though this decision was rescinded in 1856. In 1809 and 1839 the obligation to settle was reenacted.

Many musicians were adopted by nobles and made a good living as Gypsy music and songs were much appreciated. Count Orlov set up one of many Gypsy choirs formed from families living and working on the large estates, at the beginning of the 19th century, and the Tolstoy family, among others, patronized these choirs. Lev Tolstoy's brother and son both married Gypsies. Aleksei N. Aputkin wrote *The Old Gypsies* in 1870 to commemorate the love between Sergei Tolstoy and Maria Shishkin, formerly his mistress, whom he later married. In 1919 when the czarist government collapsed, some Gypsy singers accompanied their patrons to the West. One of these was V. Dimitrova. (A record of hers is pessimistically, though not realistically, entitled *La dernière des voix tsiganes.*)

There was an influx of **Lovari** and **Vlah** Romanies toward the end of the 19th century. K. Patkanov and others published works on the Gypsies and their language.

After the Revolution of 1917 and the subsequent civil war, Russia became part of the Union of Soviet Socialist Republics, until 1991.

After the political changes in 1991 and the breakup of the USSR, the situation slowly became worse for Gypsies in Russia as the curbs on open expression of racial hatred disappeared. Under Gorbachev, right-wing and nationalist groups were still kept under control, but after the succession of Boris Yeltsin, the hatred toward minorities came into the open, most potently in the shape of Vladimir Zhirinovsky, leader of the so-called Liberal Democratic party. Anti-Gypsy pogroms have been reported from Ostrov, Nyevil, Safornovo, Yeroslavni, in the Urals and near Moscow.

Some cultural activity has taken place in Russia since the political changes. For example, a dictionary of the **Kalderash** dialect was published. There are two main dialects of Romani spoken in Russia: **ha-laditko**, the dialect used in the education program of the 1930s and South Russian. A poet writing under the name Sandor uses this latter dialect. In the area around St. Petersburg, a third dialect—Livonska—is spoken.

S

SAARTO, TUULA. A contemporary writer in Finland. She has written a biography of her father-in-law, Kalle Hagert, a well-known figure in Gypsy circles, and a book for young people *Suljetut ovet* (*Closed Doors*), which aimed at dispelling the prejudice against Gypsies.

SAINTES MARIES DE LA MER. A town in France where a pilgrimage of Gypsies occurs in May every year. The two saints of the town's name are Mary Magdalen and Mary the mother of Jesus, who, according to legend, arrived by boat at the town after fleeing from Palestine after the crucifixion. They were accompanied by their Gypsy maid, Sarah, whose statue is in the church.

SAMARKAND. Timur Lenk (Tamburlaine) is said to have massacred the tribe of "Zingari" in his capital Samarkand in the 14th century, because they mutinied while he was away on an expedition. As the actual name used in the original text is apparently "Zingari"—a name not used until later in Italy for Gypsies—the victims are unlikely to have been Gypsies as we understand it. However, some scholars have thought this was a reason for the migration of Gypsies from the Middle East into Europe.

SAMPSON, JOHN. A British scholar and librarian of Liverpool University from 1892 until 1928. With the help of **Dora Yates**, he compiled the comprehensive study *The Dialect of the Gypsies of Wales* (1926), the result of his collaboration with the **Wood clan**. In 1894, he had met Edward Wood, a harpist who spoke Romani fluently, and he extended his research during a stay at Abergynolwyn. Together with Yates, he recorded folk tales and songs of the language and spent many hours with the descendants of Abraham Wood, specifically in the company of the violinist Matthew Wood. He translated some 50 verses of the Rubaiyat of Omar Khayyam (who may have been a Romany tentmaker) into Welsh Romani, with the aid of D. Macalister. Many of his articles were published in the journal of the **Gypsy Lore Society.**

SARAJEVO. Bosnia. In the years leading up to World War II, there were a few Muslim Gypsies living on the outskirts of the town, some assimilated Muslim Gypsies living among non-Gypsies in the town itself, a clan of non-Romani-speaking Christian Gypsies and some **Vlah** nomads nomadizing in the region. The situation was probably similar at the outbreak of the recent war in Bosnia. A small number still remain in the town. See also BOSNIA-HERZEGOVINA.

SARAJEVO CONFERENCE. In 1986 a scientific conference of Gypsy and non-Gypsy experts was held in what was then a peaceful town of Sarajevo. Speakers included the veteran scholar **Rade Uhlik**, who was living nearby. The conference was particularly remarkable in that Romani was used as a major language either as the language of papers or for translation. The papers of the conference were edited by Milan Šipka and have been published.

SARAJEVO PEACE CONFERENCES. The **Romany Union** decided in 1994 to sponsor a conference for peace in the Balkans. At the time it was thought that this conference could be held in Sarajevo. In the end, however, it was decided to hold it in May 1995 in Budapest. The program covered issues pertaining to the Romanies and to international relations in general. Because of the success of this conference, a second one was held in 1996. Again it was felt premature to hold the conference in Sarajevo, so instead it was held in the town of Vittoria in the Basque country.

SARAY, JOZSI. A Gypsy boy in Hungary adopted by the composer **Franz Liszt**. Liszt talks of him in his book *Des Bohémiens et de leur musique en Hongrie* (1859).

SARI, ANNELI. Contemporary singer from Finland. She is the sister of Feija and Taisto from the band **Hortto Kaalo**. Her repertoire is mainly light music by Finnish composers. She has played in France and was one of the stars at the concert that took place in Geneva during the third **World Romany Congress.**

SATTLER, JAJA (?–1944). While his family was living in a caravan in Berlin, he was sent by missionaries to study at a convent in Marburg. After this he took up missionary activities himself. Jaja translated St. John's Gospel and some of the Psalms into the **Lovari** dialect of Romani. In 1944 he was deported to the concentration camp at **Auschwitz,** where he was killed.

SCHNUCKENACH, REINHARDT (1921–   ). His musical studies at Mainz Conservatoire were stopped when he was deported by the Nazis to Poland. With Reinhardt Daweli he has formed the Schnuckenach-Reinhardt Quintet, which plays Gypsy jazz in the style of **Jean-Baptiste Django Reinhardt**.

SCOTLAND. Estimated population of Romanies, **Scottish Travellers** and **Irish Travellers**: 30,000. On the basis of the 1992 census, it appears that some 800 families live all the year round in **caravans**. In 1491 there is a record of "Spaniards" dancing before the Scottish king on the pavement at Edinburgh, although these may not have been Romanies. In 1505 a small party of Gypsies arrived—probably also from Spain—saying they were pilgrims, and were given money by James IV. They were then sent to Denmark with a letter of recommendation. A second group of dancers from Spain in 1529 undoubtedly were Romanies. The latter group danced for King James V. There is a record in 1540 of this king granting the Gypsies their right to their own laws and customs under John Faw, Duke of Little Egypt, in 1540. A year later this decree was repealed and all Gypsies were ordered to leave Scotland, allegedly because James V—who had the custom of traveling in disguise around the country—had been in a fight with three Gypsies. He died in the following year, so this law was not carried out. In 1553 John Faw was again confirmed as officially in charge of the Scottish Gypsies.

In 1573, however, a law was passed that Gypsies should either leave the country or settle down in paid work. If not, they would be imprisoned, publicly scourged and removed from the realm. A year later the law was strengthened. Gypsies were to be scourged and branded. Those who remained and did not settle down would be executed. In 1597 forced labor or banishment for life were added as punishments. The 17th century brought in heavy pressures against Gypsies and anyone who aided them. In 1608 two Scots—David Gray and Alexander Aberdere—were fined for selling food and drink to Gypsies. Noblemen who protected Gypsies on their estates were fined. In 1611 three Gypsies were brought to trial and hanged. In 1624 eight more Gypsy men were hung at Burgh Muir. Further executions took place, and then banishment became a regular treatment for Gypsies. In 1665 a Scottish company received permission to send Gypsies to Jamaica and Barbados.

In 1707 the Scottish Parliament was dissolved, and all future legislation was made in Westminster (see ENGLAND). After 1707 the existing Acts against Gypsies of England (1530, 1554 and 1562) were applied in Scotland. In 1714 two female Gypsies were executed under the provisions of the English Act of 1554, and 10 Gypsies were deported in 1715 from Scotland to Virginia in accordance with the English 1598 Act for the Punishment of Rogues, Vagabonds and Sturdy Beggars. The heavy pressure on Romanies in Scotland led to their virtual disappearance until this century. They either moved to England or hid themselves among bands of Scottish Travellers to escape punishment.

The Trespass (Scotland) Act of 1865 was introduced to control the indigenous Scottish Travellers and has been used up to the present day to move Travellers and Gypsies on from stopping places. The British **Caravan Sites Act of 1968** did not apply to Scotland, although the 1994 Criminal Justice and Public Order Act—which further criminalizes trespass—does. An Advisory Committee on Travelling People was set up in 1971. Scottish local authorities have been encouraged to build caravan sites for the Scottish Travellers and the small numbers of Irish Travellers and Romanies from England who visit the country. A target of 941 pitches was set, of which 742 had been provided by 1996. Authorities with insufficient pitches are asked to apply a toleration policy to illegally parked caravans. The present scheme by which the government gives grants is due to end in 1998. Some 50 **New Age Traveller** families live in the country. See also SCOTTISH TRAVELLERS.

SCOTTISH GYPSY/TRAVELLERS ASSOCIATION. Established in 1993 to unite Gypsies and **Scottish Travellers** to campaign for their rights. It has organized two conferences and publishes a magazine.

SCOTTISH TRAVELLERS. It is likely that there were traveling nomads in Scotland before the arrival of the Romanies. Therefore, we cannot be sure whether records in the Middle Ages refer to indigenous Scottish Travellers or Romany Gypsies. Over the centuries the two groups have mingled and intermarried, and the present-day population of Scottish Travellers is of mixed descent. They call themselves Nawkins. The Scottish Travellers have a rich tradition of singing and have preserved many ballads from the Scottish tradition. There have also been many singers, in particular the **Stewart family,** and folk storytellers this century, such as Jimmy McBeath and **Duncan Williamson**. Most Travellers speak a variety of English known as **cant,** with an "exotic" vocabulary of words from a number of sources. In the northeast of Scotland the cant is based on a Gaelic framework.

SCOTTISH TRAVELLERS' ACTION GROUP (STAG). A civil rights group operating around 1970 and cooperating with the **Gypsy Council** in England.

SCOTTISH TRAVELLERS' COUNCIL. A civil rights group initiated by the singers **Belle Stewart**, Sheila MacGregor and Cathie Higgins and active around 1985.

SČUKA, EMIL. A contemporary cultural activist in the Czech Republic who was elected secretary of the International **Romany Union** at the fourth **World Romany Congress**. He is also president of the **Rajko Djurić Foundation.** Sčuka was influential in setting up the Romen theater in Sokolov.

SEJDIĆ, RASIM (1943–1980). Poet and collector of folk tales from Yugoslavia. His poem *Gazisarde romengi violina* (*They smashed the Romanies' violin*) commemorates the concentration camp at **Jasenovac**.

SEPEDJI. The Turkish term for several Basket-maker clans in the Balkans. The Basket-makers of the Shumen area in Bulgaria and those of Turkey and Greece speak different dialects of Romani and are not related.

SERBIA. Estimated population: 425,000. It is likely that the first Gypsies to reach Serbia were shoemakers who lived in Prizren sometime around 1348. Under the **Ottoman Empire** (from 1459), the Gypsies were classed as one of the many ethnic groups in the country. No overall census figures are available for the Gypsy population in this time. The Viennese Gypsiologist Franz Miklosich reported that there were some 25,000 Gypsies in Serbia in the 1860s. At one time the Turkish rulers attempted to ban nomadism, but they were not successful. Many **Vlah** Gypsies came after the emancipation of the slaves in Romania, joining earlier immigrants from across the Danube who had by the end of the 18th century already become sedentary.

From 1878 Serbia was independent. In 1879 and 1884 the new state passed laws to prohibit Gypsies from nomadizing, and in 1891 there was an order that Gypsies who were not settled and without an occupation should be reported to the authorities. Foreign Gypsies were to be expelled. The censuses at the end of the 19th century showed around 50,000 Gypsies in Serbia. About half claimed Romany as the mother tongue, and 25 percent were Muslim.

In 1918 Serbia became part of Yugoslavia, until 1941 when it came under military rule by the German army. Soon after the German conquest of Yugoslavia, regulations forbade Gypsies in Serbia to use public transport or cafes. They had to wear an armband with the sign Z on it. At first the Germans took Gypsy men to act as hostages and then shot them in reprisal for the deaths of German soldiers at the hands of partisans. The women and children were placed in a concentration camp at Zemun (Semlin). Many were killed in gassing vans. Harald Turner—head of the German military administration—reported to Berlin that the "Gypsy problem had been solved," as he wanted to concentrate on the fight against the partisans. However, large numbers were still living outside Belgrade. The German occupying forces began to round up Gypsies in Niš in eastern Serbia and imprison them at a concentration camp at Crveni Krst. Again many were shot in reprisals for attacks on German soldiers. During the German occupation of Serbia, some 30,000 Gypsies were killed.

In 1944 Yugoslavia was reestablished as a republic. The 1971 census recorded 49,894 Romanies for Serbia (including Voivodina and Kosovo) and 396 for Montenegro, an unbelievably low figure, even allowing for the losses during the Nazi period.

In 1991–1992 Yugoslavia was split again. Only Serbia (including Voivodina and Kosovo) and Montenegro remained in the Yugoslav Republic. After 1993 the Serbian government made some efforts to get its Gypsy population to support the government. Government officials attended an official church service in Romani, and subsidies were given to newspapers. The poet **Trifun Dimić** was able to publish the New Testament in Romani as well as a first reader for schools. One cloud in the picture was the harassment of **Rajko Djurić,** who was forced to flee the country because of his opposition to Serbia's support for the Bosnian Serbs. There was also an attack by skinheads on Gypsies in Kraljevo in September 1996.

For the periods 1918–1941 and 1944–1991, see YUGOSLAVIA.

SERBOIANU, POPP. A priest. Serboianu set up a nationwide Gypsy organization in 1933 in Romania, the Asociatia Generala a Tiganilor din Romania (General Association of the Gypsies of Romania). One of his committee, **Lăzărescu Lăzurică,** broke away and set up the rival General Union of the Gypsies of Romania. Serboianu continued to be active in the Oltenia region, together with the poet Marin Simion. In 1933 he set up a Chimney Sweeps Guild that acted as a front for Gypsy civil rights activities. A conference was planned for the Romanies of Oltenia for late 1934, but before this took place, there was a further split, this time between Serboianu and Simion. Serboianu's influence then waned. In 1934 Lăzurică resigned from the presidency of the General Union and **Gheorghe Niculescu,** a flower dealer from Bucharest became president. Simion joined Niculescu's organization and helped to set up the magazine *O Rom.* Lăzurică then allied himself once more with Serboianu, but Niculescu remained the most powerful Gypsy leader, and his association continued work until 1940. The nomadic Gypsies did not take part in either of the two organizations but recognized as their leader the Kalderash Bulibaşa Gheorghe Mihutescu.

SETTELA. A Gypsy girl in Holland whose picture, peering through the door of a boxcar, has symbolized in many books the deportations to concentration camps during the Nazi period. Originally thought to be Jewish, she has recently been identified as a Romany. She was taken to **Auschwitz** on May 19, 1944 and gassed two months later. A Dutch TV film has been made about her short life.

SHAKESPEARE, WILLIAM. English playwright. By Shakespeare's time, Gypsies were well known throughout England, and the playwright could make references to them in his plays. He sometimes calls them **Egyptians** and sometimes Gypsies. In *Othello* (first performed in 1604) Desdemona talks of a handkerchief that "an Egyptian gave to my mother." It has been suggested that the name of the character Caliban in *The Tempest* comes from a Romani word meaning "blackness."

SHELTA. (i) Another name for Irish Travellers' **cant**. (ii) One of the sources of vocabulary for this cant. It is a secret vocabulary from the Middle Ages formed by changing the first consonant of a word. An example is the word *feen* (man) from Irish *duine*. The name *Shelta* itself is probably formed from the Irish word *béarla*, which originally meant "language."

SHERO ROM, SZERO ROM (Romany chief). The leader of the Lowland Gypsies in Poland. In 1890 Baso was elected to this office. He founded a hereditary dynasty that continued at least until 1976. During 1946 his grandson, Felus, was deposed for breaking the **Mageripen** Code and was purified in 1950 to take up leadership again, until 1975 when he was succeeded by his second cousin.

SHUTO (ŠUTO) ORIZARI (popularly called Shutka). Shutka is a satellite town outside **Skopje** in Macedonia. It grew rapidly after the Skopje earthquake of 1963 when large numbers of Gypsies from the town were resettled there in houses donated by foreign governments. It grew as the result of a decision by Gypsies themselves to leave the old Gypsy quarter of Topana and move into the new town. By the mid-1970s Shuto Orizari had its own district council, offices, a cinema and a football ground. Some 5,000 more houses were subsequently built, assisted by the granting of free building land and flexible town planning regulations, and it became the only place in Europe where Gypsies were not a minority. The estimated population in 1977 was 40,000 and is now double this. The inhabitants are 90 percent Romany.

SICILY. The first positive reference to Gypsies on the island dates from 1485 and refers to a horse dealer named Michele Petta. The first Gypsies had probably arrived some years earlier and from the Balkans by sea rather than from the mainland of Italy. In 1521 Duke Giovanni came with a group of followers and a safe conduct from Charles V. This party had previously been in Spain and passed down through Italy. For some time the nomadic Gypsies enjoyed a limited form of self-government under their leaders. During the Mussolini period, some Gypsy families from Italy were deported to Sicily. The island also has a population of non-Romany Travellers known as **Camminanti**.

SIMFEROPOL. A town in the Ukraine where Gypsies settled from 1874. During the 1930s, there was a strong cultural life with a Gypsy

Club—Ugolka Demirdji (Ironworkers Circle)—and a football team. However, the Romany population of some 800 were all massacred by the German occupiers in December 1941.

SINTO (singular), SINTI (plural). The term may originate with the Indian province of Sindh, or it may be an old Indian word meaning "community." It is a clan living mainly in Germany but with some families now established in Belgium, Holland, northern Italy, Poland and Russia. It is likely that the Sinti came to German-speaking lands during the 16th century and nomadized there until the 19th century when some families moved into other countries. The dialect contains a large number of loan words from German. The Sinti suffered large losses during the Nazi period. The German organization Verband der Deutschen Sinti in Heidelberg (led by **Romani Rose**) is their main civil rights organization. Sinti organizations also operate in Holland.

The term *Sinti* is also used by the Sinti for some Gypsy clans who are not linguistically Sinti, e.g., the Istriani Sinti from the Trieste region and the **Lalore Sinti.**

SKOPJE. The capital of the Macedonian Republic with a large Gypsy population. The Folklore Institute in Skopje has set up a Romany section under the direction of Trajko Petrovski. Radio and TV broadcasts are aired in Romani. See also SHUTO (ŠUTO) ORIZARI.

SKOU, MATHIASSEN. Mathiassen was of mixed Norwegian and **Traveller** descent. He wrote a book about the traveling life, *Paa Fantestien* (*On the Gypsy Trail*), published in 1893. He then married a **Norwegian Traveller** and returned with her to become a nomad himself.

SLOVAKIA. Estimated Gypsy population: 500,000. Apart from a group passing through Spiš in 1423, the earliest record of Gypsies on the territory of present-day Slovakia is of an execution in Levoca in 1534. They were accused of starting fires in Levoca and other towns. Slovakia was part of the Austro-Hungarian Empire until 1918. **Maria Theresa** tried her assimilationist policy of settling the Gypsies, with some success. By the end of the 19th century it was estimated that around 90 percent of Slovak Romanies were settled. There were also several thousand nomadic **Vlah** Gypsies who had immigrated from Romania. The settled Gypsies in general lived in isolated settlements and pursued a range of trades, from blacksmiths and bricklayers to musicians.

In 1918 Slovakia became part of an independent Czechoslovakia. From the 1920s a strong nationalistic movement arose in Slovakia, and there was a pogrom in Pobedim in which six Gypsies were killed in 1928. The anti-Semitic Slovenska Narodná Strana (Slovak People's Party) saw Gypsies as "an ulcer which must be cured in a radical way." This party gained between 25 and 40 percent of the votes in elections in the years between the two wars and paved the way for the establishment of a puppet Slovak state after the German invasion of Czechoslovakia in 1938.

In 1940 the fascist government imposed compulsory labor on Gypsies and they were forbidden to enter parks, cafés or use public transport. The following year all Gypsies living among Slovaks were ordered to move and build themselves new isolated settlements. From many areas male adults were sent to labor camps. In 1944, after the failure of a popular uprising against the fascist regime, Gypsies were accused—in some cases, unjustly—of helping the resistance movement. Massacres of men, women and children took place in Čierny Balog, Ilija, Kriz nad Hronom, Slatina, Tisovec and elsewhere. Tomas Farkas and Anton Facuna had been active in the partisan movement and were decorated after the war.

In Slovakia more Gypsies survived the war than had in the Czech lands (Bohemia and Moravia), but discrimination continued after 1945. They are still referred to as "blacks" by the Slovaks. The Communist National Front government tried to eliminate the shanty towns (with little success) and force the Gypsies into paid employment. There was some voluntary movement in the first years of peace to the Czech lands, where they took the place of ethnic Germans who had been expelled. In 1958 the Act for the Permanent Settlement of Nomadic Persons prohibited nomadism and ordered local councils to help the integration of the ex-nomads. The Czechoslovak government tried to introduce compulsory resettlement of Gypsies from Slovakia to the Czech lands to eliminate the high concentrations of Romanies in some areas. Sterilization was also introduced as a means of controlling the Gypsies' population growth.

Slovakia became an independent state in 1993. Romanies in Slovakia are classed as a national minority. As well as their own cultural organizations, there are consultative bodies such as the Council for the Affairs of Minorities and specialized advisory bodies concerned with education and other fields. The central control of solutions to "Romany problems" was abolished by the new state and the responsibility given to local councils. Nevertheless, the national Ministry of Labor, Social Affairs and the Family issued a resolution in April 1996 on "Citizens in Need of Special Care." This saw Romanies as a problem and a burden to the state. The major Romany associations that exist have received grants since 1992. They include the Cultural Society of Citizens of Romany Origin, Romani Culture, the Association of Romany Intelligentsia and the Cultural Union of the Romany Community. Seventeen Romany associations met in 1993 and formed the Council of Romanies in Slovakia (ARSS). After an initial impetus, the council has not been very active. In 1995, therefore, six Romany parties formed a new umbrella organization, the Union of Roma Political Parties in the Slovak Republic (URPSDR). The Roma Civic Initiative (ROI) had had one seat in the regional Slovak Parliament from 1990, but it was unsuccessful in the elections of 1992 and 1995 that followed independence.

According to the 1991 census figures for Slovakia, the official population of Gypsies is only 80,627 (1.5 percent of the population of the country) but as many as four out of five have registered themselves as Hungarian or Slovak.

In 1991, a Department of Romany Culture had been established at the Pedagogical Faculty in Nitra. A Romany professional theater, **Romathan**, exists since 1992 at **Košice** and a specialist music school exists in the town. There is some broadcasting in Romani—within the Hungarian service—and six bilingual publications. Many Romany children are placed in special schools or in schools and classes where the majority of the pupils are Romany. Some efforts have been made to establish a preschool year where the Romany children can improve their knowledge of Slovak or Hungarian. In 1992–1993, some primary schools in Kosice opened bilingual classes in Slovak and Romani. On the whole, however, little attention is paid to the fact that the Romany children come to school not knowing the language of instruction.

Discrimination and prejudice continue. Slogans can be seen on the walls proclaiming "White Slovakia" or "Gypsies to the gas chambers." The Slovak National Party is openly anti-Gypsy. Prime Minister Vladimir Meciar has said that social welfare payments should be cut to stop the Gypsies having so many children, and the minister of labor accused them of not wanting to work. In this atmosphere it is not surprising that racist attacks, mainly but not always by skinheads, have been reported regularly. In July 1995 Mario Goral was killed by skinheads in Žiar nad Hronom. In the same month masked policemen beat up Gypsies in Jarovnice. In 1996 a group of skinheads armed with chains attacked Romany children from a special school after the children had attended a hockey match. In the same year Jozef Miklos died when villagers burned down his house in Hontianske Nemce. In December 1996 a skinhead murdered Gustav Balaz and wounded his son at Handlova. Twenty skinheads attacked and killed a Romany in Prievidza in 1997. The Slovak government has been accused of indifference to these attacks. See also CZECHOSLOVAKIA.

SLOVENIA. Estimated Gypsy population: 9,000. The country has been independent since 1991. The first report of Gypsies on the territory of present-day Slovenia dates from 1453 and refers to a smith. During World War II part of Slovenia was annexed to Germany and the Gypsies living there were taken to concentration camps.the 1971 Yugoslav census recorded 977 Romanies. A recent report from the Institute for Nationality Questions in Ljubljana gave the figure of 5,300 for the Gypsy population. They were living in three regions: Prekmurje and the borders of Austria and Hungary, Dolnesjska (southeast of Lubljana) and Gorenjska-Alta Carniola near Bled. Only 509 were registered as having work, and only 25 percent of the children were at school. The rate of mortality was higher than for the Slovenian population. For the periods 1918–1941 and 1945–91, see YUGOSLAVIA.

SMITH, CHARLES. A contemporary poet (in English and Romani English) and civil rights worker. He is currently chairman of the **Gypsy Council for Education, Culture, Welfare and Civil Rights**.

SMITH, CORNELIUS (1831–?). The father of **Rodney Smith and** grandfather of **Reverend George Bramwell Evens.** His parents were caners and basketmakers and were married in Cambridgeshire. He himself was a craftsman and musician who was converted to being an active Christian at a revivalist meeting in Notting Hill, London. He wrote a short autobiography, entitled *The Life Story of Cornelius Smith*, during the 1890s.

SMITH, LADY ELEANOR. A 20th-century writer in England and a champion of the Gypsy cause. Her writings include *Red Wagon*, *Tzigane, Caravan,* and her autobiography *Life's a Circus.* She supported the right of the Gypsies to come to Epsom for the **Derby** race week.

SMITH, GEORGE. A 19th-century English preacher who wanted to settle the Gypsies. He saw the Gypsy way of life as requiring reform through education and improved sanitary conditions. His books on the subject were *Gipsy Life: Being an Account of Our Gipsies and Their Children, with Suggestions for Their Improvement* (1880), and the antiromantic view of Gypsy life in *I've Been a Gipsying.* The **Moveable Dwellings Bills,** which he tried to promote in Parliament, failed to be adopted.

SMITH, PHOEBE. A contemporary folk singer from the south of England. She has a large repertoire of English folk songs and has been recorded by several collectors.

SMITH, RODNEY (1860–1947). The son of **Cornelius Smith**. Born in
East Anglia and known as Gypsy Smith, he was a Methodist preacher
who could stir a crowd of 10,000 by his speechmaking and attracted
popularity with his vocal recordings of hymns. He wrote many religious pamphlets and received the Medal of the British Empire. His
brother, Ezekiel, worked with the Railway Mission for many years
and wrote hymns, and his son, Hanley, was a Methodist minister at
Sutton Coldfield. His autobiography, written in 1902, *Gipsy Smith:
His Life & Work,* was published by the Religious Tract Society
(1902).

SMITH, "ROMANY." See REVEREND GEORGE BRAMWELL
EVENS.

SMOLEN, MIKULAS. (1941–   ). Born in **Košice**, Slovakia. After a
number of jobs, he began to work for the Federation of Czech Roma
in **Brno** in 1969. Since then he has been involved particularly with
publishing. He is the director of Rompress, which used to publish the
now defunct magazine *Amaro Lav (Our Word)* and now publishes
Romano Kurko (Romany Week).

SOFIA CONGRESS. Until recently this was thought to have been a
meeting of Muslim Gypsies in 1905 to discuss certain matters relating
to the community, such as marriages. However, a fresh look at the
documents available show that one of the aims was to win the right
to vote for the Bulgarian Parliament. This was not, however, an **international congress.**

SOLARIO, ANTONIO (1382–1455). The son of a nomadic smith. Born
in Italy, he became a painter at the court of Naples.

SOLER, ANTONIO RUIZ (Antonio El Bailarín) (1921–1996). Born
in Seville, he was known as Spain's most famous and charismatic
traditional dancer, who possessed the quality of *duende*, the spirit of
flamenco. He also included in his repertoire the stamping of feet,
known as *taconeado*. Soler showed early promise by dancing publicly
at the age of four, and by the age of six, he had joined a dancing
school. Already when eight years old he had started a partnership
with another pupil, and in 1937 they left for a tour of North and South
America, performing as "Antonio and Rosario." They performed in
movies with Rita Hayworth and Judy Garland before returning to Madrid, where Antonio made his debut in 1949. The duo danced for 22
years before splitting in 1952. Soler also performed at Pablo Picasso's
80th birthday party in 1961 when the painter joined him in a rumba.

He was director of the Spanish National Ballet from 1980 to 1983 and again for a short period in 1989.

SOROS FOUNDATION (ROMA SOROS FOUNDATION). A foundation established by **George Soros**. It has set up a number of cultural programs in Eastern Europe in particular.

SOROS, GEORGE. A contemporary financier and philanthropist of Jewish-Hungarian origin who has donated money to many Romany causes.

SOVIET UNION. See UNION OF SOVIET SOCIALIST REPUBLICS.

SPAIN. Estimated Gypsy population: 700,000. The first records of Gypsies in Spain date from the 15th century and refer to companies who crossed the border from France. However, some scholars think that Gypsies had entered Spain much earlier, accompanying the Arabs when they invaded from the south. The Egyptian writer Abd-ul-Mulk, writing around 1200, advised Arabic poets in Spain (then under Arab rule) not to be "garrulous in the manner of the Zott" (the Arab term for Gypsies). Firmer evidence of their presence comes in 1425 when Don Johan of Little Egypt and Duke Thomas obtained letters of protection from King Alfonso V of Aragon. These leaders had certainly come via France.

From 1492 Spain had one government, and legislation (the *Pragmatica*) in 1499 ordered Gypsies to cease nomadizing, settle down and find a trade within 60 days and to cease traveling. If they continued to nomadize, they would be whipped, have a cut made in their ears (as an identification mark) and be forcibly bound to a master. Many did take up trades, replacing the expelled Moors as masons and bakers, for example. From 1539 Gypsies who continued to nomadize in groups were arrested, and males were used as galley slaves.

In 1633 Philip IV's government decreed that the Gypsies did not exist. They were not an ethnic group, he said, but Spanish people who had disguised themselves and made up a language. They were forbidden to speak any language other than Spanish or wear distinctive clothes. In 1695 they were, ineffectively, forbidden to have any employment other than farming. By 1746 a list of 75 towns had been drawn up, and Gypsies were—in theory—only allowed to live in the named towns.

Persecution continued. A roundup of all Gypsies was ordered in 1749. The aim was to eliminate the population completely by locking up the men and women separately and setting them to forced labor. Several hundred Gypsies were arrested and imprisoned in this campaign. Most of them were gradually released and allowed to return to their previous homes as it was realized that they performed useful services in the villages, which found themselves suddenly without a blacksmith or a baker. The last of the arrested Gypsies were finally released in 1765, after 16 years of confinement. Repression finally ceased and was replaced by a firmer policy of assimilation with the enactment of the decree of Charles III in 1783, under which the Gypsies were granted equal citizenship. The use of the word **Gitano** (Gypsy) was to be banned. The Gypsies were again forbidden to speak Romani or wear distinctive dress. Many took the opportunity of free movement to migrate to the south of France. Largely, as a result of the past penalties for speaking Romani in public, the language has died out, and Spanish Gypsies now speak a variety of Spanish with a few Romani words, known as **Caló**.

The Gypsies have continued to live in Spain on the edge of society, looked down upon by the majority population unless they are musicians or bullfighters. The Catholic Church has taken an interest in the Gypsies this century with local missions and organizing pilgrimages. Many Spanish Gypsies are, however, now turning to **Pentecostalism**.

With the fall of the Franco dictatorship in 1975, the Gypsies have been free to organize and publish magazines. However, latent anti-Gypsy racism has surfaced on many occasions. In one incident in 1984, a crowd of several hundred in Zaragoza demonstrated against the occupation of 36 prefabricated houses built for Gypsies in the Actur district. Slogans included "Fight for your rights against Gypsies." In 1986 there were attacks on the Gypsy quarter of Martos; 30 houses were set on fire and the inhabitants fled to the nearby village of Torredonjimeno. The villagers there did not allow them to stop and drove them out. The local authorities then tried to settle the evacuees in a third place, Monte Lope Alvarez, but the local population protested, and the Gypsies had to sleep in tents provided by the Red Cross, protected by the police, until alternative accommodation was found. In the district of Otxarkoaga in Bilbao in 1996, Gypsy children were denied entry to the local school, and a special school was set up for them in a disused secondary school building. Some of the Gypsy parents then boycotted the new school, in a protest against segregation.

Gypsies are among the best musicians and singers in Spain, and several of them have individual entries in this handbook, such as **Joaquín Cortes**. The economic situation has led to some young unemployed Gypsies trafficking in drugs and even beginning to experiment with the wares they sell. It is probably the only country in Europe where a serious drugs problem exists among Gypsies. On the other hand, a significant number of Romanies are going to college. **Juan**

de Dios Ramirez Heredia was a member of parliament for the Socialist Party in the Spanish and European parliaments. The Spanish royal family supported the recent **European Congress** in Seville. Other positive features are the great interest in the revival of the Romani language and links with Gypsy organizations in other countries. The Presencia Gitana association in Madrid has a wide program of educational and cultural work. Many of the local organizations are united in a network, the Union Romani, and their activities are reported in the journal *Nevipens Romani* (*Romany News*).

SPECIALIST GROUP ON ROMA/GYPSIES (MG-S-ROM). In 1995 the Committee of Ministers of the **Council of Europe** decided to set up the Specialist Group. The seven original members of the group are Outi Ojala (Finland), Carmen Santiago Reyes (Spain), Josephine Verspaget (Netherlands), Catalin Zamfir (Romania), Milcho Dimitrov (Bulgaria), Claudio Marta (Italy) and **Andrzej Mirga** (Poland). The first meeting of the group was held in Strasbourg in March 1996. The second meeting, in October 1996, considered human rights among other topics. Two members of the group took part in a fact-finding mission to Bosnia under the auspices of the Council of Europe.

SPINELLI, SANTINO. A contemporary singer and cultural worker from Abruzzia, Italy. He is editor of the journal *Them Romano* and organizer of an annual arts competition.

SPITTA, MELANIE. A **Sinti** activist who, together with Katryn Seybold, has made several documentary films about Sinti, including *Wir sind Sintikinder und keine Zigeuner* (We Are Sinti Children and Not Gypsies) and *Das falsche Wort* (The False Word). The latter deals with the question of **reparations** for Nazi crimes.

ST. GEORGE'S DAY. This day is celebrated by both Christian and Muslim Gypsies on May 5/6 according to the Orthodox calendar. Scholars have seen relics of the Indian Baisakhi (New Year's Day) rituals in the celebrations—for example, the custom in Skopje (Macedonia) of going to a river and bringing back from it bottles of water.

ST. SARAH. See SAINTES MARIES DE LA MER.

STANDING CONFERENCE FOR COOPERATION AND COORDINATION OF ROMANI ASSOCIATIONS IN EUROPE, THE. This was founded on July 30, 1994, in Strasbourg. There have been meetings at various locations, including Warsaw (January 19–20, 1996), Strasbourg (March 19–23, 1996), Brussels (July 1996) and Vienna

(November 1996). The Strasbourg meeting sent representatives to a parallel meeting of the **Specialist Group on Roma/Gypsies** of the **Council of Europe**. The November meeting took place in the **Romano Centro**, Vienna. The conference brings together some 40 Gypsy organizations.

STANDING CONFERENCE OF LOCAL AND REGIONAL AUTHORITIES. See CONGRESS OF LOCAL AND REGIONAL AUTHORITIES OF EUROPE.

STANKIEWICZ, STANISLAW. Poland. Contemporary TV producer, publisher of *Rrom p-o Drom* (*Romanies on the Road*) and a vice president (elected in 1990) of the International Romany Union.

STARKIE, WALTER. A 20th-century authority on Gypsy lore and music. He traveled widely in Europe between the two wars with his violin and has described the Gypsies he met in several books.

STENCL, A. N. A Yiddish poet based in London. In 1962 he wrote a series of sonnets dedicated to the Gypsies that he published in the magazine he edited, *Loshn un Lebn* (*Language and Life*).

STENEGRY, ARCHANGE. A musician and resistance leader during World War II. He later became the president of the Communauté Tzigane de France, which replaced the Organisation Nationale Gitane.

STEREOTYPES. We find in literature and in the popular mind many stereotypes of Gypsies. Cervantes was one of the first to introduce the theme of Gypsies stealing a child in his novel *La Gitanilla*. They teach her to dance and sing, but in her heart she remains a Spaniard. At the end of the novel she is restored to her family and married to her Spanish lover. Beautiful and handsome Gypsies appear in plays, novels and operas. We may think of Bizet's *Carmen* and D. H. Lawrence's *The Virgin and the Gypsy*.

STEWART FAMILY. Most of the musical **Scottish Travellers** named Stewart are descended from the singer Jimmy Stewart of Struan. See STEWART, BELLE; STEWART, DAVIE.

STEWART, BELLE (1906–1997). **Scottish Traveller** singer. Her husband Alex (singer and piper) and her daughters Sheila MacGregor and Cathie Higgins have become famous in folk clubs and concert halls throughout Scotland and England. Their many records include *The Travelling Stewarts* and *Festival at Blairgowrie*.

STEWART, DAVIE (ca.1901–1972). A **Scottish Traveller**, singer and musician. Davie served as an underage soldier in World War I and became a piper with the Gordon Highlanders. He earned his living as a street busker in Scotland and Ireland, playing the accordion and the pipes. After his return to Scotland, he was a well-known figure in folk clubs and made several recordings.

STOJKA, CEIJA. A **Lovari** writer and singer, living in Austria. Recently she has followed in her brother **Karl Stojka's** footsteps and taken up painting.

STOJKA, HARRI. Austria. The son of **Mongo Stojka** and nephew of **Ceija** and **Karl Stojka.** Harri is a guitarist in the rock, reggae and heavy-metal styles. His first LP record was *Off the Bone,* and he has made about a dozen records since then. He has played in various rock bands such as Gipsy Love and Harri-Stojka Express. His song "I Am So in Love with You" made the Austrian Hit Parade. Together with his father he made one CD, *Amari luma* (*Our World*) (1994), which is in quite a different style from his other recordings.

STOJKA, HOJDA. See AMENZA KETANE.

STOJKA, KARL (1931–   ). Artist and writer. A brother of **Ceija Stojka,** Stojka has had paintings exhibited in the United States and Europe.

STOJKA, MONGO. Musician in Vienna. He has recently produced the CD *Amari Luma* (*Our World*) with his son **Harri Stojka**. In 1994 this appeared as a CD with five numbers, but the second edition—in 1996—contained 10 songs. The music is modern, but the lyrics are all in Romani.

STOW-ON-THE-WOLD FAIR. A popular gathering for Gypsies in England. In 1476 a royal charter was granted for the fair. Gypsies have been attending it since about 1890. The fair takes place in May and October, and trading is on a Thursday. The Gypsies arrive in **caravans** on the preceding Sunday or Monday and leave on the Friday. In May there are some 400 caravans; in October, about 100. From 1990 the local authorities have been trying to stop Gypsies attending the fair in their caravans.

SUCURI, LJATIF (ca.1915–1945). Ljatif was a prominent Gypsy in Kosovska-Mitrovica in Kosovo, Yugoslavia, at the time of the occupation of the country by Albanian fascist forces. On several occasions

Sucuri intervened with the Albanian police chief to stop Gypsies from being killed. The police chief was to tell the German authorities in Yugoslavia that there were no Gypsies in the town, only Muslims. At the end of the war, collaborators, trying to cover up their own activities, denounced Sucuri to the partisans who took him away, without checking the allegations, and shot him.

SUMMER SCHOOLS. (i) The Romani language summer schools) (Nilajesqi Skola) organized by **Marcel Cortiade** and **Rromani Baxt**. The first was held in Belgrade in 1989 and the eighth in 1996 in St. Andriu de Sangonis, France. They bring together young and not-so-young Romanies from different countries who wish to advance their knowledge of the language and dialects. (ii) Other language summer schools have been held in Scandinavia and the Balkans, principally for younger Romanies.

SUNDT, EILERT. A Norwegian pastor who in 1848 obtained a government grant to study the problem of **Travellers**. His religious beliefs led him to believe that they would be better off in work-houses than travelling the roads. In 1863 Sundt reported that out of 425 Travellers who had been "reformed" (i.e., settled), approximately 100 had gone back to nomadism. In 1869 the work was taken from Sundt and given to a department of the church. See also NORWAY.

SVARTA PÄRLOR (Black Pearls). A musical group formed by members of the **Roma Ensemble** of Poland, which emigrated to Sweden around the 1970s.

SVETSKY. In spite of occasional references found in books on Gypsies, these are circus families, not Gypsies or **Travellers**, in the Czech and Slovak Republics.

SWANN REPORT. The 1985 report of a British committee investigating education chaired by M. Swann. It found that, although more Gypsy children were attending school, they were suffering discrimination and bullying from other pupils.

SWEDEN. Estimated Gypsy population: 16,500 (not including non-Romany **Travellers**). In 1512 Gypsies crossed from Denmark to Sweden, even though at the time Swedish nationalists were fighting to free the country from Denmark. In 1515 there were more immigrants, this time from Estonia. In 1523 Gustav Vasa became king of an independent Sweden, and two years later he wrote to the Gypsies, telling them to leave the country. During the second half of the 16th century, a number of Gypsies did leave and migrated to Finland. In 1560, the Lutheran Archbishop Petri told the priests not to baptize or bury Gypsies. This was changed in 1586 when priests were told they should baptize children, teach parents the Christian faith and encourage them to settle down. However, in 1594 the Synod of Linköping reversed this, and the previous policy was readopted.

In 1637 a new law was passed saying all Gypsies must leave the country, otherwise the men would be executed and the women expelled by force. In this law the word *Zigenare* was used for the first time for Gypsies. Previously they had been called **Tattare** (in various spellings). In 1642 and 1662 the law was strengthened. However, no cases are known of Gypsies being executed in Sweden under these laws. Finally, in 1748 a new decree was published banishing Gypsies who had not been born in Sweden. It is thought that a substantial number of Romanies stayed in Sweden and merged with the local nomadic population, forming the group now called *Tattare* or *Resande* (Travellers).

In 1860 entry restrictions in Sweden were lifted resulting in a new immigration, principally of **Vlah** Gypsies. Under the 1914 Deportation Act, Gypsies could be deported or refused entry. In fact, those already there were allowed to stay. The 1922 census in Sweden recorded 250 Gypsies and 1,500 Tattare. The wartime 1943 census listed 453 Gypsies. The government repealed the 1914 Deportation Act in 1954, and limited immigration began. In 1960 the state took responsibility for housing Gypsies, and nomadism for practical purposes ended. At the time there were about 100 sedentary and 125 nomadic families. By 1965 only 4 percent of the Gypsies remained in **caravans**.

In 1963 **Katerina Taikon** published her first book, *Zigenarska,* the story of her childhood. She later took up the campaign for the admission of **Kalderash** Gypsies from France and Spain. The government decided to set up a policy of "organized importation" of Gypsies—a form of quota. In recent years considerable numbers of Gypsies have arrived from Eastern Europe and Yugoslavia, outnumbering the descendants of those Vlah Romanies who arrived at the end of the 19th century. Many hundreds of Finnish Gypsies have also immigrated to Sweden. The education authorities have introduced mother-tongue teaching in Romani and special classes for adults to improve their education. A number of Gypsies take part in these programs as teachers or assistants. Both the Gypsies and the Tattare have set up self-help organizations. Finnish Gypsies in Sweden are represented by the Finska Zigenarrådet, the oldest body, founded (as Stockholms Finska Zigenarförening) in 1972, and the Gypsy Pentecostal church is also active.

SWEDISH TRAVELLERS. It is thought by some experts that a substantial number of Romanies stayed in Sweden after the expulsion order of 1748 and merged with the local nomadic population, forming the group now called **Tattare** or *Resande (***Travellers***)*. The Swedish Travellers today speak a language with Swedish grammar, and many words borrowed from Romani. They call this language *rommani*. The 1922 census in Sweden recorded 1,500 Tattare. In recent years the Tattare have set up a self-help organization.

SWITZERLAND. Estimated Gypsy population (including **Jenisch**): 32,500. Between 1418 and 1422, Gypsies came to Basle, Bern and Zurich as pilgrims with letters of recommendation. They were given food and wine and then escorted out of the towns. In 1471, however, the parliament of the Swiss Confederation, meeting in Lucerne, expelled Gypsies from the land. In 1510 the penalty of hanging was introduced for any Gypsies found in Switzerland. This edict was repeated six times in the years up to 1530. In 1532, however, a company of 300 Gypsies appeared on the outskirts of Geneva. It evidently took some years before all the Gypsies were finally expelled, as is indicated by a decree in Graubünden in 1571 ordering any Gypsies who were captured to be sent to be galley slaves. One wonders whose galleys these would be. During the following centuries, very few Romanies came to Switzerland, and as late as the middle of the 20th century they were still being turned back at the borders—even Romanies in cars intending to pass through the country in transit. The second **World Romany Congress** was, nonetheless, held in Geneva.

For many years no Romanies lived in Switzerland, and there are very few even today. However Switzerland has a large population of indigenous Jenisch nomads and seminomads. Early this century the authorities began to take away the children of Jenisch families and bring them up in orphanages or give them to Swiss foster parents. Often the children were told their parents were dead and vice versa. When news of this program became public, there was great indignation. Many of the children who were taken away—now grown up—have refound their Jenisch identity. An organization known as Scharotl (Caravan) publishes a magazine of the same name.

SZASZCZAVAS BAND. A Gypsy band from Transylvania. They have made several recordings.

SZEGÖ, LÁSZLÓ. A contemporary translator, teacher and poet in Hungary.

SZTOJKA, FERENCZ. In Hungary, he was one of the first Gypsies to write literature in Romani, toward the end of the 19th century.

T

TABOR. Romany word for "clan" or "camp." It is of Slav origin.

TAIKON, JOHAN DIMITR (1879–?). Coppersmith and storyteller. Born in Bullnäs, Sweden, he traveled in Russia and Scandinavia. Taikon's stories were recorded by the Gypsiologist Carl Herman Tillhagen and published as *Taikon berättar*. These and other material he produced were the basis for the study of the Coppersmith (**Kalderash**) dialect of Romani by Olof Gjerdman and Erik Ljungberg.

TAIKON, KATERINA (1932–1995). A writer and civil rights activist in Sweden. She became well known as a children's writer with her semi-autobiographical books about a Gypsy girl, Katitzi. Taikon's involvement in politics began when a group of Gypsies coming from France were interned at the border and refused entry to Sweden. After pressure, they were let in, and the Swedish government agreed to a program of organized immigration. Taikon edited the magazine *Zigenaren*.

TAIKON, ROSA. The sister of **Katerina Taikon** and a contemporary artist, metalworker and jeweler. Both she and her sister have written poetry.

TARAF. The name given to village bands in Romania. The word is of Arabic origin. Many of the tarafs are Gypsies, such as Taraful Soporu de Cimple, Taraf de Carancebes (from Banat) and **Taraf de Haidouks.**

TARAF DE HAIDOUKS. A Gypsy band from the village of Clejani in Romania. They have made successful tours to Western Europe, including a performance at the Womad Festival in England in 1991 and Routes de Tsiganes in Paris. They have made several recordings.

TARNÓW. A town in Poland where the **museum** has a strong Gypsy section, originating in an exhibition of 1979. It has been built up by the curator **Adam Bartosz**.

TAROT CARDS. The tarot cards were invented in Italy in the 15th century and used as a game. In the 18th century they became popular for fortune-telling and have been adopted by some Gypsy fortune-tellers.

TARTARS/TATARS. A Turkic people. Until the 16th century a large independent Tartar state existed in west Asia that at one time reached into Europe as far as Romania. Some historians think that the Tartars had Gypsy slaves and brought them to Romania around the 13th century, where both they and some of the captors themselves—after the defeat of the Tartars—became slaves of the Romanians.

TATERE. A pejorative term used for **Norwegian Travellers** who prefer to be called *Reisende* (**Travellers**). The name Tatere was first used for both indigenous Travellers and Romanies in Norway and Denmark because of confusion with the **Tartars,** who made incursions into Europe in the Middle Ages. See NORWAY.

TATTARE. A pejorative term used for **Swedish Travellers**, who prefer to be called *Resande* (**Travellers**). The name was first used for indigenous Travellers and Romanies because of confusion with the **Tartars,** who made incursions into Europe in the Middle Ages. See NORWAY.

TCHATCHIPEN (Truth). An organization based in Toulon, working for the promotion of Romany culture. The president is Michel Zanko and the secretary, Bernadette Pennes.

TEATR ROMA. A theater in Sofia from 1947 to 1951 when it was closed by the government. The director was **Manush Romanov.**

TEATR ROMEN. The theater was founded in Moscow during the encouragement of Romany culture by Joseph Stalin. Its aim was to replace the stereotypical romantic Gypsy figure by a new image of Gypsies taking part in the building of socialism. The theater was meant to help the "assimilation, sedentarization and education of nomadic peoples." It officially opened in April 1931 and was assisted by the Moscow Jewish Theatre and the actor Moshe I. Goldblatt, who became its director. Popular songs and sketches were presented for censorship to the commissariat of enlightenment (ministry of culture), to convince them that Gypsies were conducting an appropriate course of action. The theater was also to fight the popular stereotype of Gypsies. Three Gypsy writers worked with the company, Bezliudsky, **Aleksandr German** and **I. Rom-Lebedev**. German's *Life on Wheels* was one of the first plays to be performed at the theater. In 1933 a performance of *Carmen* was in the repertoire.

The Teatr Romen toured Siberia and the Soviet Far East after much of the western USSR was taken over by the Germans early in World War II. It returned later with the advancing Soviet army across the

Caspian Sea and, with the Luftwaffe above, performed to soldiers at Rostov, showing its commitment to the combat. Two actors joined the war effort and were decorated for bravery. This theater encountered accusations of "nationalistic deviation" but survived the later suppression of Gypsy culture.

The repertoire of the theater varies from political plays encouraging Gypsies to give up the nomadic life and settle on collective farms to world classics. Plays with songs and dance have always been a feature of the repertoire, and the artists have included many popular singers.

TELEPHONE LEGAL ADVICE SERVICE FOR TRAVELLERS (T-LAST). Founded in Wales in 1995 by the Cardiff Law School as a three-year project. It aims to provide not only a telephone legal advice service for Britain, as the name suggests, but also to develop a network of legal practitioners and to publish research about the needs of **Travellers** and Gypsies. Its first conference took place in March 1997. It has begun to publish a newsletter called *Travellers' Times*.

TELEVISION. The first regular TV broadcasts in Romani were from Pristina (in Kosovo) from around 1985, and other Yugoslav stations (Novi Sad and Prizren) followed later. In recent years a number of TV stations have broadcast regularly in Romani or in the national language but for Gypsy viewers. They include Bratislava, Bucharest, Budapest and **Skopje**.

THEATER. Apart from the long-established **Teatr Romen** in Moscow, Romany drama companies are a phenomenon of the post-1945 years. Three major professional theater groups are now playing in or largely in the Romani language: **Pralipe, Romathan** and Teatr Romen. For original plays in Romani, see DRAMA.

THEATER ROMANCE. Based in Kiev, it performs in Russian and Romani. In November 1996 it made a guest visit to Vienna.

THESLEFF, ARTHUR. A Finnish diplomat who wrote a comprehensive survey of the situation of the Gypsies in Europe at the end of the 19th century. It was printed in 1901, and much of it was later reproduced in the journal of the **Gypsy Lore Society.** Thesleff also compiled a Romani dictionary based on an earlier word-list.

TIEFLAND. Leni Riefenstahl, a filmmaker in Nazi Germany, took 68 Gypsies from Marzahn internment camp and 50 from the Salzburg camp to use as extras in the film *Tiefland* in April 1942.

TINKER. (i) A worker with tin, often nomadic. The profession goes back many centuries in Europe. There are references to persons with the surname or trade of tinker in England from around 1175. In 1551–1552 the Act for Tinkers and Peddlers was passed in England. It is likely that the traveling tinkers in England were absorbed by the Romanies when they arrived in the country. Shakespeare refers to Henry V being able to speak with every tinker in his tongue; some have seen this as a reference to the **cant** of **Irish Travellers**. (ii) A pejorative name for **Travellers** in Ireland and Scotland.

TIPLER, DEREK (ca.1940–1990). A radio and TV journalist in England. Later, while working for Radio Vatican, he decided that his mission was to translate the Bible for his own people. He then traveled with Italian Gypsies and set to work on the translation, earning money by playing in restaurants. He died of a heart attack after completing only one gospel (Mark), which has been published. He was an occasional contributor to the journal of the **Gypsy Lore Society.**

TRANSDNIESTRIA. During World War II, the German and Romanian armies conquered the Ukraine as far as the River Bug. Romanian troops were responsible for security up to the River Dnieper, and a new name was invented for the territory between the Dniester and Dnieper, Transdniestria.

Some of this newly occupied area in the East was used by the Romanians as a dumping ground for Gypsies as the Germans had used Poland. In the years 1941–1942 some 25,000 Gypsies were to be transported across to the other side of the Dniester. The government plan was to start by expelling the nomadic Gypsies from the Romanian homeland. To those to whom the policy was applied, it brought disruption of family life, suffering, hardship, hunger and death.

Between June and August 1942, over 11,000 nomads were evacuated to the East. Although no danger to Romanian blood—since they lived isolated socially from majority society—they had their own horses and wagons and just needed guards to accompany them on the journey east, so the movement could be carried out with little effort. In a few towns in Transylvania, the German-speaking villagers resisted attempts to deport "their" Gypsies. Clinic (Kelling) and Ungurei (Gergeschdorf) were amongst the villages where the Romanies remained unharmed. Policemen on horseback forced the Gypsy chiefs from Profa, Tirgu Jiu and elsewhere to set off with their extended families eastward. Mihai Tonu and Stanescu Zdrelea each led 40 families. A few leaders set off willingly, not knowing what awaited them. On arrival they had to build huts for themselves. Some dug holes to sleep in and broke up the wagons to use as a roof and protection against the weather. The rest of the wagon was gradually burned as fuel to keep warm. The horses were eaten. Conditions were hard that first winter. At night the temperature dropped and every morning frozen bodies were to be found. It is said that 1,500 died after one freezing night. The nomads had been able to take their gold with them. At night they would creep out of the camp at night to exchange gold for food in the neighboring villages. Those who had no gold had to beg. Although some were surrounded with barbed wire, the camps were guarded ghettos rather than labor camps, and for much of the time the inmates could leave not only to shop but also to celebrate weddings and baptisms in Russian Orthodox churches nearby.

The deportation of settled Gypsies followed. In May 1942 the Ministry of Internal Affairs ordered that 12,500 settled Gypsies "dangerous to public order" should be deported across the Dniestr and this measure was carried out in September of that year. General Constantin Vasiliu was in charge of the operation, with nine trains at his disposal. Dispatched from Bucharest in cattle trucks with only the possessions they could hold, the journey took some weeks with stops and starts, and because of the cold nights, lack of blankets and inadequate food supply, many died of hunger and exposure before arriving at the River Bug in the Ukraine. Those who had survived were lodged in huts and (later) made to work digging trenches. Those found with gold teeth had them pulled out. Anyone caught returning from Transdniestria to Romania was sent back and interned at Tiraspol.

The policy of transporting the Gypsies into the Ukraine aroused opposition among the local German officials. The Nazi governor of the Ukraine wrote on the subject to the Minister for Occupied Eastern Territories in Berlin in August 1942. After this a letter was sent from the minister to the Foreign Office in Berlin, dated September 11, 1942, pointing out the danger that these Gypsies would try to settle on the east bank of the Bug and would then be a bad influence on the Ukrainian population. The minister said the area set aside for Gypsies was in fact populated by ethnic Germans and asked the Foreign Office to persuade Romania to change its policy. During 1943, the deportations decreased in number. After this, the Gypsies in Romania remained comparatively free. As far as we know, no further large-scale activity against them took place, and many served in the army.

Toward the end of 1943, after the Germans had been driven back over the Bug with their Romanian allies, the guards fled, and Gypsies took the opportunity to try to return to Romania. Weakened by months of hunger and cold, many children and old people did not survive this return journey. The survivors eventually reached Dabuleni, Profa, Tirgu Jiu and the other towns from which they had been driven.

After the war when the Romanian People's Court appointed an investigation committee to look into war crimes, it took a very unfavorable view of the treatment of the deportees. Ion Antonescu, the fascist dictator, said at his trial that the Gypsies had been deported because they had robbed people during the curfew and because the Governor of Transdniestria needed workers. He was executed for war crimes. It is now thought that 19,000 Gypsies had perished in the East.

TRANSPORTATION. Many European countries transported Gypsies to their colonies as one way of removing them from their territory. In 1648 Sweden proposed to deport the Gypsies to its colony in America—Delaware. This plan was not carried out. Gypsies were, however, transported from England and Scotland to North America and Australia, and from Portugal to Africa and South America.

TRAVELLERS. A term used in this dictionary and elsewhere for industrial nomadic groups who are not of Indian origin. In many countries in Europe, there are indigenous nomadic or seminomadic groups. They include the **Camminanti** of Sicily, the Karrner of Austria, the **Jenisch** of Germany and Western Europe, the Resande (or Reisende) of Sweden and Norway, the **Quincalleros** (or *Mercheros)* of Spain and the **Woonwagenbewoners** of the Netherlands. They live very similar lives to the nomadic Romany Gypsies, and some intermarriage has occurred over the years. Details of each group will be found under entries for the country concerned.

In Ireland and Scotland they have been called Tinkers, but they themselves prefer the name Travellers. The term *quinquis* or *quinquilleros* of Spain is the equivalent of "Tinkers" and there they prefer the name **Mercheros. Swedish Travellers** became known as *Tattare* or *Zigenare* (Gypsies) and now prefer the term *resande*. See also IRISH TRAVELLERS; NORWEGIAN TRAVELLERS; SCOTTISH TRAVELLERS.

TRAVELLERS' SCHOOL CHARITY. This United Kingdom charity supports education on site for **New Travellers'** children.

TRENT, COUNCIL OF. This conference of the Catholic Church, which ended in 1563, decreed that Gypsies could not become Catholic priests.

TROLLMANN, JOHANN "RUCKELLE" (?–1943). Light-heavyweight boxing champion of Germany. In March 1933 the reigning champion Erich Seeling was deprived of his title because he was Jewish. On June 9 the same year Trollmann fought Adolf Wilt for the title and won on points. On June 17 he, in turn, was deprived of his title for racial reasons. In 1942 he was arrested and sent to Neuengamme concentration camp, where he was shot in February 1943.

TROSTANIETS. A concentration camp in the occupied Soviet Union during World War II, in which many Gypsies died.

TSIGAN, TSIGANE, TZIGANE. The Slav and French terms for Gypsy, derived (like the German *Zigeuner*) from the Greek ***athingani*** (heretics).

TURKEY. Estimated Gypsy population: 350,000. When the Turks captured the land that forms present-day Turkey from the Byzantine Greeks, they found a substantial Gypsy population already there. Sultan Bayezid drove Romanies out of the parts of Anatolia under his control, and they came into Thracia and Serbia. Only those who were or became Muslim were allowed to stay in Turkey. Later records show the Gypsies to have an important role in the Turkish state as musicians, smiths and entertainers. The report of a celebration organized by Sultan Murad III in Istanbul in honor of his newborn son talks of a procession including 60 Gypsy smiths, pulling a cart in which three smiths were working. In a second procession in the following month, 400 Romany smiths took part, as well as broommakers, bear trainers, chimney sweeps, musicians, acrobats and dancers. In the Turkish **Ottoman Empire,** the Gypsies were generally treated as a slightly lower rank of Muslims. They paid higher taxes and were exempt from military service. In 1874 Muslim Gypsies gained equality with other Muslims in the Ottoman Empire. They were called up for military service and ceased paying special tax.

After World War II, many Muslim Gypsies moved from Greece to Turkey.

Gypsies are referred to in Turkish by the pejorative term *Çingene* and also *Kipti*. Apart from the Romanies, there are also **Lom (Posha)** and **Dom** groups—in particular in the eastern regions. An estimate for the years 1960–1970 gave a figure of 10,633 nomads. The nomads are fortune-tellers, sell crafts or work with metals. The trades of the settled Gypsies include musicians, flowersellers or porters. Kibariye is a well-known singer of popular melodies.

TZIGANE. A composition for piano and violin by the 20th-century French composer Ravel.

U

UHLIK, RADE. A 20th-century Yugoslav scholar of the Romani language. He published a number of articles on Romani and compiled a dictionary. Many of the folktales he collected are printed in the journal of the **Gypsy Lore Society.**

UKRAINE. Estimated Gypsy population: 50,000. Since 1991 the Ukraine has been an independent state. The first Gypsies arrived in what is now the territory of Ukraine in the 16th century, and a substantial Gypsy population has lived there ever since.

During World War II, the Ukraine was conquered by the Germans and many Gypsies, were killed by Task Force (***Einsatzgruppe***) D in Duma-Eli, Krasnye Yerchi, Staryi Krum, Ungut and elsewhere. A delegation of three older Crimean Tatars in the village of Asan-Bey asked the German commander to spare the Gypsies there, but the officer said he would only free them if the **Tatars** were willing to die in their place. The Gypsies were locked in a storehouse and shot.

Some anti-Gypsy pogroms since the political changes in 1991. In March 1996 a Gypsy woman was raped in Mukacevo during a police raid.

In the Ukraine three dialects of Romani are spoken: Carpathian, Ukrainian (or Servi) and **haladitko.** The poet Kazimierenka writes in the haladitko dialect. In addition, the Crimean Gypsies speak their own (Krimitka) dialect, which is close to Balkan Romani, or a dialect known as **Ursari** (which is not the same as the Ursari of Romania). The newly formed Ukrainian Association of Roma is based in Kiev.

For legislation in the period before 1991, see RUSSIA and UNION OF SOCIALIST SOCIALIST REPUBLICS.

UNION OF ROMANY WRITERS. Founded in 1991 in the Czech Reoublic under the leadership of **Margita Reiznerová**. It has about 40 members, including three from Slovakia.

UNION OF SOVIET SOCIALIST REPUBLICS (USSR) (1919–1991). Estimated Gypsy population in 1991: over 500,000. For a short time after the success of the Revolution, the Gypsies in the newly formed Soviet Union were given rights as an ethnic group in exchange for supporting communism. Nomadism was discouraged. In 1926, the Soviet Communist party's Central Executive Committee issued a decree "On Measures for Aiding the Transition of Nomadic Gypsies to a Working and Settled Way of Life." This encouraged Gypsies to adopt a settled life and accept land in each Union Republic. Gypsies who had supplied the Red Army with horses during the Revolution farmed 4,700 acres at a collective farm called Khutor Krikunovo, near Rostov. There were 51 Romany collective farms (*kolkhozi*) where all the clerical work was done in the Romani language. However, many Gypsies resisted land settlement, initiating a further settlement decree in 1928. The main factor in the resistance was the change from the tradition of working in extended family groups and inexperience in farming. The estimate for "settlers" stood at 5,000 between 1926 and 1928 out of the official census of 61,229 Gypsies.

In 1925 the All-Russian Union of Gypsies had been formed, headed by Aleksandr Taranov from Siberia, with **I. Rom-Lebedev** as its secretary. It pressed for Gypsies to be classed as a nation and achieved this status the same year. The **haladitko** dialect of Romani was approved as a language for official use within the USSR in the following year. In 1927 the influential journal *Romani Zorya* (*Romany Dawn*) published its first number. Wall posters in Romani were seen that year, and the All-Russian Union recorded 640 members. In 1929 the second number of *Romani Zorya* was published, as was a popular library series, *Biblioteka Vaše Skoli Nabut Siklyakirde Manusěnge* (Library for Schools for People with Little Education). The series included *Nevo Džiben* (*New Life*) (ed. **Aleksandr German**) and **Nikolai Pankov**'s *Buti i džinaiben* (*Work and Knowledge*). The Romengiro Lav (Romany Word) writer's circle in Moscow had among its members I.Rom-Lebedev, the teacher Nina Dudarova, the poet N. I. Pankov and G. Lebedev. Cultural clubs were set up in Simferopol and elsewhere. A first reader for schools *Džidi Buti* (*Living Things*) by Pankov and Dudarova was published the next year, as was a story *Baxt* (*Fortune*) by Rom-Lebedev and *Nevo Gav* (*New Village*), an agricultural magazine edited by Alexandr Taranov. The first four schools were opened using the Romani language.

In 1928 the first Romany Congress for the Soviet Union took place. In 1931 the Soviet policy promoted drama in the languages of national minorities, but the theatres were not to promote separate national identity. A play specially written by W. N. Wsevolojsky, *Románo Drom* (*Romany Way*), was a success that led eventually to the creation of the Gypsy **Teatr Romen** in that year.

In the period 1928–1938 an educational program flourished and in due course 86 Gypsy schools were opened and teacher-training colleges and courses established. There were over 40 Gypsy medical students at Smolensk. Alongside these educational developments were more publications—for example, Maksim Sergievski's *Grammar of Romani*, which replaced the earlier grammar by Kerope Patkanov which had been based on the Ukrainian (**Carpathian**) dialect. Sergievski and the linguist Aleksei Barannikov later published a Romani-Russian Dictionary.

In 1931 the first issue of a second journal, *Nevo Drom* (*New Way*) appeared with a 1,000-copy run and some 28 pages in size. Twelve issues appeared in 1931. N. I. Pankov translated a treatise on agricultural problems. *Nevo Drom* continued until the issue numbered 6 in June 1932, with political, literary, children's and chess sections. In 1935 Aleksander German published a number of short stories and plays, G*anka Chyamba i vavre rosphenibena* (*Ganka Čyamba and Other Stories*). Leo Tolstoy's children's stories about animals were translated into Romani as *Rosphenibena vaš Životnonenge).*

All this cultural activity came abruptly to a halt when, in 1938, Josesph Stalin decided that the Gypsies were not a nation and ordered an end to all cultural activity in Romani. The schools were closed and a number of intellectuals, such as **Averian Voitiekhovski**, were executed. Others were sent to labor camps in Siberia. Only the Teatr Romen was to survive. World War II and the **Holocaust** followed, and not until 1970 did any further publication appear in Romani in the USSR.

Soon after the invasion of the Soviet Union in 1941 by Nazi Germany, the Task Forces (***Einsatzgruppen***) and other units set about killing Jews and Gypsies. Task Force B shot and buried alive 1,000 Gypsies at Rodnya near Smolensk, while Task Force D murdered over 800 Gypsies in Simferopol in the Crimea in December 1941. Tokhmakov, who had been in charge of the Communist party's Gypsy program and who looked after the Gypsy collective farms, was executed by the Germans. Many of the deportees starved to death. Many Gypsies served in the Soviet armed forces, such as Admiral Kotlowski, while others joined the partisans. Over 30,000 Gypsies were murdered, representing about half of the population of the occupied territories.

After 1945, Stalin's rule became even more despotic. The remaining Romany collective farms were abandoned, forcing Gypsies to move to non-Gypsy farms. A number of **Sinti** Gypsies were deported by Stalin to the east alongside the Volga Germans, who were accused of collaborating with the German invaders. After Stalin's death in 1953, Nikita Krushchev, his successor, was to adopt policies in 1956 that aimed at finally destroying the nomadic traditions of the Romanies. In 1956 nomadism was forbidden by the law "On Reconciling Wandering Gypsies to Work." Some Gypsies resisted sedentarization by traveling round farms for seasonal labor or working as herdsmen moving from pasture to pasture.

The Gypsy Writers Club was set up for writers in Russian, but writing in Romani was still discouraged. The first census after World War II registered 130,000 Gypsies in the whole of the Soviet Union (including the Asian republics), but many Gypsies put themselves down as belonging to another nationality. Under Leonid Brezhnev (from 1964), some liberalization occurred in the USSR. In 1970 the first publication in Romani since 1938 appeared when **Georgi Kantea** published in the **Moldavian SSR** a collection of poems, proverbs and tales in the **Ursari** dialect. Prominent Gypsy writers in the Russian language included Kantea himself, **Aleksandr Belugins** in Moscow and Vano Romano in the Altai region. N. Satkiewicz published some of his poetry and reopened Gypsy schools in Siberia.

Romanies began to outstrip the average of population growth in the 1980s, when the census recorded 210,000 Gypsies, with 74 percent claiming Romani as their mother tongue. With the advent in 1985 of yet a new national leader, Mikhail Gorbachev, a new freedom was in the air with *glasnost* (openness) and *perestroika* (restructuring). Gypsy culture thrived but was, until 1990, prevented from international contact. Then government officials in 1990 allowed Gypsies to attend the fourth **World Romany Congress** near Warsaw (April 8–12), which heralded a growth in Soviet Romany participation in international Gypsy affairs.

For this area in the period before 1919 and after 1991, see BELARUS; ESTONIA; LATVIA; LITHUANIA; MOLDOVA; RUSSIA; UKRAINE.

UNION ROMANI. An organization linking the majority of the associations in Spain.

UNITE (UNIFIED NOMADIC AND INDEPENDENT TRANSNATIONAL EDUCATION). The aim of the organization located in the United Kingdom is to build a center that will provide supplementary education and advice to Gypsies. A site in Essex has been found, but at the time of writing planning permission has not yet been granted. The principal officer is Barrie Taylor.

UNITED KINGDOM. See ENGLAND, NORTHERN IRELAND, SCOTLAND and WALES.

UNITED NATIONS (UN). The first time the UN paid attention to Gypsies was in 1977. Then the Subcommission on the Prevention of Discrimination and Protection of Minorities of the **Economic and Social Council**'s Commission on Human Rights adopted a resolution on the protection of the Gypsies. This asked all states to accord equal rights to Roma (Gypsies). In 1991 the same subcommission noted that there was still discrimination against Gypsies, and so in 1992 the main Commission on Human Rights passed Resolution 65 on the Protection of Roma (Gypsies). This measure "invites States to adopt all appropriate measures in order to eliminate any form of discrimination against Roma (Gypsies)." The special rapporteur of the Subcommission was asked to study the problems of the Gypsies. This resolution was adopted by 43 votes to none.

URSARI. Bear trainers. The word is derived from Romanian. It is the name of several clans of Gypsies who train bears and of at least two distinct dialects of Romani.

URSITORY. (i) In **Kalderash** tradition, women spirits who appear at the birth of a child to name the child.
(ii) A novel by **Matéo Maximoff** in which the Ursitory appear.

UŠTI INITIATIVE. A program supported by **George Soros**. *Ušti* in Romani means "arise."

V

VAIDA VOEVOD III (IONEL ROTARU). Gypsy writer and activist in the years after World War II. In 1959 he was elected to the title Vaida Voevod III by members of the Romanian **Ursari** tribe. In 1960 he founded the **Communauté Mondiale Gitane** (CMG). His aims included setting up an independent state, **Romanestan**. After the French government banned the CMG, he became less active.

VERBUNKOS. A dance used by recruiting units in Hungary in the 18th and 19th centuries. It was adopted and adapted by Gypsies and then by the composer **Franz Liszt**.

VERBAND DER DEUTSCHEN SINTI. The main organization of **Sinti** in Germany, based in Heidelberg and run by **Romani Rose**. It represents the Sinti in consultations with the German government, has a documentation center and intervenes on behalf of the rights of the Sinti.

VIG, RUDOLF (?–1983). A Hungarian musicologist who collected over 3,000 Gypsy songs. Some have been issued as recordings—for example, those from Szabolcs-Szatmar County.

VLAH (OLAH/VLACH/VLAX). The description Vlah would strictly be applied to Gypsy clans and dialects of Romani that originate from Wallachia but it is used more generally in Gypsy studies for those that come from, or are still on, Romanian-speaking territory (parts of

Banat, Transylvania, Wallachia and Moldavia). These include **Kalderash** and **Lovari**. The dialects are now divided into two groups. Those of the earliest clans to leave Romania have not palatalized the sounds *ch* and *sh*. See ROMANI.

VOITIEKHOVSKI, AVERIAN (?–1938). A teacher and headmaster of the Gypsy school in Leningrad during the period when Romani culture was encouraged by the Soviet authorities. In 1938 he was executed for "anti-government activities."

VOIVODINA. Estimated Gypsy population: 55,000. The official figure in the 1971 census was 7,760. During World War II, it was occupied by Hungary, which tried to deport many of the Gypsy population into Serbia proper. Nevertheless, Gypsies remained there. The Gypsy music of Voivodina has been collected and published by Katalin Kovalczik. The organization Drustvo Vojvodina (Voivodina Association) is working for the advancement of the Romani language. Classes are held for children, and there are magazines and a TV program.

The frontier town of Sremska Mitrovica has seen an influx of Muslim refugees from Bosnia. Up to 1992 the small population was largely settled **Kalderash** Gypsies practicing the Orthodox faith. Since then the population has grown to between 5,000 and 8,000. The refugees are poor and live from hand to mouth.

VRANCKX, AGNES (Bibi Anisha). A contemporary political activist. Born in France, she became secretary of a Gypsy organization in Belgium. She then helped to set up the Common Market Gypsy Committee of the International **Romany Union** and, later, the **West European Gypsy Council**. At the time of this writing, she is living in Rajasthan and hopes to set up a Romany-**Banjara** Cultural Center.

W

WAJS, BRONISLAWA (1910–1987). Using the Gypsy name "Papsuza," she was a Romany poet in Poland. During World War II, she survived by hiding in the forests, an experience described in her poems such as *Ratvale jasva* (*Tears of Blood*).

WALES. Estimated Gypsy population: 3,000. For legislative purposes, Wales is part of the United Kingdom. Gypsies probably arrived in Wales for the first time during the 16th century. The first use of the Welsh term *Sipsiwn* for Gypsy can be found in a poem, composed by Morris Kyffin at the end of the 16th century. The first official record of Gypsies recorded in Wales dates from 1579 and refers to the arrest of Gypsies in the then county of Radnor. In 1677 a certain Abraham Wood was born in Carmarthen but returned to England. A second Gypsy also named Abraham Wood arrived in Wales around 1730 and founded the **Wood clan**. He is said to have brought the violin to Wales, and his descendants included many well-known musicians. Other families who came to Wales and spent a long time there are the Ingrams and some of the Prices and Lees. They are classed as Welsh Gypsies.

Gypsies from Europe arrived in Wales in 1906, but they were kept under strict police supervision, before being escorted back into England and deported from Hull.

Possibly because there were two competing languages (Welsh and English) and not one (English), Romani survived longer in Wales than it did in England. The last known speaker (Manfri Wood) died around 1968. **Derek Tipler** met a group of Romani-speaking Welsh Gypsies in Caernarvonshire in 1950, but it is not known whether any of them are still alive. Many of the Welsh Gypsies have moved into houses. Others continue to travel in **caravans** and visit England and Scotland. In 1996 there were 489 caravans recorded (a fall from earlier figures), of which 36 were on unauthorized encampments (i.e., the roadside). The caravan-dwelling population of Wales today includes **Irish Travellers** and, in south Wales, descendants of marriages between English and Welsh Gypsies. For legislation, see ENGLAND.

WASO. A group based in Belgium that plays Gypsy music from many countries. **Fapy Lafertin** plays on some of their recordings.

WALLACHIA. A province of Romania. The first record of Gypsies in Wallachia dates from around 1360 when a document records the transfer of slaves. Gypsies were among those who later suffered the cruelties of Vlad IV, Prince of Wallachia (known as Dracula). It is said that he had many of them boiled alive, burned and hanged. Slavery was abolished in Wallachia in 1856. See also ROMANIA.

WEISS, HÄNSCHE. A jazz musician. Though leader of a sextet, however it was with a quintet that he recorded volumes 5 and 6 of the compilation *Musik deutscher Zigeuner* (*Music of German Gypsies*).

WEISS, KUSSI. A guitarist and nephew of **Hänsche Weiss**. He plays Gypsy style and popular jazz.

WELT-ZIGLER, STERNA. A contemporary poet in France writing in French and **Sinti** dialect.

WEST EUROPEAN GYPSY COUNCIL. A relaunch in 1981 of an earlier Common Market Gypsy Council. **Agnes Vranckx** and **Giles Eynard** were the first secretaries.

WIESENTHAL, SIMON. A Jewish "Nazi hunter" who has been active in seeing that the fate of the Gypsies during the **Holocaust** is not forgotten.

WILLIAMSON, DUNCAN (1928–). **Scottish Traveller**, storyteller and singer. His tales have been published in many books. He has also recorded a cassette, *Put Another Log on the Fire,* on which he recites, sings and plays the mouth organ and jaws harp. He is now settled in a house in Fife but tours widely in Britain, entertaining in schools and festivals.

WINTERSTEIN, TITI. A **Sinti** violinist and singer living in Germany. Since 1978 his quintet has played a variety of jazz and Gypsy music in the Hungarian style. His recordings include *Djinee tu kowa ziro* (*Do You Know This Time*), *Saitenstrassen* (*String Streets*—a pun on *Seitenstrassen,* side streets) and the compilation *Best of Titi Winterstein.*

WLISLOCKI, HENRICH. A Hungarian scholar from Transylvania who studied the Gypsies in the 19th century and published a number of important books: *Vom wanderenden Zigeunervolke* (*About the Roaming Gypsy People,* 1890) and *Die Sprache der Transilvanischen Zigeuner* (*The Language of the Transylvanian Gypsies,* 1884).

WOOD CLAN. Abraham (Abram) Wood came to Wales from the west of England around 1730 with his wife Sarah and three children and set up a family base near Monmouth. He was a violinist and is said to have been the first person to play the violin in Wales. Abraham Wood had four children: Valentine (John), William, Solomon and Damaris. They married into other Gypsy clans, the Stanleys, Ingrams, or Boswells and the eldest son, Valentine, was the grandfather of the famous harpist John Wood Jones (born 1800). John Wood Jones was also a teacher of the harp to blind and lame children in a school at Carmarthen. In 1843, a year before his death, he accompanied Thomas Gruffydd to Buckingham Palace to perform on the harp before the Prince of Wales, Prince Albert, and her Majesty Queen Victoria, to their apparent satisfaction.

Other harpist descendants of Abraham Wood included John Roberts and William Lewis. The former performed before the Grand Duke Constantine of Russia at Aberystwyth in 1847 and the King of the Belgians in the following year while William Lewis was to play at the Royal Command concert in the London in 1932 and later gave performances at the Phoenix Theatre.

The great scholar of Romani, **John Sampson**, recorded the dialect, folktales and songs of the Wood clan and identified their dialect as distinct from that of the English Gypsies recorded by Leland, Smart and Crofton during the 19th century. He learned Romani from the harpist Edward Wood, a descendant of Abraham Wood, and other members of the family.

WOONWAGENBEWONERS. Indigenous **caravan** dwellers in Holland. They number some 20,000 and form a separate community with their own customs. Some speak a variety of Dutch known as **Bargoens**. After 1945 the official policy was to build caravan camps and get them to stop traveling. These camps were at first very large, with a school, shop and church. It soon became evident that these large camps caused problems; for example, there was too much competition for the same sort of work. Policy then switched to building smaller camps and breaking up the large ones.

WORLD ROMANY CONGRESS. There have been four congresses since 1945. For gatherings before 1939 see INTERNATIONAL MEETINGS.

The first World Romany Congress in 1971, with delegates attending from 14 countries, was held near London under the auspices of the **Comité International Tzigane.** It was originally intended to be a preparatory meeting to plan the first congress. However, because of the number of delegates coming and the number of countries represented, it was decided to make this meeting the first congress itself. **Grattan Puxon** was elected secretary and **Slobodan Berberski**, from Belgrade, president. During the congress, work was divided between five specialized commissions dealing with education, social problems, war crimes reparations, culture and language. It was agreed to struggle against illiteracy and that the use of Romani in schools should be officially recognized. The language commission agreed that there should be a move toward unifying the language. April 8, the opening day of the conference, was proclaimed National Day to be celebrated every year. A **national anthem** and a **flag** were adopted.

The second World Romany Congress was held in April 1978 at Geneva, Switzerland, and was attended by 120 delegates from 26 countries. The **United Nations**, the Human Rights Commission of that organization and UNESCO had representatives at the Congress who put the case for future cooperation. **Jan Cibula** was elected president replacing Berberski and **Shaip Jusuf** was elected vice president.

Yul Brynner was chosen as the honorary president and took part in the final press conference. During the congress the **Romany Union** was established

The work of organizing further Congresses was carried out by the International Romany Union or **Romany (Romani) Union**, and, under the latter name, it has been able to send a delegate to the **Economic and Social Council** of the United Nations (ECOSOC) since 1979, to represent the Gypsy people.

The third World Romany Congress was in Göttingen in May 1981, with 300 representatives from 22 countries and the support of the **Gesellschaft für Bedrohte Völker**. The history of the Gypsy people under the Nazis was confronted on the first day. **Simon Wiesenthal** and **Miriam Novitch** were among the speakers. There were. At this Congress Grattan Puxon was replaced as secretary by **Rajko Djurič**, and **Sait Balič** replaced Jan Cibula as president.

A number of books refer to a fourth Congress in Paris in 1986. This was not part of this series but a conference organized by the **Comité International Tzigane** (CIT) with the main aim of looking at the work of **reparations** carried out by the CIT and **Vaida Voevod III**.(See PARIS CONFERENCE.)

The official fourth World Romany Congress organized by the International Romany Union was held in April 1990 near Warsaw. Over 200 delegates from 18 countries were present. After a formal opening on April 8, the next day was devoted to reports from different countries. It was preceded by a Language Conference on the Standardization of the Romani Language. Language was an important point on the agenda as the congress agreed to the proposal for a new common **alphabet.** This congress had the highest number of delegates from Eastern Europe than any of the previous three. A highlight of the congress was a televised concert in which many well-known groups, took part, including **Esma Redjepova's** ensemble. Rajko Djurič replaced Sait Balič as president, and **Emil Scǔka** was elected general secretary. The membership of the commissions was fixed by elections. The following commissions were set up—Cultural, **Encyclopedia**, Language, **Holocaust/Reparations**, Education and Information. Because of lack of funds, these commissions have not been particularly active.

X

X. In the international phonetic alphabet and in most systems of writing Romani, the letter *x* represents the sound in Scottish *loch* or German *doch.*

Y

YATES, DORA. Jewish scholar who was for many years secretary of the **Gypsy Lore Society** and editor of its journal.

YUGOSLAVIA. Estimated Gypsy population of Yugoslavia in 1992 (before the breakup of the republic): one million. The first Gypsies appeared on the territory of modern Yugoslavia in the 14th century. Yugoslavia existed as an independent country from 1918 to 1941 and again from 1945 to 1992, as well as from 1992 to the present day in a reduced form consisting of Serbia (with Voivodina and Kosovo) and Montenegro only.

In the Yugoslav state set up in 1918, there was a Gypsy population of some 200,000. These were for the most part settled or seminomadic and belonged to all three religions (Catholic, Muslim and Orthodox Christian). Only in Montenegro was there a large nomadic population. Some cultural activity took place in Belgrade where there was a settled community, mostly living in separate Gypsy quarters. Three issues of a bilingual magazine *Romano Lil* (*Romany Paper*), edited by Svetozar Simić, were published in 1935.

In 1941 the German army invaded Yugoslavia, which was split into separate parts. After the liberation in 1945, the Yugoslav Federation was reestablished, as a republic. It is said that Tito (the partisan leader and president of the new republic) had promised the Gypsies who fought with the partisans that they would have their own state after the war. It was likely that this would have been carved out of Macedonia. However, this plan was dropped probably because Tito did not wish to reduce Macedonia in size in case it became the object of territorial demands by Greece and Albania. Nevertheless, in communist Yugoslavia the Gypsies were declared a national minority though their exact status varied from state to state.

Over 50,000 Yugoslav Gypsies had perished during the Nazi **holocaust**, leaving a population of perhaps 600,000 in 1945. In the 1961 census Gypsies were not counted as a separate category, but we have the figures for those who declared themselves as having Romani as their mother tongue—31,674. In the 1971 census they were recorded as one of the "other nationalities and ethnic groups" together with Jews and Greeks—a third category after *peoples* and *nationalities*.

The official Gypsy population figures for 1971 reveal only a partial picture of the situation.

Bosnia and Herzegovina	1,456
Croatia	1,257
Kosovo	14,593

Macedonia	24,505
Montenegro	396
Serbia proper	27,541
Slovenia	977
Voivodina	*7,760*
Total	78,485

These figures could be multiplied by 10 to give a more accurate estimate. In 1981 a census gave the figure of 850,000 Gypsies for the whole of Yugoslavia. This showed a rise throughout the country as Gypsies felt encouraged to declare their ethnicity. Only in Macedonia and Kosovo was there pressure on them to declare themselves as Albanians by that community. The correct figure would have been around one million.

It was to be the Romanies of Macedonia who developed the largest Gypsy community called **Shuto (Sŭto) Orizari** on the outskirts of **Skopje**. The economic restructuring of Yugoslavia during the 1960s also saw a wave of mass migration of many Gypsies to the West as the restrictions on emigration were eased. Predominantly from Bosnia-Herzegovina, Montenegro and Kosovo, the migrants moved to Germany, France and other countries. Many took jobs in factories, others nomadized in **caravans**.

The antagonisms among nationalities in the country intensified, which led Tito and the Yugoslav government to hold back the official recognition of Gypsies as a nationality (as opposed to the lower status of an ethnic group) across Yugoslavia. In 1971, however, **Abdi Faik**, the representative from Shuto Orizari in the Macedonian Parliament, was able to upgrade the status of Romanies to an officially recognized ethnic group in Macedonia. This allowed the use of the Romani flag and language, as well as time on radio and television.

The press began to refer to *Rom* instead of the pejorative *Tsigan*. Publications in Romani included local periodicals and a standard biography of Tito translated into Romani in 1978 by **Shaip Jusuf**. In 1981 Radio Tetovo began a half-hour program in Romani. Eighty local Romany associations also sprang up during this period, many focusing on cultural activities and calling themselves Phralipe (Brotherhood).

The greatest barrier for the Gypsies remained education, as most children did not finish primary school and very few went on to secondary education. Prejudice appeared in all spheres. In 1986 Muslim Gypsies were prevented from burying their dead in a Muslim cemetery in Bosnia, and officials in Slovenia tried to stop Gypsies voting in local elections. In Kursŭmlija a Gypsy woman was doused with gasoline and burned.

The reduced Yugoslav state after 1992 (Serbia and Montenegro) has a population of some 150,000–200,000 Gypsies. Two bilingual magazines still appear irregularly, *Romano Lil* (*Romany Paper*) for adults and *Čhavrikano Lil* (*Children's Paper*). The editor of the former, **Dragomir Asković,** is also active in the radio broadcasts in Romani from Radio Belgrade. The government has made some attempt to gain the allegiance of the Gypsies—for example, by holding a ceremonial orthodox service with prayers in Romani and attended by government figures. See also BANAT; BOSNIA-HERZEGOVINA; CROATIA; KOSOVO; MACEDONIA; MONTENEGRO; SERBIA; SLOVENIA; VOIVODINA.

Z

ZANKO. A chief of the **Kalderash** of southern France in the 20th century. His stories were recorded by Père Chatard.

ZIGEUNER. The old German word for Gypsies. Derived from **athinganos.** Because of the association of the term *Zigeuner* with the Nazi period, books and the press in Germany now often use the term *Rom und Sinti* to refer to all Gypsies, regardless of whether they are in fact **Rom** or **Sinti**.

ZIGEUNERBARON (Unternehmen Zigeunerbaron). This was an army operation in Yugoslavia in 1943, with no Gypsy connection. The name came from Johann Strauss's operetta of the same name.

ZIGEUNERLEBEN. The title of the writers' conference Biennale Kleinere Sprachen (Biennial for Minor Languages) held in Berlin, October 1991, which was devoted to Gypsywriters. Among those taking part were **Rajko Djurić**, **Margita Reiznerová, Philomena Franz** and Jovan Nicolic from Belgrade.

ZINGARI. The common Italian name for Gypsies, derived from **athingani.**

ZOTT. An old Arabic word used for all Indians, not just the Jats. It was used to refer to the many people of Indian origin in the Middle East in the times of the great Arab Caliphate and is still used as another name for the **Nawwar**, a Gypsy clan.

Appendix A
Gypsy and Traveller Populations in Europe
Approximate Figures

Country

Albania	95,000
Austria	22,500
Belarus	12,500
Belgium	12,500
Bosnia-Herzegovina	45,000
Bulgaria	750,000
Croatia	35,000
Cyprus	750
Czech Republic	275,000
Denmark	1,750
Estonia	1,250
Finland	8,000
France	310,000
Germany	120,000
Greece	180,000
Hungary	575,000
Ireland*	23,000
Italy	100,000
Latvia	2,750
Lithuania	3,500
Luxembourg	125
Macedonia	240,000
Moldavia	22,500
Netherlands°	37,500
Norway°	750
Poland	55,000
Portugal	45,000
Romania	2,100,000
Russia	230,000
Serbia-Montenegro	425,000

Slovakia	500,000
Slovenia	9,000
Spain	725,000
Sweden°	17,500
Switzerland	32,500
Turkey	400,000
Ukraine	55,000
United Kingdom	105,000

* Non-Romany Travellers.
° Including non-Romany Travellers.

Appendix B

Important International Resolutions Concerning Gypsies

Extracts are given here. Fuller texts can be found in Marielle Danbakli, *On Gypsies: Texts Issued by International Institutions* (Toulouse: CRDP, 1994).

- **Resolution of August 31, 1977, of the Sub-Commission (of the Economic and Social Council of the United Nations) on Prevention of Discrimination and Protection of Minorities**

The Sub-Commission appeals to those countries that have Gypsies (Romanies) within their borders to accord to these people, if they have not yet done so, all the rights that are enjoyed by the rest of the population.

- **Resolution of August 19, 1991, of the Sub-Commission**

The Sub-Commission, aware of the fact that, in many countries various obstacles exist to the full realization by persons belonging to the Romany community of their civil, political, economic, social and cultural rights, invites States that have Romany communities living within their borders to take, in consultation with those communities, all the necessary legislative, administrative, economic and social measures to ensure the de jure and de facto equality of the members of those communities and to guarantee their protection and security.

- **Resolution of March 4, 1992, of the Commission on Human Rights (of the Economic and Social Council of the United Nations)**

Protection of Romanies (Gypsies)

The Commission requests the Special Rapporteur of the Subcommission on the Prevention of Discrimination and Protection of Minorities to accord special attention to and to provide information on the specific conditions in which the Romanies (Gypsies) live.

It invites States to adopt all appropriate measures in order to eliminate any form of discrimination against Romanies (Gypsies).

- **Resolution of May 22, 1975, of the Committee of Ministers of the Council of Europe.**

The Social Situation of Nomads in Europe

All necessary measures within the framework of national legislation should be taken to stop any form of discrimination against nomads.

Camping and residence of nomads on camping sites equipped so as to promote safety, hygiene and welfare should be facilitated and encouraged.

Nomads and their children should be enabled to benefit effectively from the various existing provisions for vocational guidance, training and retraining.

- **Recommendation of February 22, 1983, of the Committee of Ministers of the Council of Europe**

On Stateless Nomads and Nomads of Undetermined Nationality

Each state should take appropriate steps to facilitate in relation to stateless nomads or nomads of undetermined nationality [entering or on its territory] the establishment of a link with the state concerned.

- **Recommendation of February 2, 1993, of the Parliamentary Assembly of the Council of Europe.**

On Gypsies in Europe.

The Assembly recommends that the Committee of Ministers initiate the following measures:

Introduce the teaching and study of Gypsy music at several schools of music in Europe.

Special education should be paid to the education of women and mothers with their younger children.

Member states should ratify the 4th Protocol to the European Convention on Human Rights, which guarantees freedom of movement and is, as such, essential for travellers.

A mediator for Gypsies should be appointed by the Council of Europe.

- **Resolution of May 24, 1984, of the European Parliament (of the European Communities)**

On the situation of Gypsies in the Community

The Parliament calls on the government of Member States to eliminate any discriminatory provisions which may still exist in their legislation, to co-ordinate their approach to the reception of Gypsies, to make it easier for nomads to attach themselves to a State, and to draw up programmes to be subsidised from Community funds to be drawn up aimed at improving the situation of Gypsies.

- **Resolution of May 22, 1989 of the Council of the European Communities**

On School Provision for Gypsy and Traveller Children

The Council and the Ministers for Education will strive to promote support for educational establishments, experiments with distance learning, the training and employment of teachers of Gypsy or Traveller origin wherever possible, the encouragement of research on the culture, history and language of Gypsies and Travellers.

Bibliography

Table of Contents

Serbia
Slovakia
Slovenia
Spain
Sweden
Switzerland
Turkey
Ukraine
United Kingdom
Wales
Yugoslavia

IX. PRESS
   1. Learned Journals and Newsletters
   2. Periodical Press

X. WEB SITES

XI. DISCOGRAPHIES

INTRODUCTION

The bibliography is arranged by classes and subclasses. With very few exceptions, only works published after 1945 have been included. For historical works, one should consult George Black's *A Gypsy Bibliography* (Edinburgh: Gypsy Lore Society, 1914). A supplementary list was published in 1940 in the *Journal of the Gypsy Lore Society* (3d series) 19 nos. 1–2, 20–33. Translations are given for titles in Russian and less common languages. Books are only entered once. A book dealing with the history or present-day situation of one country only will be found under that country's heading, not under "History." However, many other titles are listed by subject (e.g., health, music). Books and articles dealing with more than one of the countries that make up the United Kingdom will be found under that heading. There are separate headings, however, for England, Scotland and Wales, where titles deal only with one of the countries making up the United Kingdom. Northern Ireland will be found under Ireland.

   Apart from Black for the classical literature, Diana Tong's *Gypsies: A Multidisciplinary Annotated Bibliography* (New York: Garland, 1995) gives good coverage of material in English though it is not comprehensive on works in other languages.

   A good overall introduction is Angus Fraser's *The Gypsies* (Oxford: Blackwell, 1992). For the modern period the various works by Jean-Pierre Liégeois should be consulted.

Nearly all works written up to 1939 deal with Gypsies as an exotic race. An exception was the substantial number of books written in Romani in the early years of the Soviet Union. After 1945 there is a wider coverage of themes and an increase in books written by Romanies themselves. Again, until the end of World War II, the *Journal of the Gypsy Lore Society* (*JGLS*), is the only serious publication and is a rich source of information. Anyone embarking on a study of Gypsies should first leaf through the *JGLS* to see what has been written on the themes that interest them. After 1945 more learned journals appear, in particular *Études Tsiganes* and *Lacio Drom*. They, too, are a valuable source of information on a variety of topics. A selection of recent articles from all three journals has been included. As regards the different clans, the Kalderash and Manouche are those that have the best descriptions. In fact many books and articles about Gypsies only write about the Kalderash.

The section on the Holocaust contains many titles and is one of the largest. Although in the first years after 1945 very little was written about the fate of the Gypsies, this lapse has been remedied in recent years, particularly with books dealing with individual towns in Germany. The only overall picture of the Holocaust period will be found in Donald Kenrick and Grattan Puxon's *Destiny of Europe's Gypsies* (London: Heinemann, 1972). This has an index and detailed references. The updated edition under the title *Gypsies under the Swastika* (Hatfield: University of Hertfordshire Press, 1995) is more for the general reader and has no references. A three-volume work on the Holocaust entitled *The Gypsies during the Second World War* is being prepared in Paris by the Centre de Recherches Tsiganes and is being published in parts (University of Hertfordshire Press, 1997–).

There are no comprehensive works on literature written by Gypsies, whether in Romani or other languages, but some articles are listed in the relevant section.

Currently a large number of bilingual periodicals are being published in Eastern Europe. However, many of them are irregular, and sometimes financial difficulties have led to a gap in their appearance.

Addresses are provided for a number of publications that are informative, rather than literary, and that have a track record of reliability. This listing should not be seen as reflecting in any way on the quality of those for which no address is given.

I. GENERAL

1. Overall Studies

Acton, T. A. ed. *Gypsy Politics and Traveller Identity*. Hatfield: University of Hertfordshire Press, 1997. (Proceedings of the ESRC Romany Studies Seminar Series vol. l).

Acton, T. A., and G. J. Mundy, eds. *Romani Culture and Gypsy Identity.* Hatfield. University of Hertfordshire Press, 1997 (Proceedings of the ESRC Romany Studies Seminar Series vol. 2).

Andersen, Kirsten. *Sigøjnere.* Copenhagen: Munksgaard, 1971.

Asséo, Henriette. *Les Tsiganes, une destinée européenne.* Paris: Gallimard, 1994.

Bodi. Zsuzsanna, ed. *Readings of the 1st International Conference on Gypsy Ethnography (Budapest 1993).* Studies in Roma (Gypsy) Ethnography. vol. 2. Budapest: Mikszáth Kiadó, 1994. In English and Hungarian.

Bogaart, Nico, et al. *Zigeuners.* Amsterdam: El Sevier, 1980.

Djuric, Rajko. *Seobe Roma* (Romany Migrations). Belgrade: BIGZ, 1987.

Earle, Fiona, et al. *A Time to Travel? An introduction to Britain's newest Travellers.* Lyme Regis, UK: Enabler, 1994.

Gronemeyer, Reimer, and Georgia Rakelmann. *Die Zigeuner, Reisende in Europa.* Cologne: Dumont, 1988.

Hemetek, Ursula and Mozes Heinschink, eds. *Roma. Das unbekannte Volk.* Munich: Boehlau, 1994.

Hohmann, Joachim, ed. *Handbuch zur Tsiganologie.* Frankfurt am Main: Lang, 1996.

———. *Zigeuner und Zigeunerwissenschaft.* Marburg: Guttandin Hope, 1980.

Hundsalz, Andreas. *Stand der Forschung über Zigeuner und Landfahrer.* Stuttgart: Kohlhammer, 1978.

Karpati, Mirella, ed. *Zingari ieri e oggi.* Rome: Centro Studi Zingari, n.d. (Also in German as *Sinti und Roma: Heute und Gestern*).

Liégeois, Jean-Pierre. *Roma, Gypsies and Travellers.* Rev. ed. Strasbourg: Council of Europe Press, 1994. (Also in French as *Roma, Tsiganes, Voyageurs.*)

Lo-Johansson, Ivar. *Zigenare.* Stockholm: Prisma, 1963.

Mayall, David, ed. "Gypsies: The Forming of Identities and Official Responses." *Immigrants and Minorities.* 2, no. 1 (March 1992) (special edition).

Nordström-Holm, Gunni and Armas Lind. *Om zigenare.* Stockholm: SI Pocket, 1982.

Nordström-Holm, Gunni and Björn Myrman. *Vi kallar dem Zigenare.* Stockholm: Alfabeta, 1991.

Maur, Wolf in der. *Die Zigeuner: Wanderer zwischen den Welten.* Vienna: Molden, 1969.

Mroz, Lech. *Cyganie.* Warsaw: Ksiazka i Wiedza, 1971.

Osella, Carla. *Zingari, storie di un popolo sconosciuto.* Turin: 1985

Rehfisch, F. ed. *Gypsies, Tinkers and Other Travellers.* London: Academic Press, 1975.

Rostás-Farkas, György. *Cigányságom vállalom.* Budapest: TIT, 1992 (Essays on Romani culture in Hungarian.)

Salo, Matt, ed. *100 Years of Gypsy Studies.* Cheverly, Md.: Gypsy Lore Society, 1990. (Papers from the 10th Annual Meeting of the GLS, 1988).

Šipka, Milan, ed. *International Symposium: Romani Language and Culture.* Sarajevo: Institut za Proučavanje Nacionalnih Odnosa, 1989. (Papers of the 1986 Sarajevo Seminar.)

Thesleff, Arthur. *Report on the Gypsy Question.* 1901 (reprinted in *JGLS* new series).

Vossen, Rüdiger, ed. *Zigeuner.* Frankfurt am Main: Ullstein, 1983.

Willems, Wim. *Op zoek naar de ware Zigeuner* (Looking for the real Gypsies). Utrecht: van Arkel, 1995.

Wiliams, Patrick, ed. *Tsiganes: identité, évolution.* Paris: Etudes Tsiganes, 1989. (Papers of the 1986 Etudes Tsiganes seminar.)

Wedeck, H. E., and Wade Baskin. *Dictionary of Gipsy Life and Lore.* London: Owen, 1973.

2. Bibliography

Binns, Dennis. *A Gypsy Bibliography.* Manchester: Dennis Binns, 1982 (with later supplements).

Black, G. F. *A Gypsy Bibliography.* London: Constable, 1913.

Collie, Michael, and Angus Fraser. *George Borrow: A Bibliographical Study.* Winchester: St. Paul's Bibliographies, 1984.

da Costa, Elisa Maria Lopes. *Os Ciganos: Fontes bibliograficas em Portugal.* Madrid: Presencia Gitana, 1995.

Franzese, Sergio. "Internet e gli Zingari." In *Lacio Drom 33* (1997) nos. 3–4, 40–45.

Gmelch, G., and S. B. "Ireland's Travelling People: A Comprehensive Bibliography." *JGLS* (3d series) 3 (1978): 159–69.

Gronemeyer, Reimer. *Zigeuner in Osteuropa: eine Bibliographie zu den Ländern Polen, Tschechoslowakei und Ungarn: mit einem Anhang über ältere Sowjetische Literatur.* Munich: Saur, 1983.

Hohmann, Joachim S. *Neue deutsche Zigeunerbibliographie: Unter Berücksichtigung aller Jahrgänge des "Journal of the Gypsy Lore Society."* Frankfurt am Main: Lang, 1992.

Hovens, Pieter, and Jeanne Hovens. *Zigeuners, Woonwagenbewoners en reizenden: een bibliografie* (Gypsies, Caravan-dwellers and travellers: A Bibliography). Rijswijk: Ministry of Cultural Affairs, Recreation and Social Welfare, 1982.

Leeds University. *Catalogue of the Romany Collection.* Edinburgh: Nelson, 1962.

Neacsu, Dana. *Roma and Forced Migration: An Annotated Bibliography*. New York: Open Society Institute, 1997.

Ortega, José. *Los Gitanos: Guia bibliográfica y estudio preliminar*. Manchester: Binns, 1987.

Tong, Diane. *Gypsies: A Multidisciplinary Annotated Bibliography*. New York: Garland, 1995.

Tyrnauer, Gabrielle. *Gypsies and the Holocaust: A Bibliography and Introductory Essay*. 2d ed. Montreal: Institute for Genocide Studies, 1991. (A version of this work appears in *Genocide, A Critical Bibliographic Review*. ed. Israel Charney. *3, The Widening Circle of Genocide*. [New Brunswick N.J.: Transaction, 1994].)

University of Liverpool. *A Catalogue of the Gypsy Books Collected by the Late Robert Andrews Scott Macfie, Sometime Editor and Secretary of the Gypsy Lore Society*. Liverpool: University of Liverpool Press, UK, 1936.

3. Demography

Arnold, Hermann. *Fahrendes Volk*. Neustadt: Pfälzische Verlaganstalt, 1980. (Revised edition of his *Randgruppen des Zigeunervolkes*, 1975.)

Brown, Marilyn R. *Gypsies and Other Bohemians: The Myths of the Artist in Nineteenth-Century France*. Ann Arbor, Mich.: UMI Research Press, 1985.

Charlemagne, Jacqueline. *Populations Nomades et Pauvreté*. Paris: Presses Universitaires de France, 1983.

Liégeois, Jean-Pierre, and Nicolae Gheorghe. *Roma/Gypsies: A European Minority*. London: Minority Rights Group, 1995.

Rishi, Padmashri W. R. *Roma: The Panjabi Emigrants in Europe, Central and Middle Asia, the USSR and the Americas*. Patiala: Punjabi University, 1976.

Vaux de Foletier, François de. *Le monde des Tsiganes*. Paris: Berger-Levrault, 1983.

Webb, G. E. C. *Gypsies: The Secret People*. London: Barrie Jenkins, 1960. (Reprinted Greenwood Press, 1974.)

Wilson, Nerissa. *"Gypsies and Tinkers," Gypsies and Gentlemen: The Life and Times of the Leisure Caravan*. London: Columbus Books, 1986.

4. Travel and Description

Croft-Cooke, Rupert. *Moon in My Pocket*. London: Sampson, Low Marston, 1984.

Fonseca, Isabel. *Bury me Standing*. London: Chatto Windus, 1995. (Also in German as *Begrabt mich Aufrecht*.)

Harvey, Denis. *The Gypsies: Waggon-time and After*. London: Batsford, 1979.

McDowell, Bart. *Gypsies, Wanderers of the World*. Washington, D.C.: National Geographic Society, 1970.

Tomasevic, Nebojsa, and Rajko Djuric. *Gypsies of the World*. London: Flint River Press, 1988.

Ward-Jackson C., and D. Harvey. *English Gypsy Caravan*. Rev. ed. Newton Abbot, UK: David Charles, 1986.

II. History

1. General

Bartoloměj, Daniel. *Dějiny Romu* (History of the Gypsies). Olomouc, Czech Republic: Univerzita Palackéhou, 1994.

Crowe, David. *A History of the Gypsies of Eastern Europe and Russia*. New York: St Martin's, 1994.

Crowe, David, and John Kolsti, eds. *The Gypsies of Eastern Europe*. Armonk, N.Y.: Sharpe, 1991.

Fraser, Angus. *The Gypsies*. Oxford: Blackwell, 1992.

Gilsenbach Reimar. *Weltchronik der Zigeuner. Pt. 1*. Frankfurt am Main: Lang, 1994.

Liégeois, Jean-Pierre. *Gypsies. An Illustrated History,* trans. Tony Berrett. London: Al Saqi Books, 1985. (Translation in part of Liégeois, *Tsiganes*.)

———. *Tsiganes*. Paris: La Découverte, 1983.

Nicolini, Bruno. "La chiesa cattolica e gli Zingari." In M. Karpati (ed.). *Zingari ieri e oggi*ed. ed. M. Karpati. Rome: Centro Studi Zingari, n.d.

Vaux de Foletier, François de. *Mille ans d'histoire des Tsiganes*. Paris: Fayard, 1970.

2. Early migration and Indian Origins

Hancock I. *The Indian Origins and Westward Migration of the Roma*. Manchaca, Tex: Romany Union, 1997.

Kenrick, Donald. *Gypsies, from India to the Mediterranean*. Toulouse: CDRP, 1993. (Also available in French, Greek, Spanish, Italian.)

Rishi, W. R. *Roma: The Punjabi Emigrants in Europe*. Patiala, India: Punjabi University, 1976.

Singhal, D. P. *Gypsies: Indians in Exile*. Meerut, India: Archana, 1982.

Soulis, G. "The Gypsies in the Byzantine Empire and the Balkans in the late Middle Ages." *Dumbarton Oaks Papers* 15 (1961).

3. History to 1939 (excluding the Holocaust)

Haley W. "The Gypsy Conference at Bucharest." *JGLS* (3d series) 13 (1934).

4. Holocaust (1933–1945)

Acković, Dragoljub. *Stradanja Roma u Jasenovcu*. Belgrade: NIGP "ABC GLAS" DD, 1994.
———. *Roma Suffering in Jasenovac Camp* (Translation of prior title). Belgrade: Stručvna Kniga, 1995.
Alt, Betty, and Silvia Folts. *Weeping Violins*. Kirksville, Mo.: Thomas Jefferson University Press, 1996.
Ayass W., et al. *Feinderklärung und Prävention* Berlin: Rotbuch, 1988.
Beckers, Jan, ed. *Me hum Sinthu. Ik ben Zigeuner* (I am a Gypsy). The Hague: Horus, 1980.
Berenbaum, M., ed. *A Mosaic of Victims*. New York: New York University Press, 1989; London: Tauris, 1990.
Bernadac, Christian. *L'Holocauste oublié: le massacre des Tsiganes*. Paris: France-Empire, 1979.
Bulajić, Milan. *Ustaski zlocini genocida* (Ustashe Criminal Genocide). Belgrade: RAD, 1988.
Dlugoborski, Waclaw, ed. *50-lecie zaglady Romów w KL Auschwitz-Birkenau* (50th Anniversary of the Massacre in Auschwitz-Birkenau Concentration Camp). Oswiecim: Stowarzyszenie Romów w Polsce, 1994. (In Polish and German.)
Dokumentationzentrum Deutscher Sinti und Roma. *Kinder und Jugendliche als Opfer des Holocausts*. Heidelberg: Dokumentationzentrum, 1995.
Duna, Williams A. *Gypsies: A Persecuted Race*. Minneapolis: Duna Studios. 1984.
Fings, Karola, and Frank Sparing. *"z. Zt. Zigeunerlager": die Verfolgung der Düsseldorfer Sinti und Roma im Nationalsozialismus*. Cologne: Volksblatt, 1992.
Fings, Karola, et al. *Einziges Land, in dem Judenfrage und Zigeunerfrage gelöst: Die Verfolgung der Roma im faschistisch besetzten Jugoslawien 1941–1945*. Cologne: Rom, n.d.
Friedman, Ina. "Bubili: A Young Gypsy's Fight for Survival." In *The Other Victims: First-Person Stories of Non-Jews Persecuted by the Nazis*. Boston: Houghton Mifflin. 1990.

Gilsenbach, Reimar. *Oh Django, sing deinen Zorn.* Berlin: BasisDruck, 1993.

Günther, Wolfgang. *Ach Schwester, ich kann nicht mehr tanzen: Sinti und Roma im KZ Bergen Belsen.* Hanover: SOAK, 1990.

―――. *Zur preussischen Zigeunerpolitik seit 1871.* Hanover: ANS, 1985.

Hancock, Ian. *The Pariah Syndrome.* Ann Arbor, Mich.: Karoma, 1987.

Heuss, Herbert. *Darmstadt, Auschwitz: Die Verfolgung der Sinti in Darmstadt.* Darmstadt: Verband deutscher Sinti und Roma, 1995.

Hohmann, Joachim. *Robert Ritter und die Erbe der Kriminalbiologie.* Frankfurt am Main: Lang, 1991.

―――. *Zigeuner und Zigeunerwissenschaft: ein Beitrag zur Grundlagenforschung und Dokumentation des Völkermords im "Dritten Reich."* Marburg: Guttandin Hoppe, 1980.

Holy, Dusan and Ctibor Nečas. *Žalující píseň.* Strážnicã: Ústav Lidové Kultury, 1993.

Johansen, Jahn Otto. *Sigøynernes Holocaust.* Oslo: Cappelen. 1989. (Original Norwegian edition.)

―――. *Zigenarnas Holocaust.* Stockholm: Symposion, 1990 (Swedish edition).

Kenrick, Donald, and Gratton Puxon. *The Destiny of Europe's Gypsies.* London: Heinemann Educational, 1972. (Also available in French, German, Italian, Japanese. For two editions in Romani, see Puxon and Kenrick below.)

―――. *Gypsies under the Swastika.* Hatfield: University of Hertfordshire Press, 1995. (A revised edition of *Destiny of Europe's Gypsies,* also available in French and Spanish.)

Kladivová, V. *Konečná Stanice Auschwitz-Birkenau.* Olomouc, Czech Republic: Univerzita Palackého, 1994.

Krausnick, M. *Wo sind sie hingekommen?* Stuttgart: Bleicher, 1995.

Lessing, A. *Mein Leben in Versteck.* Düsseldorf: Zebulon, 1993.

Lifton, Robert Jay. *The Nazi Doctors: Medical Killing and the Psychology of Genocide.* New York: Basic Books, 1986.

Lipa, Jiri. "The Fate of Gypsies in Czechoslovakia under Nazi Domination." In M. Berenbaum. *A Mosaic of Victims,* ed. M. Berenbaum. New York: New York University Press, 1990.

Müller-Hill, Benno. *Murderous Science: Elimination by Scientific Selection of Jews, Gypsies, et al., Germany 1933–1945,* trans. George R. Fraser. New York: Oxford University Press, 1988.

Nazi Genocide in Poland Seminar (1983). Papers by Ciechanowski, Galinski, Wilczur and Zabierowski, translated and reprinted in *Lacio Drom* 20 (May, June 1984) nos. 2, 3.

Nečas, Ctibor. *Českoslovenští Romové v letech 1939–1945* (Czechoslovak Gypsies in the Years 1939–45). Brno: Masaryková Univerzita, 1994.

————. *Nad osudem česých Cikánů a slovenských cikanů v letech 1939–1945* (On the fate of the Czech and Slovak Gypsies). Brno: Univerzita J. S. Purkyňe, 1981.

————. *Nemůžeme zapomenout: našti bisteras* (We cannot forget). Olomouc, Czech Republic: Univerzita Palackého, 1994.

Pape, Marcus. *A Nikdo vám Nebude Věřit: dokument o koncentračním táboře Lety u Písku* (Nobody will believe you: Documents about the Lety Concentration Camp). Prague: GplusG, 1997.

Parcer J., ed. *Los Cyganów w KL Auschwitz-Birkenau—Das Schicksal der Sinti und Roma im KL Auschwitz-Birkenau*. Oswięcim: Stowarzyszenie Romów w Polsce. 1994

————. ed. *Memorial Book. The Gypsies at Auschwitz-Birkenau*. Munich: Saur, 1993.

Pedersen, F. *Skyd Zigeunerne*. Copenhagen: Carnet, 1990.

Peschanski, Denis. *Les Tsiganes en France 1939–1946*. Paris: CNRS, 1994.

Puxon, Grattan, and Donald Kenrick. *Bibahtale bersa* (Unhappy Years). London: Romanestan, 1990. (New edition, Madrid: Presencia Gitana, 1996.)

Rose, Romani, and Walter Weiss. *Sinti und Roma im "Dritten Reich": Das Programm der Vernichtung durch Arbeit*. Göttingen: Lamuv, 1991.

Sigot, Jacques. *Ces Barbelés oubliés par l'histoire*. Bordeaux: Wallada, 1994.

Sijes, B. A. *Vervolging van Zigeuners in Nederland. 1940–1945*. The Hague: Martinus Nijhoff, 1979.

Thurner, E. *Nationalsozialismus und Zigeuner in Osterreich*. Vienna: Geyer, 1983.

Tyrnauer, G. "A Sinto Survivor Speaks." In *Papers from the 6th and 7th Annual Meetings of the Gypsy Lore Society*. New York: Gypsy Lore Society, 1986. (Also in *Social Education* 55.2, Feb. 1991.)

Vexler, Y. "J'étais médecin des Tsiganes a Auschwitz." *Monde Gitan*, 27 (1973). 1–10.

Wagenbaar, Aad. *Settela*. Holland, Amsterdam: Arbeiderpres, 1996.

Wippermann, W. *Das Leben in Frankfurt zur NS Zeit*. Frankfurt am Main: Kramer, 1986.

Yoors, Jan. *Crossing*. New York: Simon Schuster, 1971.

Zimmermann, M. *Rassenutopie und Genozid: Die nationalsozialistische "Lösung der Zigeunerfrage."* Hamburg: Christiansverlag, 1996.

————. *Verfolgt, vertrieben, vernichtet: Die nationalsozialistische Vernichtung gegen Sinti und Roma*. Essen: Klartext, 1989.

5. History from 1945—General

Auzias, Claire (ed.). *Les familles Rom d'Europe de l'Est*. Paris: ALIZE, n.d.

Braham, Mark. *The Untouchables: A survey of the Roma people of Central and Eastern Europe*. Geneva: United Nations High Commissioner for Refugees, 1993.

Brearley, Margaret. *The Roma/Gypsies of Europe: A Persecuted People*. London: Institute for Jewish Policy Research, 1996.

Kocze, Angela. *The Roma of Central and Eastern Europe: Legal Remedies or Invisibility*. Warsaw: OSCE, 1996.

Schenk, Michael. *Rassismus gegen Sinti und Roma*. Frankfurt am Main: Lang, 1994.

Svanberg, Frederik Folkeryd-Ingvar. *Gypsies (Roma) in the Post-totalitarian States*. Stockholm: Olof Palme International Center, 1995.

6. History 1945–1990—Eastern Europe under Communism

Anon. *Destroying Ethnic Identity. The Gypsies of Bulgaria*. New York: Human Rights Watch, 1991.

McCagg, W. "Gypsy Policy in Socialist Hungary and Czechoslovakia 1945–1989."*Nationalities Papers* 19, no. 3 1991. 313–36.

Silverman, Carol. "Bulgarian Gypsies: Adaptation in a Socialist Context." *Nomadic Peoples* (1987).

Sus, Jaroslav. *Cikánská otázka v CSSR*. Prague: 1961.

III. Politics

1. General

Acton, Thomas. *Gypsy Politics and Social Change: The Development of Ethnic Ideology and Pressure Politics among British Gypsies from Victorian Reformism to Romany Nationalism*. London: Routledge Kegan Paul. 1974.

Adams, Barbara, Judith Okely, David Morgan, and David Smith. *Gypsies and Government Policy in England: A Study of the Travellers' Way of Life in Relation to the Policies and Practices of Central and Local Government*. London: Heinemann, 1975.

Bauer, Rudolph, Josef Bura and Klaus Lang eds. *Sinti in der Bundesrepublik: Beiträge zur sozialen Lage einer verfolgten Minderheit*. Bremen: Universität Bremen, 1984.

Fienborg, Gunoula, et al. *Die Roma—Hoffen auf ein Leben ohne Angst*. Hamburg: Rowohlt, 1992.

Geigges, Anita, and Bernhard W. Wette. *Zigeuner Heute: Verfolgung und Diskriminierung in der BRD.* Bornheim-Merten: Lamuv, 1979.

Liégeois, Jean-Pierre, et al. *Gypsies and Travellers: Socio-Cultural Data, Socio-Political Data.* Strasbourg: Council for Cultural Cooperation, 1987.

Matras, Yaron, and Ian Hancock. *Rezoluciji e EUROM-eske.* Hamburg: Rom Cinti Union, 1990.

Soest, George von. *Zigeuner zwischen Verfolgung und Integration: Geschichte, Lebensbedingungen und Eingliederungsversuche.* Weinheim: Beltz, 1979.

Zürcher-Berther, Maria-Luisa. *Nomades Parmi les Sédentaires: Problèmes Posés par un autre Mode de Vie.* Basel: Helbing Lichtenhahn, 1989.

2. Civil Rights Movements

Acton, Thomas. "IV Congresso Mondiale dei Rom." In *Lacio Drom* 26 (1990) no.5.

Gesellschaft für bedrohte Völker. *III. Welt-Roma-Kongress 1981.* Special double number of *Pogrom,* nos. 80, 81. (1981).

Liégeois, Jean-Pierre. *Mutation Tsigane.* Brussels: Complexe, 1976.

Lopez, Sergio Rodriguez ed. *I Congreso Gitano de la Unión Europea.* Barcelona: Instituto Romanó, 1995.

Puxon, Grattan. "The First World Romani Congress." *Race Today* (June 1971).

Rishi W. R.ed. "IV World Romani Congress." Special issue of *Roma,* nos. 33, 34. (July 1990/January 1991).

3. Law

Bergen-Schuijt, Ada van. "Buitenlandse zigeuners en de Nederlandse wetgeving . . . in 1977 en 1978." *Zigeuners in Nederland* ed. Peter Hovens and Rob Dahler. pp. 229–256. Nijmegen: Instituut voor Culturele en Sociale Antropologie, 1988.

Danbakli, Marielle ed. *On Gypsies: Texts issued by International Institutions.* Toulouse: CRDP. 1994. (Also in French.)

Doering, Hans-Joachim. *Die Zigeuner in Nationalsozialistischen Staat.* Hamburg: Kriminalistik, 1964.

Forrester, Bill. *The Travellers' Handbook: A Guide to the Law Affecting Gypsies.* London: InterChange, 1985.

Helsinki Foundation for Human Rights. *Try to Use it. It is Your Right! A practical guide on the rights of Romanies.* Warsaw: Helsinki Foundation, 1997.

Mroz, Lech. "Gypsies and the Law." In *Ethnologia Polona* 3 (1977): 175–83.

Wolfrum, Rüdiger. "The Legal Status of Sinti and Roma in Europe: A Case Study Concerning the Shortcomings of the Protection of Minorities." *Annuaire Européen/European Yearbook* 33 (1986), 75–91.

IV. Economy

Chignard, Louis. "Le système économique du voyage." *Hommes et Migrations*. (June/July 1995).

V. Society

1. Anthropology/Ethnology

Acton, Thomas and David Gallant. *Romanichal Gypsies*. UK, Hove: Wayland, 1997.

Clébert, Jean-Paul. *The Gypsies*, trans. Charles Duff. London: Vista, 1963

Dollé, Marie-Paul. *Les Tsiganes Manouches*. Sand: Dollé, 1980.

Graham-Yooll, Andrew. "In Search of Saint George."*London Magazine* (August/September 1990): 754–88.

Rao, Aparna, ed. *The other nomads*. Cologne: Böhlau, 1987.

Stewart, Michael. *The Time of the Gypsies*. Oxford: Westview, 1997.

University of Gothenburg. *The State of Ambiguity: Studies of Gypsy Refugees*. Gothenburg. University of Gothenburg Anthropological Research Series, n.d.

Williams, Patrick. *Mariage Tsigane*. Paris: L'Harmattan, 1984.

———. *Nous, on n'en parle pas: les vivants et les morts chez les Manouches*. Paris: Maison des Sciences de l'Homme, 1993.

———.ed. *Tsiganes: identité, évolution*. Paris: Syros Alternatives, 1989. (Papers of the Etudes Tsiganes conference.)

2. Children

Réger, Zita. "Bilingual Gypsy Children in Hungary: Explorations in 'Natural' Second-Language Acquisition at an Early Age." In *International Journal of the Sociology of Language* 19, 1979. (Special number on Romani Sociolinguistics.)

3. Education

Acton, Thomas, and Donald Kenrick. "From Summer Voluntary Schemes to European Community Bureaucracy: The Development of

Special Provisions for Traveller Education in the United Kingdom since 1967." *European Journal of Intercultural Studies* 1 no. 3 (March 1991): 47–62.

Anon. *Education of Travelling Children.* London: Office for Standards in Education, 1996.

Anon. *School Provision for Gypsy and Traveller Children.* Brussels: European Communities, 1996. (Not a new edition of Liégeois et al.'s study of the same title.)

Binns, Dennis. "History and Growth of Traveller Education." *British Journal of Educational Studies* 38 no. 3 (August 1990): 251–258.

Conway, Laura. *On the Status of Romani Education in the Czech Republic.* Prague: HOST, 1996. (Also available in Czech.)

Csapo, Marg. "Concerns Related to the Education of Romany Students in Hungary, Austria and Finland." *Comparative Education.* 18 no. 2 (1982): 205–19.

Dowber, Hilary. *Travellers and School: Travellers in Lewisham Talk of Their Experiences of School.* London: Lewisham Bridge, 1991.

Gustafsson, Inga. *Studies of a Minority Group's Efforts to Preserve Its Cultural Autonomy.* Stockholm: IMFO-GROUP, Institute of Education, University of Stockholm, 1973.

Krause, Mareile. *Verfolgung durch Erziehung: Eine Untersuchung über die jahrhundertelange Kontinuität staatlicher Erziehungsmassnahmen im Dienste der Vernichtung kultureller Identität von Roma und Sinti.* Hamburg: An der Lottbek, 1989.

Kyuchukov, Hristo. *Romany Children and Their Preparation for Literacy: A Case Study.* Tilburg: University Press, 1995.

Liégeois, Jean-Pierre, et al. *School Provision for Gypsy and Traveller Children: A Synthesis Report.* Luxembourg: Commission of the European Communities, 1987.

Reiss, Christopher. *Education of Travelling Children.* London: Macmillan, 1975.

Sangan, Jean-Claude. *Une École chez les Tziganes.* Paris: Droit et Liberté, 1974.

4. Religion

Ridholls, Joe. *Travelling Home: God's Work of Revival Among Gypsy Folk.* Basingstoke, England: Marshall Pickering, 1986.

Trigg, E. B. *Gypsy Demons and Divinities: The Magical and Supernatural Practices of Gypsies.* Secaucus, N.J.: Citadel, 1973.

5. Sociology

Falque, Edith. *Voyage et tradition: Approche Sociologique d'un sous-groupe Tsigane: les Manouches.* Paris: Payot, 1971.

Lucassen, Leo. "Under the Cloak of Begging? Gypsy occupations in Western Europe in the 19th and 20th century." *Ethnologia Europaea* 23 (1993): 75–94.

Rakelmann, Georgia. *Interethnik. Beziehungen von Zigeunern und Nichtzigeunern.* Münster: Literatur, 1988.

Reyniers, Alain. "Le rôle de la parenté dans la formation d'une communauté manouche." In *Etudes Tsiganes* (new series) 6 (1994) no. 2.

Tauber, E. "Studi sugli Zingari: recensione critica secondo la teoria di Gerarchia di Dumont." *Lacio Drom* 30 no. 5. (Sept.–Oct. 1994): 4–55.

Ward-Jackson, C., and D. Harvey. *The English Gypsy Caravan.* Newton Abbott: Charles. 1972, 1986.

Wippermann, Wolfgang. *Wie die Zigeuner: Antisemitismus und Antiziganismus im Vergleich.* Berlin: Elefantenpress, 1997.

6. Women

Chaderat, Sarge. *Variations Gitanes.* Paris: Flammarion, 1992.

Cipollini, Roberta, Franca Faccioli and Tamar Pitch. "Gypsy Girls in an Italian Juvenile Court." In *Growing Up Good: Policing the Behaviour of Girls in Europe,* ed. Maureen Cain. London: Sage, 1989.

Fernández, Maria Dolores, and Carmen Bajo. *Jornadas sobre la situación de la Mujer Gitana.* Granada: Asociación de Mujeres Gitanas de Granada "Romi," 1990.

Mossa. *La Gitane et son destin: Témoignages d'une jeune Gitane sur la condition féminine et l'évolution du monde gitan.* Textes présentés par Bernard Leblon. Paris: L'Harmattan, 1992.

Okely, Judith. "Gypsy Women: Models in Conflict." In *Perceiving Women,* ed. Shirley Ardener. London: Malaby, 1975.

Wang, Kirsten, ed. *Mujeres Gitanas ante el Futuro.* Madrid: Editorial Presencia Gitana, 1990.

VI. Cultural

1. Dance

Balázs, Gusztáv. *A nagyecsedi oláh cigányok tánchagyománya.* (The Dance Tradition of Vlach Gypsies in Nagyecsed). Studies in Roma (Gypsy) Ethnography, vol. 3. Budapest: Magyar Néprajzi Társaság, 1995.

Dunin, Elsie. "Dance change in the Context of the Gypsy St. George's Day, Skopje. Yugoslavia 1967–1977." *Papers from the 4th and 5th Annual Meetings of the Gypsy Lore Society,* ed Joanne Grumet. pp. 110–20. New York: Gypsy Lore Society, 1982.

2. Folk Arts

Dummett, Michael. "The Gypsies and the Tarot." In *Traveller Education* 17 (1982). (Reprinted from M.Dummett, *The Game of Tarot from Ferrara to Salt Lake City.* London: Duckworth, 1980.)

3. Linguistics

a. General

Bakker Peter, and M.Cortiade, eds. *In the Margin of Romani: Gypsy Languages in Contact.* Holland, Amsterdam: Institute for General Linguistics, 1991.

Bakker, Peter, and Hein van der Voort. "Para-Romani Languages: An Overview and Some Speculations on Their Genesis." In *In the Margin of Romani: Gypsy Languages in Contact.* ed. P. Bakker and M. Cortiade. pp. 16–44.

Boretzky, Norbert. *"Sind Zigeunersprachen Kreols?" Akten des 1. Essener Kolloqiums über Kreolsprachen und Sprachkontakte (1985),* ed. Boretzky, Enninger and Stolz. pp. 43–70. Bochum: Brockmeyer, 1985.

Hancock, Ian. "The Development of Romani Linguistics." In *Languages and Cultures: Studies in Honor of Edgar C. Polomé.* ed. M. Jazayery and W. Winter. Holland, Amsterdam: Mouton, 1988.

Hübschmannová, Milena. "Bilingualism among the Slovak Rom." In *International Journal of the Sociology of Language.* 19 (1979).

Kenrick, D. S. "Report on the Warsaw Linguistics Conference." *Roma* 33/34.

Matras, Yaron, ed. *Romani in Contact.* Amsterdam: Benjamin, 1995.

Matras, Yaron, ed. *The Typology and Dialectology of Romani.* Holland, Amsterdam: Benjamin, 1997.

b. Grammars and description

Acton, Thomas, and Donald Kenrick eds. *Romani Rokkeripen To-Divvus.* (The contemporary English Romani dialect.) London: Romanestan, 1984. (In English.)

Bakker, Peter. "Basque Romani: A Prelimary Grammatical Sketch of a Mixed Language." In Bakker and Cortiade, *In the Margin of Romani: Gypsy Languages in Contact.* pp. 56–90. Amsterdam: Institute for General Linguistics, 1991.

Boretzky, Norbert. *Romani: Grammatik des Kalderas-Dialekts mit Texten und Glossar.* Wiesbaden: Harrassowitz, 1994.

Borrow, George. *Romano Lavo Lil.* (Romani Wordbook). London: Murray, 1874. (Many reprints since.)

Cech, Petra, and Mozes Heinschink. *Sepecides. (Romani).* Munich, Unterschleissheim: Lincom Europa, 1996.

Daroczi, József Choli and Feyer Levente. *Zhanes Romanes?* (Do you Know Romani). Budapest: Cigany Nielkónvy, 1988.

Friedman, Victor. "Problems in the codification of a standard Romani literary language." In *Papers from the 4th and 5th Annual Meetings of the Gypsy Lore Society* ed. Joanne Grumet. New York: GLS, 1985.

Gjerdman, Olof and Erik Ljungberg. *The Language of the Swedish Coppersmith Gipsy Johan Dimitri Taikon.* Uppsala: Lundequist, 1963.

Haarmann, Harald. *Spracherhaltung und Sprachwechsel als Probleme der interlingualen Soziolinguistik: Studien zur Gruppenmehrsprachigkeit der Zigeuner in der Sowjetunion.* Hamburg: Busje, 1980.

Halwachs, Dieter, et al. *Roman: The Dialect of the Burgenland Romanies).* Munich, Unterschleissheim: Lincom Europa. 1997.

Hancock, Ian. *Grammar and Dictionary of the Hungarian-Slovak Romani Language.* Manchaca, Tex: Romany Union, 1990.

———. *Handbook of Vlax-Romani.* Columbus, Ohio: Slavica, 1985.

Holzinger, Daniel. *Romanes (Sinti).* Munich, Unterschleissheim: Lincom Europa. 1997.

Igla, Birgit. *Das Romani von Ajia Varvara.* Wiesbaden: Harrassowitz, 1996.

Iversen, R. *Secret Languages in Norway.* Pts. 1 and 2. Oslo: Norske Videnskapsakademi, 1944, 1945.

Kepeski, Krume, and Šaip Jusuf. *Romani Gramatika-Romska Gramatika.* Skopje: Naša Kniga, 1980. (Bilingual, Macedonian and Romani.)

Kochanowski, Jan. *Gypsy Studies.* 2 vols. New Delhi: International Academy of Indian Culture, 1963.

Kochanowski, Vanya (Jan). *Parlons Romanes.* Bordeaux: Wallada, 1995.

Macalister, R. A. S. *The Secret Languages of Ireland.* Cambridge: Cambridge University Press, 1937.

Pobozniak, T. *Grammar of the Lovari Dialect.* Krakow: Polska Akademia Nauk, 1964.

Russell, A. "Scoto-Romani and Tinklers' Cant." *JGLS* (New series) 8 (1914–1915): pp. 11–79.

Sampson, John. *The Dialect of the Gypsies in Wales, Being the Older Form of British Romani Preserved in the Speech of the Clan of Abram Wood.* Oxford: Clarendon, 1992. (Reprint.)

Sărau, Gheorghe. *Limba Romani.* Bucharest: Ministerul Invatamantului, 1992.

Smart, Bath Charles, and Henry Thomas Crofton. *The Dialect of the English Gypsies.* London: Asher, 1875.

Soravia, Giulio. *Dialetti degli Zingari Italiani.* Pisa: Pacini, 1977.

Tcherenkow (Cherenkov), Lev, and Mozes Heinschink. *Kalderas.* Munich, Unterschleissheim: Lincom Europa, 1996.

Toro, Rita Paola. "Il Gergo dei Camminanti." *Lacio Drom.* 27 (1991) nos. 3/4

Ventzel, T. V. *The Gypsy Language,* trans S. S. Gitman. Moscow: Nauka, 1983. (Also available in German as *Die Zigeunersprache.* [Leipzig: Enzyklopädie, 1980].)

c. Dictionaries

Barthelemy, André. *Dictionnaire du Tsigane Kalderash.* Paris: Barthelemy, n.d.

Boretzky, Norbert and Birgit Igla. *Wörterbuch Romani-Deutsch-Englisch.* Wiesbaden: Harrassowitz, 1994.

Calvet, Georges. *Dictionnaire Tsigane-Français, dialecte kalderash.* Paris: L'Asiathèque, 1993.

Demeter, R. S. and P. S. *Gypsy-Russian and Russian-Gypsy Dictionary. (Kalderash dialect).* Moscow: Russky Yazyk, 1990.

Endt, Enno. *Bargoens Woordenboek.* Amsterdam: Rap, n.d.

Hübschmannová, Milena et al. *Romsko-Česky a Česko-Romsky kapesní slovník.* (Czech-Romani Pocket Dictionary). Prague: Státní Pedagogické Nakladatelství, 1991.

Koivisto, Viljo. *Romano-Finitiko-Angliko laavesko liin.* (Finnish-Romani-English dictionary). Helsinki: Painatuskeskus, 1994.

Mija, J. *Romčina do vrecka* (Slovak-Romani pocket dictionary). Kosice: 1995.

Rishi, W. R. *Multilingual Romani Dictionary.* Chandigarh: Roma, 1974.

―――. *Romani-Punjabi-English Dictionary.* Patiala: Language Department, 1981.

Rostas-Farkas, György and Ervin Karsai. *Cigány-magyar, magyar-cigány szótár* (Hungarian-Romani Dictionary). Budapest: Kossuth Könyvkiadó, 1991.

Sărau, Gheorghe. *Mic dicţionar Rom-Român* (Small Romani-Romanian dictionary). Bucharest: Kriterion, 1992.

Uhlik, Rade. *Srpskohrvatsko-Romsko-Engleski rječnik* (Serbocroat-Romani-English dictionary). Sarajevo: Svjetlost, 1983.

Valtone, Pertti. *Suomen Mustalaiskielen etymologinen sanakirja* (Romani-Finnish-English Etymological Dictionary). Helsinki: Suomalaisen Kirjallisuuden Seura, 1972.

Wolf, S. *Grosses Wörterbuch der Zigeunersprache.* Hamburg: Helmut Buske, 1993.

4. Literary Criticism

Acković D. "Le journal Romano Lil." *Études Tsiganes.* (new series) 7 (1995) no. 1. 123–132.

Binns, Dennis. *Children's Literature and the Role of the Gypsy.* Manchester: Travellers' School. 1984.

Courthiade, M. "Jeunes poètes roms de Cassove." In *Etudes Tsiganes.* 28 (1982) no. 3 and 29 (1983) no. 1.

Djurić, Rajko. "Gli Inizi di una nuova Letteratura." In *Zingari ieri e oggi* (Also available in German). ed. Mirella Karpati, Rome: Centro Studi Zingari, n.d. 175–79.

———. *Roma und Sinti im Spiegel der deutschen Literatur.* Frankfurt am Main: Lang, 1995.

Kenrick, Donald and Gillian Taylor. "The Portrayal of the Gypsy in English Schoolbooks." In *Internazionale Schulbuchforschung.* 6 no. 1, 38–47.

Kommers, Jean. *Kinderroof of Zigeunerroof* (Stealing Children or Stealing Gypsies). Amsterdam: Van Arkel, 1993.

Leblon, Bernard. *Les Gitans dans la littérature espagnole.* Toulouse: France-Ibérie Recherche, 1982.

Niemandt, Hans-Dieter. *Die Zigeunerin in den Romanischen Literaturen.* Frankfurt am Main: Lang, 1992.

Panebianco, Candido. *Lorca e i Gitani.* Rome: Bulzoni, 1984.

Reyniers A. "Quelques élements pour une histoire des médias Tsiganes." In *Etudes Tsiganes* (new series) 7 (1995) no. 1, 141–46.

5. Literature

a. Anthologies

Balić, Sait, et al. *Jaga. Vatre* (Fires). Leskovac: Napredak, 1984. (Poetry in Romani and Serbian.)

Bari, Karoly, ed. *Tüzpiros Kígyócska/Feurige kleine rote Schlange.* Debrecen: Gondolat, 1985. (Romani and German editions.)

———, ed. *Le vešeski dej* (The Forest Mother). Budapest: Országos Közmövelödési Központ, 1990. (Folktales and poetry in Romani and Hungarian.)

Daróczi, József Choli. *Romane Poetongi Antologia.* Budapest: Ariadne Foundation, 1995. (Poetry in Romani, English and Hungarian.)

Djurić, Rajko. *Märchen und Lieder europäischer Sinti und Roma.* Frankfurtam Main: Lang, 1997.

Rostás-Farkas, György, ed. *Maladyipe. Találkozás* (Meeting). Budapest: Müfordítások, 1993. (Poetry in Romani and Hungarian.)

b. Autobiography and Biography

Boswell, Silvester Gordon. *The Book of Boswell: Autobiography of a Gypsy,* ed. John Seymour. London: Gollancz, 1970.

Cannon, Jon, and the Travellers of Thistlebrook. *Travellers: An Introduction.* London: Emergency Exit Arts/Interchange Books, 1989.

Delaunay, C. *Django Reinhardt.* London: Cassell, 1961.

Dybing, Svein, and Terje Gammelsrud. *Raya.* Oslo: Tiden, 1983.

Franz, Philomena. *Zwischen Liebe und Hass: Ein Zigeunerleben.* Freiburg: Herder, 1985.

Joyce, Nan. *Traveller: An Autobiography,* ed. Anna Farmar. Dublin: Gill Macmillan, 1985.

Lowe, Richard, and William Shaw, eds. *Travellers: Voices of the New Age Nomads.* London: Fourth Estate, 1993.

Loveridge, Guy. *Biography of Bramwell "Romany" Evens.* Huddersfield: Loveridge, 1995.

Maximoff, Matéo. *Ce Monde qui n'est pas le mien.* Paris: Concordia, 1992.

———. *Dites-le avec des Pleurs.* Paris: Concordia, 1990.

———. *Routes sans Roulottes.* Paris: Maximoff, 1993.

Nikolic, Miso. *Und dann zogen wir weiter.* Klagenfurt: Drava, 1997.

Nussbaumer-Moser, Jeanette. *Die Kellerkinder von Nivagl.* Basel: Friedrich-Reinhardt, 1995.

Reeve, Dominic. *Smoke in the Lanes.* London: Constable, 1958.

———. *No Place Like Home.* London: Phoenix House, 1960.

Sampson, Anthony. *The Scholar Gypsy.* London: Murray, 1997.

Sandford, Jeremy. *Gypsies.* London: Secker and Warburg, 1973.

Šebková, Hana, Edita Zlanayová and Milena Hübschmannová. *Fragments Tsiganes: Comme en Haut, ainsi en Bas.* Paris: Lierre Coudrier, 1991.

Skogholt, P. and K. Lilleholt. *En for hverandre: Sigoynere Milos Karol og Frans Josef forteller* (One for all. Gypsies Milos Karol and Frans Josef Relate). Oslo: Gyldendal, 1978.

Stojka, C. *Reisende auf dieser Welt.* Vienna: Picus, 1992.

———. *Wir leben im Verborgenen.* Vienna: Picus, 1988.

Tremlett, G. *The David Essex Story.* London, 1974.

Tschawo, Latscho. *Die Befreiung des Latscho Tschawo: Ein Sinto-Leben in Deutschland.* Bornheim-Merten: Lamuv, 1984.

Wang, Kirsten. *The Story of Tio Carlos.* Frankfurt am Main: Lang, 1996.

Whyte, Betsy. *The Yellow on the Broom: The Early Days of a Traveller Woman.* Edinburgh: Chambers, 1979.

Williamson, Duncan. *The Horsieman: Memories of a Traveller 1928–1958.* Edinburgh: Canongate, 1994.

Winterstein, Adolf Boko. *Zigeunerleben: Der Lebensbericht des Sinti-Musikers und Geigenbauers,* ed. Erich Renner. Frankfurt am Main: Büchergilde Gutenberg, 1988.

Wood, Manfri Frederick. *In the Life of a Romany Gypsy.* London: Routledge Kegan Paul, 1979.

Yates, Dora. *My Gypsy Days: Recollections of a Romany Rawnie.* London: Phoenix House, 1953.

Yoors, Jan. *Crossing: A Journal of Survival and Resistance in World War II.* New York: Simon & Schuster, 1971.

c. Folktales and Folk Poetry

Berki, János. *Tales of János Berki Told in Gypsy and Hungarian,* ed. Veronika Görög-Karády. Budapest: MTA Néprajzi Kutató Csoport, 1985.

Copoiu, Petre. *Povesti Tiganesti. Rromane Paramica* (Romany tales, ed. Gheorghe Sarau. Bucharest: Kriterion, 1996.

Dememeter, R. *Obrazoy Folklora Cygan-Kelderarej* (Collection of the Folklore of the Kalderash Gypsies). Moscow: Nauka, 1981.

Gjerde, Lars and Knut Kristiansen. *"The Orange of Love" and Other Stories: The Rom-Gypsy language in Norway.* Oslo: Scandinavian University Press, 1994.

Grabócz, Gábor, and Katalin Kovalcsik. *A Mesemondo Rostás Mihály/ Mihály Rostás: A Gypsy Story Teller.* Budapest: MTA Néprajzi Kutató Csoport, 1988.

Groome, Thomas E. *Gypsy Folk-tales.* London: Hurst Blackett, 1899.

Hübschmannová, Milena, ed. *Romske Pohádky* (Romany Tales). Prague: Odeon, 1973.

Jagendorf, M. A., and C. H. Tillhagen. *The Gypsies' Fiddle and Other Gypsy Tales.* New York: Vanguard, 1956.

MacColl, Ewan, and Peggy Seeger. *Till Doomsday in the Afternoon: The Folklore of a Family of Scots Travellers, the Stewarts of Blairgowrie.* Manchester: Manchester University Press, 1986.

———. *Travellers' Songs from England and Scotland.* London: Routledge Kegan Paul, 1977.

Mode, Heinz, and Milena Hübschmannová, eds. *Zigeunermärchen aus Aller Welt.* Leipzig: Insel, 1983.

Nagy, Olga. *A havasi sátaro:. David Gyula mesel.* (The ten [fingers] of a Gypsy of the Alps. Tales Told by Gyula David). Budapest: MTA Néprajzi Kutató Csoport, 1988.

———. *Barangolásaim varázslatos tájban.,* Székeludvarhely, Hungary: Erdélyi Gondolat Könyvkiadó, 1994.

Osella, Carla. *Racconti Zingari.* Turin. 1978.

Sampson, John, ed. *Gypsy Folk Tales.* London: Robinson, 1984. (Reprint from 1933 ed.)

Serra, Maria João Pavao. *Filhos da Estrada e do vento: contos e fotografias de ciganos Portugueses.* Lisbon: Assirio Alvim, 1986.

Szegö, László. *Cigány bölcsödal* (Gypsy Lullaby). Budapest: Móra, 1980. (Songs in Romani with Hungarian translations.)

————. *Csikóink kényesek*. Budapest: Europa Könyvkiadó, 1977. (Songs in Romani with Hungarian translations.)

Taikon, Katerina, ed. *Zigenerdikter* (Gypsy Poems). Stockholm: FIB's Lyrikklubb, 1964.

Tillhagen, Carl Herman. *Taikon erzählt Zigeunermärchen*. Zurich, Artemis,1948. (Translation of *Taikon Berättar* [Stockholm: Norstedt, 1946].)

Tong, Diane. *Gypsy Folk Tales*. San Diego, California: Harcourt Brace Jovanovich, 1989.

Williamson, Duncan. *May the Devil Walk Behind Ye*. Edinburgh: Canongate, 1989.

Williamson, Duncan and Linda. *A Thorn in the King's Foot*. London: Penguin, 1987.

d. Literature in Romani

Balić, Sait, ed. *Po Tito* (About Tito). Niš, Yugoslavia.: Prosveta, 1980. (Essays.)

Dimić, Trifun, trans. *Nevo Sovlahardo Cidipe*. (New Testament). Novi Sad, Yugoslavia: Dobri Vest, 1990.

Djurić, Rajko. *A i U. A thaj U.* Belgrade: Narodna Knjiga, 1982. (Poems in Romani and Serbian.)

————. *Bi kheresko bi limoresko: Bez doma bez groba.* (Without a House, without a Grave). Belgrade: Nolit, 1979. (Poems in Romani and Serbian); also in French as *Sans maison sans tombe*. [Paris: L'Harmattan, 1990].)

————. *Les disciples d'Héphaistos*. Troyes: Librairie Bleue, 1994. (Selected poems in French.)

————. *Zigeunerische Elegien*. Hamburg: Helmut Buske, 1989. (Poems in German and Romani.)

Gjunler Abdula. *Bizoagor/Eindeloos* (Without End). Oss, Holland: Gjunler, 1995. (Bilingual Dutch/Romani.)

Jusuf, Šaip, trans. *Amen sam e Titoske: O Tito si Amaro.* (We Are Tito's. Tito Is Ours). Ljubljana: Univerzum, 1978. (Translation from Slovenian.)

Manuš, Leksa (Aleksis Belugins), trans. "Ramayana." In special double number of *Roma,* nos. 31–32 (July 1989/January 1990).

Maximoff, Matéo, trans. *E Nevi Vastia* (New Testament). Paris: Societé Biblique Française, 1995.

Metkov, Sulyo, trans. *Neevo Zakon* (New Testament). Sofia: Adventist, 1995.

Olah, Vlado. *Khamori luludi: slunecnice* (Sunflower). Prague: MMM, 1996 (Bilingual Romani/Czech.)

Papusza (Bronislawa Weiss). *Piesni Papuszy*. (Songs of Papusza). (In Romani and Polish.) Wroclaw: Ossolinski, 1956.

Wlislocky H., ed. *Volksdichtungen der siebenbürgischen und südungarischen Zigeuner.* Vienna: Graeser, 1890. Romani and German.)

e. Literature in Other Languages (by Gypsy Authors)

Baltzar, Veijo. *Brännande väg* (Burning Road). Borgå: Norstedt, 1969. (Translated from the Finnish original *Polttava tie.*)

Binns, Dennis, ed. *Gavvered All Around* (Anthology of Poetry). Manchester: Manchester Travellers' Education Service, 1987.

Jayat, Sandra. *Nomad Moons,* trans. Ruth Partington). St Albans: Brentham Press, 1995. (A selection from *Lunes nomades* and other collections.)

Lakatos, Menyhért. *Bitterer Rauch.* Stuttgart: Deutsche Verlags-Anstalt. 1979. (German translation of *Füstös Képek* [Budapest: Könyvkiadó].)

Maximoff, Matéo. *Condamné à survivre.* Paris: Concordia, 1984.

———. *Prix de la Liberté.* Paris: Concordia, 1981.

———. *Septième Fille.* Paris: Concordia. 1982 (new edition).

———. *The Ursitory.* London: Chapman Hall, 1949. (Translated by Brian Vesey-FitzGerald from the French original *Les Ursitory.*)

———. *Vinguerka.* Paris: Concordia, 1987.

Smith, Charles (Charlie). Not All Wagons and Lanes. Aveley: Smith, 1996. (Poems.)

———. *The Spirit of the Flame: Poems by Charlie Smith.* Manchester: Manchester Travellers Education Service, 1990.

Spinelli, Santino, ed. *Baxtalo Drom—Felice Cammino* (Happy Road). Lanciano, Italy: Them Romano/ Tracce, 1995. (Anthology in Italian and Romani.)

f. The Holocaust in Fiction

Florence, Ronald. *The Gypsy Man.* New York: Villard, 1985.

Kanfer, Stefan. *The Eighth Sin.* New York: Random House, 1978.

Kosinski, Jerzy. *The Painted Bird.* New York: Bantam, 1965.

Ramati, Alexander. And the Violins Stopped Playing. New York: Franklin Watts, 1986.

Stancu, Zaharia. The Gypsy Tribe, trans. Roy MacGregor—Hastie. London: Abelard-Schuman, 1973.

g. The Gypsy in World Literature

Cervantes, Miguel de. *The Gipsy Maid: Six Exemplary Novels,* trans. Harriet de Onis. Woodbury, N.Y.: Barron's Educational, 1961.

Christie, Agatha. *Endless Night.* New York: Pocket Books, 1969.

Eliot, George. "The Spanish Gypsy." In *The Writings of George Eliot,* vol. 18. Boston: Houghton Mifflin, 1908. (Reprinted by AMS Press [New York n.d.].)

Florence, Ronald. *The Gypsy Man.* New York: Villard, 1985.

Freud, Jonathan. *Uppbrott.* Stockholm: Carlssons. 1993.

Garcia Lorca, Federico. *Gypsy Ballads,* trans. Langston Hughes. *The Beloit Poetry Journal,* Chapbook No. 1. (Fall 1951). Beloit, WSC: Beloit College, 1951.

Hugo, Victor, *Notre-Dame de Paris* (The Hunchback of Notre Dame). Various editions.

Lawrence, D. H. *The Virgin and the Gipsy.* New York: Bantam, 1970. (Reprint from 1925).

Márquez, Gabriel Garcia. *One Hundred Years of Solitude.* New York: Avon, 1971.

Mérimée, Prosper. *Carmen, and other stories,* trans. Nicholas Jotcham. Oxford: Oxford University Press, 1989.

Podgorets, Vidoe. *Beloto Tsiganche* (The White Gypsy). Skopje: Naša Kniga, 1988.

Pushkin, Alexander. "Gypsies." In *The Bronze horseman: Selected Poems of Alexander Pushkin,* trans. D. M. Thomas. New York: Viking, 1982. Also in *Selected Verse,* trans. John Fennell. London: Penguin. 1994. (Reprint Bristol: Classical Press, 1991) and *Selected Works in Two Volumes.* Vol. 1. Poetry. Moscow: Progress Publishers, n.d. (The poem "The Gypsies," trans. by I. Zheleznova.)

Scott, Walter. *Guy Mannering or the Astrologer.* London: Soho, 1987. (Reprint from 1815 ed.)

h. Music and Theater

Acton, Thomas, Rosy Denaro and Bernard Hurley, eds. *The Romano Drom Song Book.* Oxford: Romanestan, 1971.

Barrios, Manuel. *Gitanos, Moriscos y cante flamenco.* Seville: Rodríguez Castillejo, 1989.

Beissinger, Margaret. *The Art of the Lautar: The Epic Tradition of Romania.* New York: Garland, 1991.

Bobri, Vladimir. "Gypsies and Gypsy Choruses of Old Russia." *JGLS.* (3d series). 40, nos. 3–4 (1961): 112–20.

Brune, John. "Songs of the Travelling People." In *Folksongs of Britain and Ireland,* ed. Peter Kennedy. London: Cassell, 1975.

Davanellos, Nick. "Les Tsiganes et la musique démotique grècque." In *Tsiganes: Identité, Evolution.* Paris: Etudes Tsiganes, 1989.

Davidová, Eva and Jan Žižka. *Folk Music of the Sedentary Gypsies of Czechoslovakia.* Budapest. Magyar Tudományos Akadémia, 1991.

Equipo, Alfredo. *El Flamenco y los Gitanos: una aproximación cultural.* Granada: Universidad de Granada, 1978.

Gillington, Alice E., and Dowsett Sellars. *Songs of the Open Road: Didakei Ditties and Gypsy Dances.* Norwood, P A: Norward, 1973. (Reprint of 1911 ed.)

Haederli, Freddy. *Django Reinhardt. Discography.* Geneva: Haederli, 1996.

Hemetek, Ursula, et al. *Romane Gila: Lieder und Tänze der Roma in Österreich.* Vienna: Institut für Volksmusikforschung an der Hochschule für Musik und darstellende Kunst, 1992.

Kovalcsik, Katalin, ed. *Ernö Király's Collection of Gypsy Folk Music from Voivodina.* Budapest: Magyar Tudományos Akadémia, 1992.

———. *Vlach Gypsy Folk Songs in Slovakia.* Budapest: Magyar Tudományos Akadémia, 1985.

Lajtha, Lázsló. *Instrumental Music from Western Hungary: From the Repertoire of an Urban Gipsy Band,* ed. Bálint Sárosi, trans. Katalin Halácsy). Budapest: Akadémiai Kiadó, 1988.

Leblon, Bernard. *El cante flamenco, entre las musicas gitanas y las tradiciones andaluzas.* Madrid: Cinterco, 1991.

———. *Gypsies and Flamenco.* Hatfield: University of Hertfordshire Press, 1995. (Also available in French.)

——— *Musiques tsiganes et flamenco.* Paris: L'Harmattan. 1990.

Lemon A. "Roma (Gypsies) in the USSR and the Moscow Teatr Romen." In *Nationalities Papers* 14, no. 3, 1991.

Liszt, Franz. *The Gypsy in Music.* (English translation of *A czigányokrol és a cigány zenérol Magyarországon,* Pest: Heckenast, 1861). 1926.

Mitchell, T. *Flamenco Deep Song.* New Haven, CONNT: Yale University Press, 1995.

Rasmussen, Ljerka Vidić. "Gypsy Music in Yugoslavia: Inside the Popular Culture Tradition." *JGLS.* (5th series) 1, no. 2 (August 1991).

Sárosi, Bálint. *Cigányzene.* Budapest: Gondolat, 1971 (German translation, Zurich: Musikbuch, 1977: English translation, *Gypsy Music.* Budapest: Corvina, 1978.)

———. "Gypsy music." In *The New Grove Dictionary of Music and Musicians,* ed. S. Sadie. London: Macmillan, 1980.

Seton, Marie. "The evolution of the Gypsy theatre in the USSR." In *JGLS* (3rd series) 14: 66–72.

Stanley, Denise and Rosy Burke. *The Romano Drom Song Book.* Warley, England: Romanestan, 1986. Uffreduzzi, Marcella, ed. *Canti Zigani.* (2nd ed.) Genoa: Sabatelli Editore, 1973.

i. Painting

Balázs, János. *A Hungarian Gipsy Artist.* Budapest: Corvina, 1977.

Dzurko, Ruda. *Ich bin wieder Mensch geworden,* ed. Milena Hübschmannová. Leipzig: Stiepenheuer, 1990.

Stojka, Karl. *Ein Kind in Birkenau*. Vienna: Stojka, 1990.
———. *The Story of Karl Stojka: A Childhood in Birkenau,* ed. Sybil Milton. Washington, D.C.: U.S. Holocaust Memorial Council, 1992. (English edition of the prior title.)

j. Photography

Carret, Marie-Jose, and Claude Carret. *Les Anges du destin*. Trézélan, France: Filigranes, 1996.
Koudelka, J. *Gypsies*. London: Hale, 1975.
Szuhay, Péter, and Antónia Barati. *Pictures of the History of the Gipsies in Hungary in the 20th century*. Budapest: Néprajzi Museum, 1993.

VII. Health

Takman, John. *The Gypsies in Sweden: A Socio-Medical Study*. Stockholm: LiberFörlag, 1976.

VIII. Country by Country Listing

Albania

Anon. *No Record of the Case: Roma in Albania*. Budapest: European Roma Rights Center, 1997.
Hasluck, Margaret. "The Gypsies of Albania." In *JGLS* (3d series) 17 (1938), nos 2, 3, 4.

Austria

Cahn, Claude. *Divide and Deport: Roma and Sinti in Austria*. Budapest: European Roma Rights Center, 1996.
Fennesz-Juhasz, Christiane et al. "Sprache und Musik der Österreichischen Roma und Sinti." *Grazer Linguistische Studien* 46 (1996): 61–110.
Mayerhofer, Claudia. *Dorfzigeuner.*(2d ed.) Vienna: Picus, 1988.
———. "Gli Ungrika Roma del Burgenland. *Lacio Drom* 21 (1985), no. 6.

Belgium

Cuijle, J. H. *Zigeuners in Vlaanderen*. Antwerp: Ecclesiola, n.d.
Mijs, J. "Een bank vooruit. Onderwijs in Belgie." *Drom* 10, no. 4. (December 1995).

Tambour L. "Roma in Belgium: Past and Present." *Roma,* 3 no. 1. (January 1977).

Bulgaria

Anon. *Children of Bulgaria: Police Violence and Arbitrary Confinement.* New York: Human Rights Watch, 1966.

————.*Increasing Violence against Roma in Bulgaria. (*pamphlet) New York: Human Rights Watch, 1994.

————. *Police violence against Gypsies. (*pamphlet). New York: Human Rights Watch, 1993.

Marushiakova, Elena and Veselin Popov. *Tsiganite v Balgaria.* Sofia: Klub 90, 1993 (Translated into English as *Gypsies (Roma) in Bulgaria* [Frankfurt am Main: Lang, 1997].)

Silverman, Carol. "Bulgarian Gypsies: Adaptation in a Socialist Context." *Nomadic Peoples,* 21–22 (1986): 51–62.

Tomova, Ilona. *The Gypsies in the Transition Period.* Sofia: International Center for Minority Studies, 1995.

Croatia

Hrvatić, N., ed."Education and Upbringing of Romany Children in Croatia." Special edition of the journal *Romano Akharipe* (1994).

Cyprus

Kenrick, Donald, and Gillian Taylor. "Gypsies of Cyprus." *Roma* 24 (Jan. 1986).

Mene, Asik. "Interview." Translation from *Kibris* in *Drom* 10 (1995), no. 4.

Czech Republic

Anon. *Roma in the Czech Republic: Foreigners in Their Own Land.* New York: Human Rights Watch, 1996.

Conway, Laura. *Report on the Status of Romani Education in the Czech Republic.* Prague: HOST, 1996.

Czechoslovakia

Anon. *Struggling for Ethnic Identity: Czechoslovakia's Endangered Gypsies.* New York: Human Rights Watch, 1992.

Davidová, Eva. "The Gypsies in Czechoslovakia." *JGLS* (3d series). 69, nos. 3–4 (1970): 84–97 and 70, nos. 1–2, (1971): 39–54.

Hübschmannová, M. "Birth of Romani Literature in Czechoslovakia." *Cahiers de Littérature Orale* 30. (1991): 91–98.
Kostelancik, David. "The Gypsies of Czechoslovakia: Political and Ideological Considerations in the Development of Policy."*Studies in Comparative Communism* 22, no.4 (1989): 307–21.
Ulc, Otto. "Integration of the Gypsies in Czechoslovakia." *Ethnic Groups* 9, no. 2 (1991): 107–17.

Denmark

Albert, Jorn. *Sigøjnere er et folk.* (Gypsies are a People). Copenhagen: Forum. 1983.
Bartels E. and B. Brun. *Gypsies in Denmark.* Copenhagen: Munksgaard, 1943.
Enevig, Anders. *Sigøjnere i Danmark.* Copenhagen: Fremad, 1969.
———. *Tatere og rejsende* (Nomads and Travellers). Copenhagen: Fremad, 1965.

England

Birtill, Angie. *Rights for Travellers.* London: Irish Women's Centre, 1995.
Dodds, Norman N. *Gypsies, Didikois and Other Travellers.* London: Johnson, 1966.
Kenrick, Donald, and Sian Blakewell. *On the Verge: The Gypsies of England.* London: Runnymede Trust, 1990.
Mayall, David. *English Gypsies and State Policies.* Hatfield: University of Hertfordshire, 1996.
———. *Gypsies-Travellers in Nineteenth-Century Society.* Cambridge: Cambridge University Press, 1988.
Sibley, David. *Outsiders in Urban Society.* Oxford: Blackwell, 1981.

Finland

Grönfors, Martti. *Blood Feuding among Finnish Gypsies.* Helsinki: University of Helsinki Department of Sociology, 1977.

France

Vaux de Foletier, François de. *Les bohémiens en France au 19e siècle.* Paris: Lattès, 1981.
———. *Les Tsiganes dans l'Ancienne France.* Paris: Connaissance du Monde, 1981.

Germany

Geigges, A., and B. Wette. *Zigeuner heute.* Bornheim-Merten: Lamuv, 1979.

Hohmann, Joachim, ed. *Sinti und Roma in Deutschland.* Frankfurt am Main: Lang, 1995.

Hohmann, Joachim. *Verfolgte ohne Heimat. Geschichte der Zigeuner in Deutschland.* Frankfurt am Main: Lang, 1990.

Lucassen, Leo. *Die Zigeuner: die Geschichte eines polizeilichen Ordnungsbegriff in Deutschland 1700–1945.* Cologne-Weimar-Vienna: Böhlau, 1996.

Margalit, Gilad. *Antigypsyism in the Political Culture of the Federal Republic of Germany.* Jerusalem: Hebrew University Vidal Sassoon Centre for the Study of Antisemitism, 1996.

Martins-Heuss, Kirsten. *Zur mythischen Figur des Zigeuners in der Deutschen Zigeunerforschung.* Frankfurt am Main: Hagg Herchen, 1983.

Opfermann, Ulrich. *Dass sie den Zigeuner-Habit ablegen.* Frankfurt am Main: Lang, 1996.

Rinser, Luise. *Wer Wirft den Stein? Zigeuner sein in Deutschland: eine Anklage.* Stuttgart:Weitbrecht, 1985.

Schenk, Michael. *Rassismus gegen Sinti und Roma.* Frankfurt am Main: Lang, 1994.

Greece

Bereris, Petros. "Information File. Greece." *Interface* 13 (Feb. 1994).

Holland

Cottaar, Annemarie. *Kooplui, Kermisklanten en ander Woonwagenbewoners.* Amsterdam: Het Spinhuis, 1996.

Cottaar, Annemarie, et al. "The Image of Holland: Caravan Dwellers and Other Minorities in Dutch Society." *Immigrants and Minorities.* 2, no. 1 (March 1992).

———. *Mensen van de Reis, Woonwagenbewoners en Zigeuners in Nederland 1868–1995.* Zwolle: Waanders, 1995.

Hovens P., and R. Dahler eds. *Zigeuners in Nederland.* Nijmegen: Instituut voor Culturele en Sociale Antropologie, 1988.

Lucassen, Leo. *En Men noemde hen Zigeuners.* Amsterdam: Stichting IISG/SDU, 1990.

Van Kappen, O. *Geschiedenis der Zigeuner in Nederland.* Assen: Van Gorcum. 1965.

Willems, Wim and Leo Lucassen. "A Silent War: Foreign Gypsies and

Dutch Government Policy, 1969–89." *Immigrants and Minorities* 2, no. 1 (March 1992).

Hungary

Anon. *Rights Denied: The Roma of Hungary*. New York: Human Rights Watch, 1966.
———. *Struggling for Ethnic Identity: The Gypsies of Hungary*. New York: Human Rights Watch, 1993.
Hajdu, Mihaly. "Gypsies, 1980." *Hungarian Digest* 6 (1980): 28–34.
Karsai, Lászó. *A Cigánykérdés Magyarorzágon 1919–1945: út a Cigány holocausthoz*. Budapest: Scientia Hungariae, 1992.
Kovats, Martin. "The Roma and Minority Self-Governments in Hungary." *Immigrants and Minorities* 15, no. 1. (March 1996).
Szabó, György. *Die Roma in Ungarn*. Frankfurt am Main: Lang, 1991.
Vekerdi, Jozef. "The Gypsies and the Gypsy Problem in Hungary." *Hungarian Studies Review* 15, no. 2 (1988): 13–26.
Wagner, Francis "The Gypsy Problem in Postwar Hungary." *Hungarian Studies Review* 14, no. 1 (1987): 33–43.

Ireland

Gmelch, George. *The Irish Tinkers: The Urbanization of an Itinerant People*. Menlo Park, Calif.: Cummings, 1977.
McCann May, et al., eds. *Irish Travellers, Culture and Ethnicity*. Belfast: Institute of Irish Studies, 1994. (Papers from a conference in 1991.)
Paris, C., et al. *A Review of Policies Affecting Travellers in Northern Ireland*. Coleraine: Magee College, 1995.

Italy

Luciani, A. "Zingari a Roma nel 1700." *Lacio Drom* 31, no. 6. (Nov.–Dec. 1995).
Martelli, Vladimyr. "Gli Zingari a Roma dal 1525 al 1680." *Lacio Drom* 32, nos. 4–5. (Aug.–Oct. 1996.)
Piasere, Leonardo, ed. *Italia Romaní*. Rome: CISU di Colamartini Enzo, 1996.

Macedonian Republic

Barany, Zoltan. "The Romas in Macedonia." *Ethnic and Racial Studies* 18 (1995): 515–31.

Norway

Flekstad, K. *Omstreifere og sigøynere* (Travellers and Gypsies). Oslo: Aschehoug, 1949.

Hanisch, Ted. *Om sigøynersporsmalet* (On the Gypsy Question). Oslo: Institutt for Samfunnsforskning, 1973.

Midboe, O. *Eilert Sundt og fantesaken* (Eilert Sundt and the Nomad Question). Oslo: Universitets Forlaget, 1968.

Schlüter, Ragnhild. *De Reisende* (The Travellers). Oslo: Gyldendal, 1993.

Poland

Ficowski, Jerzy. *Cyganie na polskich drogach*. Krakow: Wydawnictwo Literackie, 1985.

———. *Gypsies in Poland: History and Customs*. Warsaw: Interpress, 1991. (Also in German and Polish.)

———. *Wieviel Trauer und Wege*. Frankfurt am Main: Lang, 1992.

Postolle, Angele. "Who are the Romanian Roma Living in Poland? *CPRSI Newsletter*. 3, no. 3 (1997).

Portugal

Coelho, Francis Adolpho. *Os Ciganos de Portugal: com um estudo sobre o calao*. Lisbon Imprensa Nacional, 1892.

Nunes, Olimpio. *O Povo Cigano*. Porto: Livrari Apostolado da Imprensa, 1981.

Serra, Joao Pavao. *Filhos da Estrada e do Vento: contos e fotografias de Ciganos Portugeses*. Lisbon: Assirio Alvim' 1986.

Romania

Anon. *Destroying Ethnic Identity: The Persecution of the Gypsies in Romania*. New York: Human Rights Watch, 1991.

———. *Lynch Law: Violence against Roma in Romania*. New York: Human Rights Watch, 1994.

———. *Sudden Rage at Dawn: Violence against Roma in Romania*. Budapest: European Roma Rights Center, 1996.

Beck, Sam. "Ethnicity, Class and Public Policy: Tiganii/Gypsies in Socialist Romania." In *Papers from the Vth Congress of Southeastern European Studies. Belgrade,* ed. K. K. Shangriladze, and E. Townsend. pp. 19–38. Columbus, Ohio: Slavica, 1984.

———. "The Origins of Gypsy Slavery in Romania." In *Dialectical Anthropology,* no. 14 (April 1989): 53–61.

———. "Racism and the Formation of a Romani Ethnic Leader (Gheorghe Nicolae)." In *Perilous States,* ed. G. Marcus. pp. 165–91. Chicago: University Press, 1993.

Block, Martin. *Die materielle Kultur der rumänischen Zigeuner.* Revised J. Hohmann. Frankfurt am Main: Lang, 1991.

Nicolae, Gheorghe. "Origin of Roma's Slavery in the Romanian Principalities." *Roma* 7, no. 1. (1983): 12–27.

Remmel, Franz. *Die Roma Rumäniens.* Vienna: Picus, 1993.

Russia

Gilsenbach, Reimar. "Roma in Russia: A Community Divided." *Transition. Open Media Research Institute Reports* 1, no. 4. Prague: OMRI, (March 1995).

Gilsenbach, Reimar, with Ljalja Kuznetsova (photographs). *Russlands Zigeuner.* Berlin: BasisDruck, 1994.

Scotland

Duncan, Tom. *Neighbours' views on official sites for travelling people.* Glasgow: Planning Exchange, 1996.

Gentleman, Hugh, and Susan Smith. *Scotland's Travelling People: Problems and Solutions.* Edinburgh: HMSO, 1971.

MacRitchie, D. *Scottish Gypsies under the Stewarts.* Edinburgh: Douglas, 1894.

Neat, Timothy. *The Summer-Walkers: Travelling People and Pearl Fishers of the Highlands of Scotland.* Edinburgh: Canongate, 1996.

Secretary of State's Advisory Committee. *Scotland's Travelling People: Reports.* Edinburgh: HMSO, 1974– (irregular).

Serbia

Vojvodanska Muzej. *Etnološka Grada o Romima: Ciganima i Vojvodine.* Novi Sad: Vojvodanska Muzej, 1979.

Slovakia

Anon. *Time of the Skinheads: Denial and Exclusion of Roma in Slovakia.* Budapest: European Roma Rights Center, 1997.

Horváthová, Emilia. *Cigáni na Slovensku.* (Gypsies in Slovakia). Bratislava: Vydavatelstvo Slovenskej Akadémie Vied, 1964.

Mann, Arne. *Neznami Romovia* (The Unknown Romany Story). Bratislava: Ister Science Press, 1992.

Slovenia

Strukelj, Paula. *Romi na Slovenskem*. Ljubljana: 1980.

Spain

Alfaro, Antonio. *The Great Gypsy Round-Up*. Madrid: Presencia Gitana, 1993. (Also available in French and Spanish.)
Calvo Buezas, Tomás. *España racista? Voces payas sobre los Gitanos*. Barcelona: Anthropos, 1990.
Garcia, José Manuel Fresno. "La situation sociale de la communauté gitane d'Espagne." *Ethnies* 8 (1993), no. 15.
Leblon, Bernard. *Les Gitans d'Espagne: prix de la différence*. Paris: Presses Universitaires de France, 1985.
———. *Los gitanos de España. el precio y el valor de la diferencia*. Barcelona: Gedisa. 1987. (Spanish trans. of prior title.)
Leon-Ignacio. *Los Quinquis*. Barcelona: Ediciones 29, 1974.
Lopez de Menses, A. *La immigración gitana en España en el siglo XV*. Madrid: Martinez Ferrandi Archivero, 1968.
Luna, José Carlos de. *Gitanos de la Bética*. Madrid: EPESA, 1951.
Ortega, Maria Helena Sánchez. *Dieser wichtige Zweig der Landesordnung: Zur Geschichte der Zigeuner in Spanien bis zum Ende des 18 Jahrhunderts*. Frankfurt am Main: Lang. 1993.
———. Los Gitanos españoles. Madrid: Castellote, 1977.
———. *La Inquisición y los Gitanos*. Madrid: 1988.
Ramírez Heredia, Juan de Dios. *En Defensa de los Míos: Qué sabe Vd. de los Gitanos?* Barcelona: Ediciones 29, 1985.
———. *Nosotros los Gitanos*. Barcelona: Ediciones 29, 1972.
———. *Vida Gitana*. Barcelona: Ediciones 29. 1985.
Yoors, Jan. *The Gypsies of Spain*. New York: Macmillan, 1974.

Sweden

Heymowski, A. *Swedish Travellers and Their Ancestry*. Uppsala: Almquist Wiksell, 1969.
Taikon, Katerina. *Förlat att vi stör*. (Excuse the Disturbance). Stockholm: 1970.
Tillhagen, Carl-Hermann. *Zigenarna i Sverige*. Stockholm: Natur Kultur, 1965.
Trankell. A. *Kvarteret Flisan* (The Flisan district). Stockholm: Nordstedt Soner, 1973.

Switzerland

Thodé-Studer, Sylvia. *Les Tsiganes suisses: la marche vers la reconnaissance*. Lausanne: Réalités Sociales, 1987.

Turkey

Rooker, Marcia. "Field Report from Turkey." *Roma Rights* (Spring 1997): 33–35.

Ukraine

Anon. *The Misery of Law: The Rights of Roma in the Transcarpathian Region of Ukraine.* Budapest: European Roma Rights Center, 1997.

United Kingdom

Acton, Thomas, and David Gallant. *Romanichal Gypsies.* Hove: Wayland, 1997.

Hawes, Derek, and Barbara Perez. *The Gypsy and the State.* (2d ed.) Bristol: Policy Press, 1996.

Ministry of Housing and Local Government. *Gypsies and Other Travellers.* London: HMSO, 1967.

Okely, Judith. *The Traveller-Gypsies.* Cambridge: Cambridge University Press, 1983.

Vesey-Fitzgerald, Brian. *The Gypsies of Britain.* Newton Abbott: David Charles, 1973.

Wales

Davies, J. Glyn. "Welsh sources for Gypsy History. *JGLS* (3d series) 9, 64–86.

Jarman A. O. H., and Eldra. *Y Sipsiwn Cymreig.* Cardiff: University of Wales Press, 1979.

———. *The Welsh Gypsies.* Cardiff: University of Wales Press, 1991. (Rev. English ed. of prior title.)

Yugoslavia

Vukanović, Tatomir. *Romi (Tsigani) u Jugoslaviji.,*Vranje, Yugoslavia: Nova Jugoslavia, 1983.

IX. Press

1. Learned Journals and Newsletters

This list includes current journals of Gypsy studies and regular newsletters.

(O) Drom. P.O. Box 16875, 1001 RJ, Amsterdam, Holland. (Dutch). (publication suspended.)

Études Tsiganes. 2, rue d'Hautpoul, 75019 Paris, France (French).

Interface. Centre de Recherches Tsiganes. Université Rene Descartes. 106 quai de Clichy, Clichy, France F 92110. (Editions include English and French.)

Journal of the Gypsy Lore Society (JGLS). There have been five series. The second is known as the New Series. The third series was the longest with 52 volumes. The fifth series is published from the United States. 5607 Greenleaf Rd., Cheverly, M D. 20785.

Lacio Drom. Centro Studi Zingari, 22 Via dei Barbieri, Rome, Italy 00186 (Italian).

Roma. 3290/15-D, Chandigarh 160 015, India (English).

Romnews. Roma National Congress. Simon-von-Utrecht Str. 85, Hamburg, D-20359, Germany (English).

Romano Dzaniben. Prague (Czech and Romani).

Studii Romani. Sofia (bilingual, Bulgarian/English).

Tsiganologische Studien. Giessen (German; successor to *Giessener Hefte für Tsiganologie 1984–1960*).

2. Periodical Press

This list includes only magazines appearing since 1945. Pre-1939 magazines will be found mentioned in the dictionary under the respective countries and "PRESS."

Most of those listed are bilingual, in the majority language of the country and Romani.

Amaro Dives/Ditet Tona—Albania

Amaro Drom—Budapest, Hungary, journal of Pralipe

Amaro Gao—Valencia, Spain

Amaro Lav—Czech Republic

Asul de Trefla—Romania; organ of the Democratic Union of the Gypsies

Aven Amentza—Bucharest, Romania; organ of the Cultural Association Aven Amentza

CPRSI Newsletter—Warsaw; English and Romani

Cigányfurö—Budapest, Hungary; edited by Attila Balogh

Dialogo Gitano—Madrid, Spain; Catholic

Divano Romano—Romania

Gazeta Romilor—Romania

Drom Dromendar—Sliven, Bulgaria

Glaso el Romengo—Romania; first issue numbered 15

Informaciaqo Lil—published in Romani (with English translations of some articles) by Romani Baxt for the Romany Union

Jekhetane—Spolu (Together)—Slovakia

Kethano Drom (Common Road)—Budapest, Hungary

Khamutne Dive—Suncani Dani (Sunny Days)—Zeleznik, Yugoslavia

Krlo e Romengo (Voice of the Romanies)—Yugoslavia; edited at one time by Rajko Djurić. Ceased to appear, then reappeared

Lacho Lav—Czech Republic. Ministry of Social Welfare

Loli Phabai—UK and Greece; three numbers only

Lungo Drom—Szolnok, Hungary

Nachin News—Scotland

Neo Drom—Romania

Nevi Yag—Belgium. Comité international catholique pour les Tsiganes

Nevipe—Slovakia

Nevipens Romani—Barcelona, organ of the Union Romani of Spain. Spanish; some numbers in Romano-Kaló

Nevo Drom. Novi Put—Croatia. Romapastorat

Nicovala—Romania

Nov Put (previously *Romano Esi* and *Nevo Drom)*—Bulgaria

Ocicat Romengo—Romania

Patrin—Holland/Slovakia. Romani/English

Phralipe—Budapest

Pomezia—Barcelona; organ of the Secretariado Gitano

Roma—Slovakia

Roma Rights—European Roma Rights Centre, Budapest.

Romano Barvalipen—Sofia, Bulgaria

Romano Boodos—Finland, religious magazine

Romano Drom—UK, organ of the Gypsy Council then independent (under the editorship of Jeremy Sandford), finally organ of the National Gypsy Council

Romano Glendalos—Czech Republic

Romano Ilo—Sofia, Bulgaria

Romano Kurko—Brno, Czech Republic

Romano Lil—Romske Novine—Belgrade, Yugoslavia.

Romano Lil—Berlin

Romano Lil—Slovakia

Romano Nevijpe—Murska Subota, Yugoslavia

Romipen—Bratislava, Slovakia

Romnews—Hamburg. Roma National Congress

Romologija—Voivodina, Serbia, journal of Gypsy studies

Romska Revue—Bratislava, Slovakia

Rrom p-o Drom—Bialystok, Poland

Ṣatra (Tent). Romania

Ṣatra libera. Romania

Scharotl (Caravan), organ of the Swiss Travellers
Tchatchipen—Barcelona
Te aves bahtale—Romania
Thèm Romanó—Lanciano, Italy
Traveller Education—National Gypsy Education Council, United Kingdom
Vie et Lumiere—Paris, organ of the Gypsy Pentecostal Church
Voix mondiale tzigane. Paris, Organ of the Comité International Tsigane, no longer published
Zigenaren—Sweden. Edited by Katerina Taikon, no longer published
Zirickli—Finland

X. Web Sites

Association of Gypsies/Romani International.
http://www.niia.net/~rom/
http://www.gypsies.net

European Roma Rights Center
http://www.errc.com

Gypsy Lore Society
http://gypsynet/gls/

Gypsynet (Rroma Yekhipe)
http://www.rroma.com/

Indian Institute of Romani Studies
http://www.aloha.net/-bohem/rishroma.html.

Patrin
http://www.geocities.com/Paris/5121/

Roma National Congress
htttp://www.romnews.com

RRPP
http://www.osi.hu/roma

Unión Romaní (Spain). http://www.unionromani.org
http://www.qsystems.es/gipsy/

XI. DISCOGRAPHIES

A first step into the rich world of recorded Gypsy music can be made by consulting the review pages of the British magazine *Folk Roots* and the book *World Music: The Rough Guide* (London: Rough Guides, 1994). Discographies have also appeared in *Journal of the Gypsy Lore Society* and *Études Tsiganes* (1994, no. 1).

About the Authors

Donald Kenrick has recently retired from a career as an organizer of adult education during which he pioneered basic education courses for Gypsies and training courses for those working with them. He was at one time honorary secretary of the British Gypsy Council and was an official interpreter at three World Romany Congresses. He has written extensively on the history, language and social situation of the Romanies.

Gillian Taylor was born in New Zealand but now resides in England. She is a graduate of the University of North London. She has carried out research into attitudes toward Gypsies and has set up the original database from which much of the material in this volume has been drawn.